# No One A Neutral

## Political Hostage-Taking in the Modern World

Wit

Ch

The

n Antok

Nudell

No One a Neutral
Political Hostage-Taking in the Modern World
by Norman Antokol and Mayer Nudell
Copyright © 1990 by Mayer Nudell and Norman Antokol

ISBN 0-939427-78-8
Printed in the United States of America

Published by Alpha Publications of Ohio
P. O. Box 58017
Medina, Ohio 44258   USA

Jacket illustrations and design by
Max Crace © 1990.

Library of Congress Catalog Card Number: 90-60358

# No One A Neutral
## Political Hostage-Taking in the Modern World

ALPHA PUBLICATIONS of OHIO

# TABLE OF CONTENTS

# ILLUSTRATIONS

# ACKNOWLEDGEMENTS

In writing this book, we were very fortunate to have the help and advice of a number of people whose invaluable assistance we would like to acknowledge. Our sincere thanks to: Joe Reap, Office of the Ambassador-at-Large for Counterterrorism, U.S. Department of State; Michael Guidry, President, Guidry and Associates; Robert Lukeman, Senior Assignments Editor, ABC News; Eugene Mastrangelo, Risks International Division, Business Risks International; Dr. Douglas Stuart, Director of International Affairs, Dickinson College; Lt. Col. Linda Du-Moulin, U. S. Department of Defense, and Joe Johnson, Public Affairs Officer, U.S. Embassy, Dublin, Ireland.

The contents of this book reflect our personal evaluations and assessments. Nothing contained herein should be construed to represent the views of the United States Government, the U.S. Department of State, or any other entity. We are indebted to the above-named people for their assistance, but all conclusions—along with any errors or omissions—are our entire responsibility.

# AUTHORS' NOTE

Our purpose in writing this book is to describe the growth of a particular form of kidnapping called *hostage-taking* and its relationship to contemporary terrorism. The political manifestation of this phenomenon is often in the form of barricade situations. Readers will note that, after the first chapter, we use the terms *hostage situation* and *hostage/barricade situation* somewhat synonymously. We do this because we believe that they are. As we explain, there are some differences between a kidnapping and a hostage or hostage/barricade situation. However, hostage situations—for the purposes of this book—are quite similar regardless of whether or not they involve a barricade.

We remind readers that this book is an overview. With regard to the section on hostage negotiation, we especially caution you to keep in mind that we have simplified a complex subject. Our purpose is to provide readers with only an introduction to this important topic. Our treatment of it is not all-inclusive; we have limited our discussion to areas which will not materially assist terrorists or other malefactors in their assaults on the body politic.

Finally, all readers should be aware that the many different definitions of terrorism have given rise to disagreements over what constitutes a terrorist act. This has resulted in a wide variety of statistics, many of which are contradictory. We have used those statistics which seem to us the most reliable, but we recognize that others exist. Furthermore, statistics are sometimes revised well after the fact in the light of more information or new interpretations. We believe that the statistics contained herein are accurate and will support our conclusions.

# DEDICATION

We dedicate this book to the memories of Ted Galecki and Julius Antokol, both of whom are greatly missed.

# ABOUT THE AUTHORS

**NORMAN ANTOKOL,** a former political science professor, is a foreign service officer. His overseas service includes tours in Caracas; London; Bridgetown, Barbados; and with the Multinational Force and Observers in the Sinai. For two years he was the Public Affairs Officer for the State Department's Office of Counterterrorism and Emergency Planning, as well as holding the aviation, European, and African portfolios. In August 1988, he became Deputy Director for Political Training at the School of Professional Studies of the Department of State's Foreign Service Institute, the training school for the U.S. diplomatic corps. In that capacity, he teaches political tradecraft to U.S. diplomats and coordinates the teaching of ancillary subjects.

Mr. Antokol has written previously on many facets of crisis management and other national security topics for a variety of publications with specialized and general readerships. He has addressed many government, private sector, and academic organizations on these topics.

**MAYER NUDELL** is a consultant to government and industry with many years of experience in counterterrorism, international affairs, and crisis management. He previously was a staff member of the U.S. State Department's Office of Counterterrorism and Emergency Planning, and the Executive Director of the Institute on Terrorism and Subnational Conflict. He has published extensively and has addressed academic, governmental, law enforcement, professional, business, and other organizations worldwide. He is an adjunct faculty member at the Center for Advanced Police Studies, and an instructor at the U.S. General Services Administration's Training Center.

Mr. Nudell is Chairman of the Public Safety and Human Relations Advisory Commission of the City of Falls Church, Virginia and of the Terrorist Activities Subcommittee of the American Society for Industrial Security's Washington, D.C. Chapter. He is a member of the American Foreign Service

Association, the American Society for Industrial Security, the International Association of Chiefs of Police, and the International Counterterrorism & Security Association.

BY THE SAME AUTHORS
The Handbook for Effective Emergency and Crisis Management

# INTRODUCTION

While much has been written about terrorism, *No One A Neutral* dissects one of its most insidious aspects, hostage taking. Tracing its evolution with meticulous documentation, the authors offer unique insights into the phenomenon of hostage taking. This is critical reading for those struggling for an understanding of the convolutions of terrorism.

**Herbert F. Saunders,**
**Former Deputy Director**
**of the Office of**
**Technical Service,**
**Central Intelligence Agency**

*In today's world, no one is innocent, no one a neutral. A man is either with the oppressed or he is with the oppressors. He who takes no interest in politics gives his blessing to the prevailing order, that of the ruling classes and exploiting forces.*

—George Habash

*In the 13 years since 1976, only 258 days have passed when Americans were not held hostage by terrorists somewhere in the world. Since March 1985, not a day has passed without an American in captivity. Terror is now woven into national life.*

—David Gergen

# Chapter 1
# DESCENT INTO CHAOS

The commandos quietly slipped across the fields and groves, virtually invisible black figures in the moonless night. The small Lebanese town which was their objective loomed ahead as they took up pre-determined positions. Silenced weapons at the ready, the twenty highly trained and well-briefed men prepared to assault their target.

In the town, Sheik Abdul Karim Obeid, one of the spiritual leaders of the Shiite terrorist group *Hezbollah* (Party of God), lay sleeping—unaware that his imminent abduction would mark the first time that one of the Shiites' favorite tactics would be used against him.

The commandos, members of an elite Israeli Defense Forces unit, had done their homework well. In the early morning hours of July 28, 1989, the commando team forced its way into Obeid's house and rounded up the adult members of the family. The sleeping children were locked in their room, while the adults were bound and gagged. Obeid's wife was locked in another room, while he and two other men were taken away.

From entry to exit, the entire operation lasted less than ten minutes. As the commando team departed, one of Obeid's neighbors stepped into the street and immediately was killed. Only as they left the town did they receive any hostile fire, but neither the commandos nor their prisoners were injured. A helicopter waited a short distance away, and twenty minutes later they were all safely back in Israel.

The raid was intended to provide the Israelis with a bargaining chip to negotiate the release of three Israeli servicemen believed to be held by various Shiite groups in Lebanon—an unfortunate reflection of the fact that human lives in that part of the world have come to be thought of as just another commodity to barter for advantage. But as with so many other well-conceived plans in the Middle East, this one took an unanticipated turn for the worst.

The first development following Obeid's abduction ironically affected an American. On July 31, *Hezbollah* announced the murder of one of its American hostages, Marine Lt. Col. William Higgins, who had been abducted in February 1988 while performing his duties as commander of the U.N. peacekeeping forces in Lebanon. Higgins' death had been threatened the previous day unless the Israelis immediately released Obeid. While it became apparent that Higgins had been killed months before, this response by *Hezbollah* involved the United States yet again in the intricacies of Middle Eastern politics.

Hard on the heels of the announcement of Higgins' death came a threat to kill yet another American hostage, Joseph Cicippio, if Obeid was not released. Cicippio had been abducted by *Hezbollah* (using the name Revolutionary Justice Organization) in September 1986 while working as the Comptroller of the American University in Beirut. This second threatened murder was postponed only after the Iranian government put pressure on the terrorists to rescind their threat.

As we write in October 1989, the Shiites have offered to release Cicippio in exchange for Obeid and several hundred Shiite and Palestinian prisoners presently held in Israeli jails. The Israelis, of course, want no part of any deal unless they obtain the release of their own servicemen. They have offered to widen the deal to include all foreign hostages and prisoners being held in Lebanon. The United States has been willy-nilly swept into this process, for it hopes that this incident might provide a breakthrough of sorts which will lead to a once-and-for-all resolution of hostage-taking in Lebanon.

The death of Americans for reasons only tangentially relevant to developments in Lebanon was nothing new. For a decade, the United States has suffered from indecision over how to respond to the hostage-taking of its citizens and frustration

over its inability to end this practice.[1] This frustration and indecision have been most pronounced in Lebanon—which, in
the 1980s, became the hostage capital of the world. Obeid's
abduction was just the latest in a series of events which transformed what had been the financial center of the Arab world
into a torn and bloodied nation. It is worth considering this
phenomenon in some detail, for it provides us with a point of
departure in considering how hostage-taking has evolved.

## DESCENT INTO CHAOS

Until 1975, Beirut was known as the "Paris of the Middle
East." The financial and commercial heart of the Arab world,
it—and Lebanon generally—had been able to avoid the dislo-
cations and devastations of the region. In an otherwise conflict-
ridden area, Lebanon traditionally had been viewed as an oasis
of stability. Part of the reason for this was the unusual compromises which became incorporated in its political system. A
crossroads since ancient times, modern Lebanon was an imper-
fect amalgam of various religious and national groups: Druzes,
Shiite Moslems, Christians, Maronites, Sunni Moslems, Palestinians, etc. By 1958, the competition for power had become so
deadly that civil war threatened to destroy the country and the
United States was asked to prop up the government. U.S. President Eisenhower sent in the Marines, who were able to restore
order in a relatively short period and were hailed as heros and
deliverers upon their departure.

---

[1]This frustration is shared by other countries. As of October 10, 1989,
twenty-four citizens of the U.S., Great Britain, Italy, Ireland, Belgium, Switzerland, and France were held hostage by various Shiite and Palestinian
groups. Many other citizens of the U.S., France, West Germany, India, Saudi
Arabia, Sweden, Belgium, Kuwait, Cyprus, Libya, Iran, Switzerland, and
other nations (some of them women and children) previously were taken hostage. Most were either released or killed, but the fate of some remains unknown. For further details, see Appendix A.

Out of the political competition emerged an unusual compromise based upon the relative strengths of the various groups. The country's presidency was reserved for a Christian, and the office of Prime Minister was reserved for a Moslem. Other governmental positions were similarly allocated. That provided a role for all of the groups except the Shiites and the Palestinians. These two groups, each a small minority, had no part in this political compromise.

By 1975, this structure had begun to break down for two reasons: the Palestinian takeover and the emergence of the Shiites as a political and military force. Both were reflections of the changing situation in the Middle East. Lebanon's insulation from these changes no longer existed.

## THE PALESTINIAN DIASPORA

With the establishment of Israel in 1948, large numbers of Arabs became exiles from their homeland. Adopting their version of the area's name, they became Palestinians—people without a country. They optimistically believed that their exile would be a short one, and many of them settled in the neighboring countries of Jordan and Lebanon. In each country, they were looked down upon and frequently forced to eke out a meager existence while living in "temporary" refugee camps. Some Palestinians beat the odds—achieving economic successes, accumulating wealth, and establishing businesses. Most, however, did not.

At the same time, the Palestine Liberation Organization (PLO) was developing its military and terrorist capabilities. Over time, as we will note later, some of these became world-class. They eventually turned their organizational talents to the refugee camps, and used them as bases of operation and sources of recruitment. As the PLO's influence spread throughout the refugee camps in Jordan, King Hussein came to regard it as a threat to his kingdom. In September 1970, he finally and forcibly expelled the PLO—providing a name for a new terrorist group, Black September.

Lebanon, on the other hand, never had the muscle to oust or control PLO activities. As the 1970s continued, it finally became the operational and organizational headquarters for the PLO. As its strength grew, the PLO became a country within a country. By 1975, the fragile fabric of Lebanon's "great compromise" had begun to deteriorate under this strain. Competing militias began to enforce their factional self-interest at the expense of Lebanon's national identity, and the country slipped into civil war.

By 1982, Lebanon's unwillingess or inability to keep its terrority from being used as a staging base for Palestinian incursions into Israel became intolerable for the Israelis. Using the provocation of an attack on its ambassador to Great Britain as its justification, the Israelis launched an invasion of Lebanon which rapidly brought them all the way to Beirut. Before the Israelis would withdraw two years later, the PLO had been forced out of Lebanon, at least temporarily.

## SHIITE EMERGENCE

The ouster of the PLO left something of a vacuum in the Lebanese power equation. As with all vacuums, there was a rush to fill it. Christian, Moslem, and Druze militias all vied for control, while Syria and Iran supported one or another of them for reasons of their own. This provided the other "despised minority" of Lebanon, the Shiites, with an opportunity to assert itself.

In 1982, the Shiites welcomed the Israelis as heros who would deliver them from their Sunni Moslem oppressors.[2] The Israelis

---

[2]The sources of the Sunni-Shiite friction are too involved for complete treatment here. Sunnis basically represent mainstream Islamic observance, while Shiites are a minority which the Sunnis view as heretical. Readers who wish to explore this matter are invited to consult such sources as the Public Broadcasting Service-sponsored videotape, *The Sword of Islam,* and Amir Taheri's *Holy Terror.*

did not reciprocate these warm feelings. The Shiites eventually became disenchanted with the continuing Israeli occupation of Lebanon and turned on them. Their militias and terrorist organizations (*Amal*, *Hezbollah*, Islamic Jihad, etc.)[3] began to attack the Israelis as well as their Lebanese adversaries.

The Israelis finally withdrew from Lebanon after establishing a buffer zone (the originally announced intention for the June 1982 invasion) in southern Lebanon. However, before they did, the Shiites were able to develop their military and terrorist capabilities—much at the expense of other Western countries, including the United States.


## PEACEKEEPERS AT WAR

Partly to provide a mechanism to restore order and partly as a way to ease the Israelis out of the country, the United States, France, and Italy agreed to establish a Multinational Forces (MNF) unit in Beirut in late 1982. In an attempt to repeat its successful 1958 intervention, the U.S. headed this effort. Unfortunately, what began as a well-received initiative became a quagmire which was to cost many Americans and others their lives.

Once the Shiites discovered that the MNF presence was to be a prolonged one, they cast about for ways to dislodge it. Fundamentally opposed to Western ways, the Shiites wanted to extend the Ayatollah Khomeini's Islamic Revolution to Lebanon and eliminate all Western influence. They knew, however, that direct military confrontation could not accomplish this; they turned to terrorism instead.

Beginning in 1983, a series of vehicle bomb attacks were mounted by the Shiites against U.S. and other Western targets in Beirut. The U.S. Embassy was attacked twice, resulting in

---

[3]We agree with those experts in the intelligence community who believe that Islamic Jihad is an umbrella name used by several Shiite groups for their convenience.

more than 20 American and a large number of Lebanese killed and injured. The bulk of the CIA station's officers and some visiting headquarters' officials were among the casualties.[4]

By far, the worst single incident occurred on October 23, 1983. Early that Sunday morning, the barracks of the U.S. contingent of the MNF was attacked, resulting in the deaths of 241 Marines and the injury of many more. At the same time, the French contingent's headquarters was also attacked with a vehicle bomb. Other elements of the MNF had been previously attacked while on patrol, but nothing of this magnitude had been seen before.

Similar attacks occurred in other countries, most notably Kuwait, where the U.S. Embassy and five other targets were simultaneously hit. In each instance, the Shiite terrorists threatened more such attacks until the MNF withdrew from Beirut. In 1984 the withdrawal finally occurred. To the Shiite terrorists who had been behind most of the violence in Lebanon and elsewhere, this vindicated their tactics, as the U.S. and other Western nations appeared to be leaving Lebanon under fire.

However, in winning this victory, the Shiites were left with a problem. After their attacks in Kuwait, seventeen of their colleagues were arrested, tried, and convicted. Now that there were fewer convenient Western targets for conventional attacks, they needed a new tactic.

Analyzing the implications of the 1979–81 Iranian seizure of the U.S. Embassy (which will be discussed in more detail later), some Shiite leaders recognized U.S. vulnerability to hostage-taking. In 1982, they had experimented with this tactic by seizing David Dodge, an American who was Acting Rector of the American University in Beirut. Dodge was abducted to force the U.S. to apply pressure on one of the Christian militias which had kidnapped three Iranian diplomats. After many

---

[4]This destroyed CIA activities in Lebanon. William Buckley, one of CIA's leading terrorism specialists, was assigned to rebuild the station. Buckley was kidnapped in 1984 and died while in captivity.

months, Dodge was finally released in exchange for the bodies of the three diplomats.

William Buckley, then-chief of the CIA's Beirut station, was abducted outside his residence in 1984. This time, the demand was for the release of the seventeen Shiite terrorists imprisoned in Kuwait. This was not met and the release of the seventeen would become a continuing demand of Shiite terrorists. Buckley died in captivity; intelligence sources believe as the result of torture. Although they were unsuccessful in obtaining their demand, the Shiites concluded that the U.S. could or would do nothing to retaliate.

Over the next five years, more and more innocent hostages would be taken by Shiite groups, and some would also be taken by radical Palestinian groups which benefited from the Shiite example. Appendix A contains a list of foreigners abducted during this period and reflects their status as of October 1989. Much has been written about the plight of the American hostages, but others are suffering as well. In most of the cases, those held hostage are truly innocent and, often, went to Lebanon out of a desire to help its people. Of course, this means nothing to their captors. We have selected the cases of two non-Americans, representative of many others, to illustrate clearly the cynicism of these Shiite terrorists.


## VICTIMS: BRIAN KEENAN AND TERRY WAITE


### BRIAN KEENAN

Brian Keenan was new to Lebanon. The 35 year-old British/Irish dual national had left his Belfast home in pursuit of twin interests in travel and international affairs. On April 11, 1986, he had been in Beirut for four months, teaching English at the American University. Keenan was aware of the potential danger in Beirut, but, after all, Belfast was only different by degrees and Ireland was a neutral country anyway. So, despite the concern of family and friends, he was in Beirut.

On that April day, Brian Keenan was walking to work, as usual. A car suddenly pulled up and, before he even realized what was happening, the men had forced him into it and they were off. Three and one-half years later, family and friends are still trying to learn his whereabouts, clinging to hope that he will safely return someday. There have been reports via other released hostages that Keenan is alive, and the usual rumors of his release periodically surface. For his mother and two sisters, there is only the waiting and frustration over the apparent inability of either the Irish or British governments to get him back.

## TERRY WAITE

On January 20, 1987, *Hezbollah* struck in its most cynical fashion. Church of England envoy Terry Waite, the 47-year old assistant of the Archbishop of Canterbury, was in Beirut yet again. He had been there many times before as he attempted to negotiate with Shiite groups for the release of British and American hostages. Such activity was nothing new for Waite, who was thrust into this business back in 1979, when the Church sent him on his first such mission. Then it was to Iran, where he successfully arranged for the release of several Britons being held captive. In 1985, he was similarly successful in Libya.

A religious layman, Waite had become quite knowledgeable about Islam by the latter 1980s. His many international missions had established his credentials as an apolitical humanitarian. So when Britons were made hostages in Beirut, it was not surprising that the Archbishop would ask him yet again to see what he might do. And because so many of the hostages were Americans, it was natural that his efforts would overlap into that arena as well.

In 1986, the Iran-Contra scandal in the United States touched Terry Waite. Having met several times with Oliver North, there was much speculation that he might have known of the arms-for-hostages swap and, indeed, some of his activities did coincide with these clandestine maneuvers. Waite always maintained that any involvement of his was unknowing, but the scandal may have set the stage for his abduction.

By January 1987, his credibility with the Shiite terrorists had declined and Waite felt he needed to return to Beirut to restore it. Always willing to risk personal danger, he agreed to a secret and private meeting—with whom it is impossible to say. Eluding his bodyguards, he left his hotel, and never returned. Nearly three years later, the world waits and hopes for the best.

These two incidents illustrate how terrorists attempt to capitalize on the basic humanity of Westerners to accomplish their goals. As George Habash so succinctly put it, "in today's world, no one is innocent. . . . " Kidnapping and hostage-taking directed against ordinary people have become favored tools in the shadowy war between democracy and terrorists.

## DEFINITIONS

There are a large number of criminal activities lumped together under the rubric of kidnapping. By motivation, however, they are distinct.

A kidnapping[5] is *the act of illegally holding one or more persons captive in a secret or otherwise hidden or unknown location.* It is an act of abduction with many traits. Among the criminal ones are:

(1) *White Slavery*, persons (overwhelmingly women) kidnapped for commercial prostitution.

---

[5]Kidnapping only became a U.S. federal crime in the wake of the 1932 Lindbergh baby kidnapping. Its use in the English language has been dated to the late seventeenth century by William Cassidy in his *Political Kidnapping: An Introductory Overview.* The term was developed to describe the practice of abducting children for forced labor.

(2) *Child Stealing*, resulting from marital discord or (as in the seventeenth century) for labor or prostitution.

(3) *Sexual Abduction*, for reasons other than prostitution.

(4) *Murder*, or other purpose apart from financial gain (e.g., to prevent a person from being in a certain place at a certain time, robbery, etc.)

(5) *Financial Gain*, as the result of negotiating a ransom payment or to otherwise financially benefit from a person's abduction.

(6) *To secure a source of labor*, as when seamen are "Shanghaied"[6] or when the British impressed sailors into their navy.

(7) *Hostage-Taking*, holding prisoners of war or political kidnappings such as have occurred in Latin America and the Middle East, in order to bring about or to prevent particular actions. This includes hijackings (which seek to force the authorities to agree to terrorist demands) and foiled criminal acts such as robberies (which seek to prevent the authorities from harming the criminal or impeding his escape). This is the type of kidnapping with which we primarily are concerned.

## POLITICAL HOSTAGE-TAKING

The political form of kidnapping is hostage-taking. We define this as *the act of illegally holding one or more persons captive in order to make political demands*. The most important distinction between kidnapping and hostage-taking is the question of publicity. This is the reason for its appeal to terrorists. As will be discussed later, media attention is one of the principal goals of terrorist groups. Criminals, however, only take hos-

---

[6]This term dates back to the days when San Francisco's Barbary Coast was the scene of kidnappings of sailors, who found themselves on ships destined to such exotic places as Shanghai. A captain who found himself short of deckhands might resort to this practice.

tages as a last resort (for example, when a holdup goes bad) or by accident (such as when an unexpected person interrupts the commission of a crime). Many of the hostage incidents discussed elsewhere have secrecy associated with them, but the public nature of the cases lift them out of the kidnap category.[7]

Experts—both psychological and practical—agree that there are three basic categories of hostage-takers: professional criminals, mentally disturbed persons, and terrorists. Before moving to a more detailed discussion of hostage-taking, we should briefly review each category of hostage-taker.

## CRIMINALS

Law enforcement agencies have constructed profiles of typical criminals involved in hostage-taking (often referred to by psychologists as anti-social personalities). These usually identify them as poorly educated and having had a disadvantaged youth. They are generally repeat offenders and probably have spent time in jail. Typically, they are not interested in taking hostages; rather, it spontaneously happens as the result of something going wrong during a crime.

Criminals generally take hostages as a means of preventing law enforcement authorities from arresting them. As the incident unfolds, criminals begin to realize that the safety of the hostage is their shield against the authorities. These incidents usually conclude with the criminal peacefully surrendering, after making the best possible deal.

## MENTALLY DISTURBED PERSONS

Often lumped together under the heading of "psychotics," there is no typical pattern to the actions of this type of hostage-

---

[7]In Lebanon, for example, the secrecy associated with the hostages' locations is more a function of the chaotic situation than an intentional tactic—especially since the hostage-takers continually seek to publicize the cases.

taker. Depending on the nature of their illness, the mentally disturbed may be interested in suicide, seeking help in coping, or any number of other things. They may come from poor families or wealthy ones, from disadvantaged families or socially prominent ones. Many such people are intelligent, others are retarded or have little education.

Regardless of the particular taxonomy, mentally disturbed hostage-takers are likely to act irrationally and unpredictably. This might be the result of a life-long problem or some recent event which has caused them to lose their mental balance. Time is important in dealing with such people, because they are often carrying on a titanic struggle within themselves. As this internal struggle continues, they often become tired and/or emotionally drained, making possible a peaceful resolution of the incident. (This is, of course, an extremely simple view of a complex matter.)

## TERRORISTS

This is the category of hostage-taker with which this book is principally concerned. The typical terrorist is young, highly educated, and intelligent. These individuals often come from middle- and upper-class families and frequently have benefited from college educations. Hostage-taking for them is a calculated, planned activity to further their political agenda. To make matters worse, they are prepared to die, if necessary.[8] They are certainly willing to kill for their objectives.

Hostage-taking probably is the terrorists' best attention-getter. The longer a hostage incident lasts, the more media at-

---

[8]As we know too well, some terrorists **intend** to die as part of their attacks. Such terrorists fortunately appear to be confined to Shiite Moslems in Lebanon. Such a suicidal impulse probably would qualify as a mental aberration were it not for the religious blessing accompanying such an attack. Islam generally reserves a place in Paradise for those who die in its service. However, the Shi'a doctrine—as did the Assassins of the Middle Ages—perverts this religious drive by focusing it upon secular political goals.

tention it will receive. Kidnappings are not as useful, because the required secrecy makes media access difficult and provides the authorities with more ways of controlling what access there is—although secrecy enables the kidnappers to retain considerable control over the incident.

## HOSTAGE-TAKING HISTORICALLY

The practice of taking hostages has been with us for as long as man has competed for dominance. Just as war has been a constant feature of human history, so too have there been prisoners of these wars—captives (hostages) who have been held until the hostilities ended and a mechanism for their repatriation could be arranged. Over the years, hostages came to be seen as a way to ensure the keeping of peace treaties. They were also viewed as a way to prevent the outbreak of wars between political entities which uneasily coexisted. The Romans, for example, made it a practice to "invite" the sons of tribal chiefs to live in Rome as "a gesture of goodwill." Arranged marriages were another variant on this theme. Although much of this human exchange was involuntary, much of it was the result of a common perception that a voluntary exchange of hostages made good sense.

After the fall of the Roman Empire, Europe metamorphosed politically and socially during the period sometimes called the Dark Ages. Power became extremely de-centralized until about the time of Charlemagne (9th century A.D.) The centuries which followed were typified politically by the rise of feudalism and the coalescence of political power among increasingly larger entities. This political power structure had a place for hostages.[9]

By the late eighteenth century, this political structure began to change once again, as nationalism began to replace feudal-

---

[9]The English language retains evidence of this institutionalization. Any extremely large amount of money often is referred to as a "king's ransom."

ism. As the nation-state increased in influence, the voluntary exchange of political hostages became less common, and finally disappeared altogether as a factor in international political relations.

However, in the late twentieth century, the international political arena is changing again. The nation-state is being challenged by transnational forces seeking to shape political events. The growth of international organizations (such as the United Nations), regional organizations (such as the European Community), special interest groups (such as the Organization of Petroleum Exporting Countries), and the rise of international terrorism as a major influence in world affairs have all contributed to the relative decline of the nation-state. As a concomitant development, the incidence of political hostage-taking has increased.

The modern version of hostage-taking, as practiced by terrorist groups, is a natural and logical extension of political developments and represents the latest stage of a continuing phenomenon. In many ways, it is a throwback to earlier times in which political development and international stability were lacking.

## THE EVOLUTION OF HOSTAGE-TAKING

### EARLY HOSTAGE-TAKING

From history's earliest records until the late eighteenth century, political power was de-centralized among numerous entities. Kingdoms and empires rose and fell, while city-states and other political units made appearances upon the world stage. International affairs were primarily characterized by conflicts and attempts by one or another of these political units to impose its domination upon certain geographic areas. At different times, empires such as the Persian, Macedonian, Egyptian, and

Roman successfully accomplished this. However, each was a relatively brief interruption in an otherwise conflict-ridden process.

Within this de-centralized competition, rulers vied with each other and with other aspirants to power. Kings competed with Popes and Caliphs for temporal authority. At the same time, they also needed to be concerned with groups such as the Knights Templar and the Assassins. It was a time of fuzzy lines of authority, changing loyalties, and dubious claims of political legitimacy.

This instability was institutionalized and, therefore, the responses to it were institutionalized as well. Agreements were only as permanent as the whims of those who entered into them. The concept of *pacta sunt servanda*—binding future political leaders to today's agreements—was unknown, and moral obligations were defined to fit the convenience of leaders.

In this atmosphere, it is not surprising that political leaders sought mechanisms to ensure that agreements were kept. One of the most frequent was the exchange of family members or loyal subalterns among political leaders. Reflecting the highly personal form of political rule, it was felt that this exchange of hostages would be a check upon any surprise attacks or violations of agreements. (The word "hostage" is derived from the word "host".) The reasoning was simple: hostages would be killed if something went wrong.[10] While not completely effetive, such reasoning is quite understandable and direct. Hostage exchange was a means of mitigating anarchy; it became obsolete as the world became less anarchic and politics less personal.

By the seventeenth century—beginning with the Peace of Westphalia in 1648, at the close of the Thirty Years' War—the

---

[10]As a matter of fact, it was not necessary to be a hostage for this to occur. Frequently, the bearers of bad news were summarily executed by potentates. Occasionally, so were emissaries from other potentates. This, of course, made diplomacy difficult, so rules for the protection and proper treatment of diplomats were developed and codified by the early eighteenth century.

highly personal form of political rule began slowly to give way
to more impersonal and organized forms of government. Limits
were placed on royal or executive authority as legislative assemblies became more powerful. As the eighteenth century dawned,
political power—especially in Europe—was becoming increasingly centralized in ways which outgrew the feudal system. As
the American and French Revolutions approached, a new basis
for political power made its appearance—nationalism.


## THE CRIMINALIZATION OF HOSTAGE-TAKING

Unlike previous political ideologies, nationalism provided
both a unifying and a de-stabilizing effect. Countries were now
based upon "national" characteristics such as language, cus-
toms, religion, etc. These "unifying" internal forces could also
find themselves in competition with other "unified units." The
forms of government were slow to change, but the source of their
legitimacy was not. The "divine right of kings" slowly gave
way to constitutional monarchies subject (at least in theory) to
the will of the people, expressed through legislative bodies.

The rise of nationalism and the modern nation-state changed
many traditional factors in political and international affairs—
some radically. One example of this was the change in the
character of war. Prior to the French Revolution, war was organized along feudal lines, with manpower and logistics predicated upon arrangements between lords and their vassals and
upon religious obligations. It was conducted as an actuarial activity, with the costs of mercenaries and hostages becoming
part of the risk-benefit calculus. Napoleon built his empire
upon the revolutionary fervor of the French people. For the
first time, all-out war became possible, as entire nations were
mobilized. Conscription in the national interest replaced feudal
obligations (which had provided some checks on authority).

The change of most interest to us was the diminution and,
finally, the end of hostage-taking as a normal feature of international political affairs. Because nations were now organized

on impersonal foundations, hostage-taking became obsolete as a deterrent. Standing armies, secret services, and other mechanisms grew up. Some of these (for example, large standing armies) had been impossible to sustain previously. However, as the new political unit became more established and more prosperous, international affairs became more codified and regularized. Predictability and precedent characterized these relationships and the holding of hostages was abandoned.

However, hostage-taking and kidnapping did not disappear from the scene. Criminals and other malefactors discovered that these practices could be of direct use to them. Slavers, organized criminals, short-handed sea captains, and similar groups regularly employed these tactics in their operations. Additionally, there are many accounts of individual kidnappings for ransom in all parts of the world.[11] That such tactics were criminal (not political) is further evidenced by the fact that they were not a part of revolutionary arsenals. While murder, arson, bombings, and other violent acts were commonly accepted revolutionary tactics, kidnapping and hostage-taking were not. Thus, when the Russian anti-Tsarist revolutionaries attacked, they directly did so against government officials.[12]

Thus, for a period of approximately 200 years, the international political arena was relatively unaffected by kidnappings or hostage-takings. Of course, isolated events provided exceptions to this generalization in contacts with "peripheral" areas such as North Africa (the Barbary pirates), the Caribbean (mainly piracy again), and Latin America. By the middle part

---

[11]While child stealings and other abductions were reported, for example, in the United States by the mid-1800s, the first recorded ransom kidnapping seems to have occurred in 1874. See Ernest Alix's *Ransom Kidnapping in America, 1874–1974* (Southern Illinois University Press). In addition, there are exceptions to the rule, as when the British extended their naval recruiting internationally through the impressment of foreign sailors—one of the causes of the War of 1812.

[12]In fact, in more than one case, operations were aborted because of the risk of injury to bystanders or family members of the target.

of the twentieth century, what was once an accepted tool of international political relations had become a predominantly criminal endeavor. As with other aspects of political life, this would change. The latter part of the twentieth century has witnessed the emergence of a world in which the nation-state is no longer the single dominant political factor.

## POLITICAL CRIMINALITY AND HOSTAGE-TAKING

With the conclusion of the Second World War, the world was dominated by a handful of great powers, with two superpowers at the top. This state of affairs began to unravel as the large European colonial empires broke up and large numbers of new countries were added to the international community. For a time, the superpowers continued to exercise their domination, but, for a variety of reasons, the world increasingly became multi-polar. The international community moved away from the easily understood divisions between colonial powers and colonies, great and secondary powers, and between the northern and southern hemispheres—as the "First, Second, Third, and Fourth Worlds" struggled to accommodate each other.[13]

Many of the great powers were in economic or political chaos, but they had survived the war intact and victorious. However, the political tensions of the Cold War caused those few great powers which could afford it to develop their military and industrial bases to such an extent that they developed into superpowers, and for approximately twenty years they effectively dominated world political and economic affairs.

---

[13]Loosely speaking, the "First World" is that of the free and democratic countries of Western Europe, the United States, Canada, Japan, Australia, New Zealand, etc. The "Second World" consists of the Communist countries of Eastern Europe, the Soviet Union, China, etc. The "Third World" is commonly understood to be the new, non-aligned, developing countries of Africa, Asia, and Latin America, while the "Fourth World" is a relatively new term coined to identify many Third World nations whose economic problems are so great that they make other Third World countries' economies look sound.

At the same time, a number of non-traditional political actors assumed importance in world affairs. Some were intended to serve as catalysts for world peace (e.g., the United Nations), while others were the result of regional cooperation (the European Community) or shared interests (the Organization of Petroleum Exporting Countries). Still others reflected the darker side of the struggle for ethnic, national, or religious independence (here we refer to international terrorist organizations). As a whole, they further undermined the viability of the nation-state in international affairs by providing additional power centers whose influence and significance could not be overlooked.

In fact, what seems to be happening in the late twentieth century is a reversion to pre-modern international politics as the nation-state loses much of its previous dominance. A concomitant development of this process has been the reintroduction of hostage-taking as a feature of international political affairs via the activities of terrorist groups. This reflects a criminalization of political action. Terrorism fundamentally is political crime.[14] Hijacking is theft and hostage-taking, assassination is murder, etc. When it comes to hostage-taking, kidnapping is the operative equivalent—an activity which is universally illegal. In fact, many nations (for example, the United States) have little or no terrorism legislation as such, believing that their ordinary criminal laws are sufficient. What we may be witnessing in the latter part of the twentieth century—and events in Lebanon seem to support this view—is the reversion to a more primitive and unstable form of politics based upon personalities, where the personal ties of the sovereign to his family or vassals have been replaced by the symbolic ties of a government to its citizens. This has led to the renewed use of involuntary hostages as a political tactic.

---

[14]We have heard all the arguments over how to define terrorism and the refrains such as "one man's terrorist is another man's freedom fighter." However, whatever one's definition, terrorism involves an activity which would be considered criminal were it not for its political rationalization.

But it is not enough to simply condemn hostage-taking and to point out that terrorists have transformed a criminal activity back into a political one. That does not contribute much to our understanding of the phenomenon.

Whatever the answer, we believe that it is useful to understand what hostage-taking has come to mean in today's world. Doing so requires a look at the past.

# Chapter 2
# REVOLUTION AND RANSOM

As long ago as 81 B. C., a kidnapping took place involving no less a figure than Julius Caesar. The future dictator of Rome was on his way to the island of Rhodes when he was overtaken and captured by a pirate ship. Brought before the captain, he was informed that the price of his freedom would be twenty talents. Caesar, then just an ambitious young politician, was offended by the paltriness of the sum and insisted that the ransom be increased to fifty talents (about twelve thousand pieces of gold). This the pirate captain was happy to do, and the ransom was duly borrowed from relatives and friends. Once released, Caesar raised a private navy and hunted down his former captors. He got back his money and had all the pirates crucified, which undoubtedly was a fairly effective way to discourage the practice.

A millennium later, another well-known figure of history found himself in a similar situation. In 1192, Richard the Lion-Hearted, having concluded a treaty with Saladin and left the Third Crusade, was shipwrecked in the Adriatic. Attempting to make his way across Europe in disguise, he was taken prisoner by Duke Leopold of Austria, who turned him over to Emperor Henry VI of the Holy Roman Empire. Eventually 150,000 marks were pledged as ransom, and Richard was released in March 1194.

Then as now, hostage situations didn't always end happily. In 1532, Francisco Pizarro captured the Inca leader Atahuallpa after a battle for the city of Cajamarca. Pizarro offered to release his prisoner if he would fill the chamber in which he was being held with gold and silver—surely one of the highest ransom demands in history. This was done, requiring 13,265 pounds of gold and 26,000 pounds of silver—enough to make every one of Pizarro's followers wealthy for life. Pizarro, however, fearing to let his captive go, instead charged him with the

murder of his own brother and had him put to death by stran-
gulation. Even 450 years ago, the word of a hostage-taker was
not to be trusted.

American history furnishes its own examples of hostage-
taking and ransom demands. Immediately following independence, the fledgling United States faced a crisis with the Muslem
states of the North African coast. Barbary pirates were harass-
ing American shipping, and British protection, which the colo-
nists had enjoyed prior to the Revolution, was at an end. Over
a twenty-year period, treaties with Algiers, Tunis, and Tripoli
cost the United States close to a million dollars—mainly for
the ransom of American sailors who had been captured by the
Corsairs.

The treaties were violated with regularity, however, and in
1801 the Pasha of Tripoli repudiated his agreement outright and
declared war on the United States. There followed a four-year
naval war, ending with a treaty signed on June 4, 1805. Notwithstanding South Carolina Congressman Goodloe Harper's
famous 1798 response to French demands for payment to stop
raiding U.S. ships—"millions for defense, but not one cent for
tribute"—the U.S. paid more than sixty thousand dollars for
the release of American prisoners. The Pasha, for his part, gave
his "guarantee" of future safe passage. It would require ten
more years, and another show of American naval strength, before this would become a reality.

A generation later, in 1835, the U.S. Navy warship *Vin-
cennes* was dispatched to the island of Ngercheangel, in the
Western Pacific, to try to ransom three shipwrecked American
sailors. The ransom demanded was two hundred muskets and a
supply of powder, which the Americans were prepared to pay.
This would have had a fearful effect on the balance of power
among the warring villages of the area and, in the end, the
ransom was paid in axes, chisels, and similar kinds of tools.

In more recent times, the aftermath of the Bay of Pigs fiasco (1961) saw the payment of what effectively was a ransom to Fidel Castro. Cuba was holding more than a thousand
prisoners, whom Castro offered to exchange for a substantial

price. Unofficial intermediaries negotiated a settlement, which amounted to about fifty-three million dollars worth of food and medical supplies. The Cuban dictator described this as an "indemnity" paid for the damage his country had suffered, but the reality was that it was paid as the price of retrieving the prisoners. Senator Barry Goldwater described it as giving in to international blackmail.

## THE PAST AS PROLOGUE

Hostage-taking is a very old phenomenon and a very new one. Old, because the practice of trading captured soldiers and kidnapped royalty for money or political concessions was well known in ancient and medieval times. New, because the current practice of considering nearly everyone an appropriate target has only been a part of a grand revolutionary strategy for about twenty years. In the past, ransoms or political favors were demanded for diplomats or other government figures, or they grew out of a failed military action. In both cases, there was a direct connection between the captive and the ones on whom the demands were being made. A hostage found himself in his situation as a result of his official relationship to the rulers of his country.

Starting around the late 1960s, however, this began to change. The ranks of political hostages began to include third-country diplomats, businessmen, tourists, innocent bystanders, and even whole planeloads of uninvolved individuals. As the term "terrorism" was added to the contemporary political lexicon, ever greater numbers of people found themselves potential targets. The impact of terrorism was that kidnappings and hostage situations were now taking place with a wider audience in mind. Publicity and general intimidation were now the goals, and nearly everyone was considered fair game.

The days when only military prisoners and policy-makers could be held for political concessions were over. The new strategy made everyone a target. Beginning a little more than twenty years ago, a whole new element once again had to be factored into foreign policy considerations. The question is, why?

## FOCO: THE GUERRILLA BECOMES A TERRORIST

The roots of political hostage-taking in the modern world, and of terrorist activity in general, are to be found in the theory of revolution. Karl Marx taught that there is an historically inevitable process through which capitalism must lead to the eventual alienation of the working class. He believed that the socialist revolution would ultimately occur when conditions were ripe; when the workers were sufficiently alienated and the corruption of the capitalist system had properly been exposed. For Marx, this was not the result of individual desires, but an immutable law of history. The triumph of the working class was built into the logic of human development.

Marx's ideas went through several refinements in the twentieth century, most notably those of Lenin and Mao. By the time of the anti-colonial revolutions of the 1950s and 1960s, his doctrine had been transmuted. The socialist revolution, at least in the Third World, was something that could be brought on— that is, its inevitability could be accelerated—through the force of arms. What was needed was a focal point from which the revolution could be induced. The rural areas of the underdeveloped world were to provide this focus.

The model for this concept was Castro's victory in Cuba. The experience of his years of guerrilla warfare, using the Cuban countryside as a base, provided Ché Guevara with the outline of a guerrilla manual and a new concept of revolution— the *foco*, or focal point. Further systematized by Régis Debray in his *Revolution Within the Revolution*, the idea took hold among Latin American insurgents. A revolution could be launched from the rural areas even where the supposedly necessary pre-conditions of orthodox Marxism had not yet occurred. Later, it would be said that "Vietnams would be created in Latin America."

Castro's example notwithstanding, the theory just could not be made to work. Guevara himself was a miserable failure in Bolivia and paid with his life there in 1967.[1] After that, aspiring revolutionaries began to reject the ideas of Debray, and to look instead at the possibilities of the urban areas. There was to be a new bible for the late 1960s: the work of the Brazilian Carlos Marighella, entitled *Minimanual of the Urban Guerrilla*. Rural guerrilla warfare was about to become modern urban terrorism, as the *foco* shifted to the cities.

## URBAN TERRORISM

In reality, the idea was not altogether new with Marighella. It had first appeared during the days of the Algerian revolt against France. Abane Ramdane, a resistance leader, made the conscious decision to shift his campaign to the urban areas of Algeria. He reportedly remarked that the murder of ten Frenchmen in the desert would go unnoticed, while the killing of a single Frenchman on a busy city street would be covered in the international media.

The shift to the cities, however, meant a major shift in tactics. Guerrilla warfare essentially is a branch of standard warfare, one which emphasizes small decentralized groups, ambushes, hit-and-run engagements, and the element of surprise. In the countryside, where large troop movements are difficult and standard military operations are unwieldy, most of the traditional advantages of superior numbers and firepower are neutralized. If the terrain is really favorable, as in Vietnam, an insurgent group can maintain itself indefinitely. The aim

---

[1]There are those who claim that Castro did not expect Guevara to succeed in Bolivia and that he sent him there in order to get him out of Cuba, where his revolutionary zeal was becoming a problem for Fidel.

is a war of attrition and the ultimate demoralization of the larger force.

In the city, though, such a strategy cannot work. Transportation and communication are too readily available to the authorities, and it is very difficult for a guerrilla band to stay long out of reach. However complex a city may be, it is not a Vietnamese jungle, and all of its terrain is accessible. Directly engaging the authorities—ambushing the government's forces and then melting away—is no longer an option.

The result was the birth of contemporary terrorism. Ambushes and running military engagements gave way to bombings, arson, murder, and the taking of hostages. The rhetoric remained military and legalistic. The new urban guerrillas, the terrorists, spoke sententiously of "executions" and "people's campaigns"—but the targets necessarily were not, at least not exclusively. The aims of urban guerrilla warfare, i.e., terrorism, were threefold: to undermine and demoralize the forces of authority; to precipitate oppressive countermeasures, increasing the discontent of the populace and (theoretically) hastening the ultimate "revolt of the masses"; and, perhaps most important of all, to gain the widest possible publicity for the cause. This, then, was the basis of the gospel according to Carlos Marighella.

Marighella and his disciples quickly realized that the taking of hostages would reap even greater returns than mere bombing or murder alone. It would contribute to the accomplishment of all the goals mentioned above, with a few other side benefits thrown in as well. Hostages could be exchanged for terrorists who previously had been imprisoned—usually referred to as "political prisoners" or "revolutionary comrades" in the tortured argot of the terrorist. They could be used to raise ransom money and thereby further the financing of the terrorists' objectives. And because political kidnappings or hostage/barricade incidents are ongoing situations full of inherent threat and drama, they would provide an almost unparalleled source of publicity for the group responsible.

## CONTEMPORARY POLITICAL KIDNAPPING

The earliest contemporary political kidnappings, which took place during Castro's struggle in Cuba, were undertaken almost entirely for publicity; no specific demands were made. In 1958, race driver Juan Manuel Fangio was abducted just before he was to participate in a race. The incident generated the desired publicity, and Fangio was released unharmed. Shortly after, forty-five U.S. citizens were taken hostage under the direction of Raul Castro to protest the U.S. maintenance of the Batista government's planes at Guantanamo. As in the previous case, no demands were made and the hostages were released unharmed.

Castro eventually realized that taking hostages *en masse* was more efficient than capturing them singly, and this, coupled with his recognition of the vulnerability of civil aviation, led to the first Cuban hijackings. Three planes were hijacked during this period, but again there were neither ransoms nor releases demanded. (Airplane hijacking ultimately became a major part of the strategy of some groups, particularly after its adoption by Palestinian terrorists. Prior to Marighella's codification of urban guerrilla operations, it was only a minor piece of the overall picture.)

Given that the intellectual founder of this new approach was a Brazilian, it is perhaps not surprising that the first successful application of Marighella's theories was the kidnapping of the U.S. ambassador to Brazil, Charles Burke Elbrick, on September 4, 1969.[2] Ambassador Elbrick was taken from his car by

---

[2]Hostage-taking as part of a terrorist strategy actually made its first appearance in two separate incidents in Guatemala in 1968, but we relegate these to a footnote because, in both cases, the intended hostages were killed without actually being kidnapped. On January 16, 1968, U.S. Army Colonel John D. Webber and U.S. Navy Lieutenant Commander Ernest A. Munro were shot to death from a passing car. Webber was commander of the U.S. Military Group in Guatemala and Munro headed its naval section. The episode is believed to have been the responsibility of the *Fuerzas Armadas Rebeldes* (FAR), which claimed responsibility for the killings the following day.

four men on a street in downtown Rio de Janeiro. The kidnappers left behind a ransom note demanding the publication of its manifesto, the release of fifteen prisoners by the Brazilian government, and provision for their flight to another country. If these demands were not met within forty-eight hours, the note said, Ambassador Elbrick would be "executed."

The kidnapping was carried out by two left-wing Brazilian groups, the *Movimiento Revolucionario do Outubre 8* (MR-8) and the *Acao Libertadora Nacional* (ALN). The Brazilian government gave in to their demands and, on September 5, broadcast the groups' manifesto. The next day, the fifteen prisoners were released and flown to Mexico. The following day, Ambassador Elbrick was released by his captors, whom he described as having been fully prepared to carry out their threats had their demands not been met. The theories of Carlos Marighella had been shown to work.

The lesson learned, it quickly was put into practice in various parts of Latin America. On March 6, 1970, U.S. labor Attaché Sean Holly was seized by the *Fuerzas Armadas Rebeldes* (FAR) on a main street in Guatemala City. The terrorists demanded the release of four of their imprisoned comrades in return for Holly's release. The government of Guatemala quickly agreed, and within two days, two of the four were released and given political asylum in the Costa Rican Embassy. All four

---

On August 28, 1968, U.S. ambassador to Guatemala, John G. Mein, was en route to the Embassy when his car was forced to the curb, blocked in, and surrounded by several young men with weapons. Ambassador Mein jumped from the car, but was shot down as he tried to escape. A communique issued by the FAR the next day stated that the ambassador was killed "while resisting political kidnapping." It is believed that the FAR had intended to try to exchange Mein for their imprisoned Commandant Camilo Sanchez.

While both these incidents pre-date the kidnapping of Ambassador Elbrick, neither actually brought about a genuine hostage situation, with demands for ransom or release of prisoners. We therefore consider the Brazilian episode as the beginning of the application of Marighella's theory.

received safe conduct to Mexico.[3] Holly was held for a total of thirty-nine hours, then released at a church in a working-class district of the city. The whole affair took less than two days, but once again the taking of a hostage had proven to be an effective tactic in the "revolutionary struggle."

Emboldened by success, the FAR kidnapped the West German ambassador to Guatemala, Count Karl von Spreti, a mere three weeks later. On March 31, Ambassador von Spreti was forced from his car by armed men in downtown Guatemala City. This time, the terrorists demanded the release of seventeen political prisoners, including five who were charged with responsibility for the earlier kidnapping of Sean Holly. The other twelve included prisoners accused of killing several politicians and policemen. The Papal Nuncio was contacted to serve as intermediary.

On April 2, the Guatemalan government announced that it would not agree to the kidnappers' demands; no prisoners would be released. Indeed, since some of the prisoners had already been tried and convicted, the government argued that they couldn't be released by executive order in any event. Instead, political and labor activities were ordered suspended, personal rights were shoved aside, and the military was authorized to interrogate anyone it considered suspicious.

The West German government protested this refusal to accede to the kidnappers' demands, and on the morning of April 3, a delegation of foreign ambassadors met with the Guatemalan Foreign Minister to urge that the prisoners be released. Meanwhile, the FAR upped its price to twenty-five prisoners and a ransom of seven hundred thousand dollars. The West German government reportedly offered to provide the money, but the Guatemalan government remained adamant. On April 5, the body of Ambassador von Spreti was found in an abandoned house, fatally shot in the head.

---

[3]The kidnappers were incorrect in thinking that all four were in jail in the first place. Even terrorists apparently can make mistakes.

While the results were disastrous for Count von Spreti, and almost as bad for relations between West Germany and Guatemala, it was hardly a victory for the theories of Carlos Marighella. The FAR found itself isolated from the masses it had expected to incite, and it became the target of a crackdown by the authorities. The fate of urban guerrilla warfare in Guatemala suggested that the theory would have to be refined and adapted somewhat more carefully.

Meanwhile, in the three weeks between the release of Sean Holly and the murder of Count von Spreti, there were three more political kidnappings in Latin America. Two of these, in Brazil and the Dominican Republic, achieved their aims, while the third, in Argentina, failed.[4]

The first of these incidents, just three days after Holly's release in Guatemala, took place—perhaps not surprisingly—in Brazil. On March 11, the Japanese Consul General in São Paulo, Nobico Okushi, was taken from his car en route to his home. The kidnappers, who identified themselves as members of the Popular Revolutionary Vanguard (*Vanguarda Popular Revolucionaria*), demanded the release of five individuals from prison and their safe conduct to another country. They also demanded that the government call off the manhunt it had begun or Okushi would be killed.

As in the Burke case six months earlier, the Brazilian authorities announced that they would meet the terrorists' demands. They further agreed to an additional demand, a guarantee of humane treatment for all prisoners in Brazilian jails. On March

---

[4]There was a fourth attempt, also in Argentina, on March 29, when the Soviet Assistant Commercial Attaché was overpowered in a garage in Buenos Aires. Fleeing from the police, the terrorists' car collided with another vehicle and the attempt was foiled. Since one of the kidnappers was a Deputy Police Inspector, however, and the plot was the brainchild of a Soviet-hating right-wing organization, it is difficult to know precisely what the group intended. This incident does not fit in with the others detailed here, but it is interesting to note how tactics and ideas can be copied—even by organizations with radically different goals.

14, the five prisoners were released and allowed to leave for Mexico. Ten hours later, Okushi was released unharmed. The doctrine of Marighella was two-for-two in his native Brazil.

Ten days later, the U.S. Air Attaché in the Dominican Republic, Air Force Lieutenant Colonel Donald J. Crowley, was kidnapped from a polo field next to a hotel in Santo Domingo. The abductors, who identified themselves as members of the United Anti-Reelection Command (a group attempting to keep incumbent President Joaquin Balaguer from serving another term), demanded that twenty-one prisoners be released in a public ceremony in Santo Domingo's main square. Crowley's release would take place ten hours after the ceremony, the kidnappers' note promised.

The Dominican Republic's government agreed to the release of the prisoners, but it refused both the public ceremony and the ten-hour delay preceding Crowley's release. The two sides eventually reached a compromise, and twenty prisoners were placed on board an airplane under the protection of the Mexican Embassy, accompanied by the auxiliary Archbishop of Santo Domingo, to be permitted to leave only upon the appearance of Lt. Col. Crowley. On March 26, Crowley was released unharmed, and the twenty former prisoners took off for Mexico. In light of this and the Okushi incident, it is hardly surprising that the FAR thought it could get away with the demands it presented for the return of Ambassador von Spreti only a week later in Guatemala.

## THE TACTIC SPREADS

While the successes of these few weeks in March 1970 marked a turning point in the history of political hostage-taking, there was one notable exception. On March 24, the same day that Lt. Col. Crowley was being abducted in the Dominican Republic, a left-wing guerrilla group in Argentina tried its hand at a terrorist kidnapping. The *Frente Argentina de Liberación* (Argentine Liberation Front), a splinter group of the Argentine Communist Party, abducted Paraguayan Consul Waldemar Sanchez in the town of Ituzaingo. His safety was promised in exchange for the release of two of the group's imprisoned members, and a deadline was set for 10:00 p.m. the following night.

The Argentine government refused these demands, apparently with the approval of Paraguayan President Stroessner (who had arrived in Argentina on March 25 to begin a scheduled vacation). The government insisted that one of the alleged prisoners was not even in custody, while the other was a criminal and could not be released. The kidnappers responded that if their terms were not met they would not only kill Sanchez, but also undertake the "execution" of "all managers of American businesses." The Argentine authorities stood firm, repeatedly broadcasting over the next two days that they would not be coerced into releasing prisoners. Faced with this intransigence, the kidnappers released Sanchez on March 28, explaining this action in "humanitarian" terms. The emerging tactic of political kidnapping was still gaining strength in Latin America, but Argentina and Guatemala were not yet fertile breeding grounds.

Had all the responses to the demands of terrorists been so uncooperative, it is impossible to guess what the ultimate outcome would have been. There were other failures as well, but there were enough successes along the way to encourage practitioners of this new revolutionary credo. In Brazil particularly, political kidnapping became a specialty of left-wing revolutionary organizations. An attempt was made on April 5 to abduct U.S. Consul General Curtis Cutter in Porto Alegre. Although the attempt was unsuccessful, Cutter was shot in the back and only narrowly escaped fatal injury.

Undaunted, terrorists struck again in Brazil on June 11, this time kidnapping West German Ambassador Ehrenfried von Hollenben. The terrorists, members of the Popular Revolutionary Vanguard and the National Liberation Action, demanded the release of forty prisoners in return for the Ambassador. The Brazilian government agreed, and von Hollenben was released on June 16. The lesson learned—at least as far as operations in Brazil were concerned—the same two groups attacked the Swiss Ambassador, Giovanni Enrico Bucher, on December 7 of the same year. This time, they demanded the release of seventy prisoners. Once again, the Brazilian government acceded to the kidnappers' demands, and the seventy were released on January 14, 1971, and given political asylum in Chile. Ambassador Bucher was released two days later, after nearly six weeks of captivity.

The implications of the Brazilian experience, if not that of Argentina, were soon felt in neighboring Uruguay. On July 31, 1970, the *Movimiento de Liberación Nacional* (MLN) undertook three simultaneous and separate kidnappings. (The MLN is better known as the *Tupamaros*; they were named after the leader of the last Inca revolt against the Spaniards during the late eighteenth century, Tupac Amaru.) One of the three captives taken that day was U.S. diplomat Michael Gordon Jones. He managed to leap from the kidnappers' vehicle and make it to safety, thereby escaping the fate which befell the others. The second victim was Brazilian Consul Aloysio Mores Dias Gomides. The third victim was U.S. Public Safety Adviser Daniel A. Mitrione. Both originally were offered in exchange for the release of approximately 150 imprisoned *Tupamaros*.

The Uruguayan government, however, had apparently been more impressed by the Argentine example than the Brazilian, and absolutely refused to negotiate. Instead, the police launched a massive manhunt throughout Montevideo and arrested twenty accused terrorists. The *Tupamaros* announced they would "execute" Mitrione if their demands were not met, and to strengthen their hand, they abducted another American, Claude Fly, on August 7. Fly, an agricultural adviser, was taken from his office in the Ministry of Agriculture on the outskirts of Montevideo.

In the face of continued governmental intransigence, the *Tupamaros* realized that they would have to either back down or carry out their threats. As a result, Mitrione's body was found in an abandoned car on August 10, his wrists bound with wire and several bullets in his back and neck. A *Tupamaro* leader later explained that they "had to" kill him in order to preserve the taking of hostages as a political tool. Thus was demonstrated one of the practical drawbacks of the new urban guerrilla theory: if the other side won't negotiate, a terrorist group may feel compelled to take an action which it neither intends nor wants.

The killing of Daniel Mitrione was a major setback for the Uruguayan left (and, as it turned out, for democracy in that country as a whole). The *Tupamaros* previously had enjoyed a rather romantic image—men whose ends were admirable even if their means were violent. The murder of an innocent man, who left behind a wife and nine children, shocked the public's sensibilities and vastly undercut the *Tupamaros'* popular support. With Fly and Dias Gomides still in the kidnappers' hands, the Uruguayan legislature voted to temporarily suspend many individual rights, and a massive search for Mitrione's murderers was begun. In September, the *Tupamaros* issued a statement rather lamely attempting to justify their actions, but it was clear that the tide of public opinion was turning against them.

Making the best of a bad job, the kidnappers dropped their demand for the release of prisoners (which by now clearly was not a possibility), and asked instead for a ransom of two hundred fifty thousand dollars for the safe return of the Brazilian Consul. The money was paid, and Dias Gomides finally was released on February 21, 1971. Claude Fly, meanwhile, suffered a heart attack during his captivity, and the *Tupamaros* (after abducting a cardiologist from a medical convention in Montevideo to examine him) released him on March 2. Another death at that point was the last thing they needed.

However, the *Tupamaros* still had one outstanding practical problem. During the negotiations over Fly and Dias Gomides, the group had attempted to gain greater leverage by kidnapping the British ambassador, Sir Geoffrey Jackson, on January 8, 1971. By March it was obvious that no prisoners were going to be released. The other hostages had all been either killed or freed, and the government was continuing its crackdown. The *Tupamaros* had little hope of receiving any concessions, yet they could neither kill Jackson nor return him without suffering a devastating loss of face.

The situation dragged on like this for more than eight months. Finally, in early September, 106 of the prisoners on the *Tupamaros'* list somehow escaped on their own. Three days later, undoubtedly relieved to have been shown a way out of the impasse, the kidnappers released Ambassador Jackson. They quickly explained that there was no longer any reason to hold their hostage, as their comrades were no longer in prison. The net result of all this was a public relations disaster for the *Tupamaros*. Unsuccessful as hostage-takers, they turned, in 1972, to a campaign of murderous assaults on police and military personnel. The government declared an ''internal state of war'' and virtually wiped out the entire *Tupamaro* network. Nonetheless, despite the magnitude of these setbacks, the tactics of Marighella had shown enough success in Latin America to have become an entrenched part of the political landscape by 1972.

## STRATEGIC AND TACTICAL MODIFICATIONS

The experience of Argentina suggests the flexibility of this new approach and the adaptability of its advocates. As we have seen, the Argentine government had shown itself unwilling to exchange prisoners for hostages, so the local terrorist groups changed both their targets and their demands. The forerunner of the new strategy was the kidnapping of an executive at the Swift Meat Packing plant in Rosario, Stanley Sylvester. He was also the British honorary consul in that city. Sylvester was taken outside his home by the *Ejército Revolucionario Popular* (ERP) on May 23, 1971. The kidnappers demanded not a prisoner exchange this time, but $62,500 in ''gifts'' of food and clothing to the poor. The Swift Company agreed, and Sylvester was released unharmed a week later.

The implications of this victory, when coupled with the defeat suffered in the earlier Sanchez case, was not lost on Argentina's terrorists. Large companies were easier to do business with than was the government, and money ransoms were easier to obtain that were political concessions. This doesn't really seem much different from the actions of any number of common criminals over the years, considerably pre-dating the revolutionary theories of Guevara and Marighella, but the rhetoric remained political. Money was to be taken in exchange for hostages in order to "finance the revolution" and help "alleviate the suffering of the masses."

On March 22, 1972, the ERP attempted to combine fundraising with political demands in the kidnapping of Oberdan Sallustro, a Fiat executive in Buenos Aires. The demands for Sallustro's release included a ransom of one million dollars (to be paid in the form of "gift packages" to poor school children around the country), the release of fifty imprisoned comrades, safe passage to Algeria, and the reinstatement of some 250 employees who had lost their jobs as the result of their participation in a labor dispute at the Fiat factory in Cordova. Fiat was willing to pay the ransom, but was prevented from doing so by the Argentine government, which decided on a much tougher line.

Argentine authorities warned the Fiat Company that they would be prosecuted if they didn't immediately break off ransom negotiations with the ERP. A manhunt was then mounted and, on April 10, police found the hideout where Sallustro was being held. A shootout took place, resulting in the arrest of four terrorists. Unfortunately, moments before the police could effect his rescue, Sallustro was murdered by his captors. This failure notwithstanding, the willingness of Fiat to come to terms and the near-payment of such a large ransom virtually ensured that Argentine terrorists would soon try again.

Almost a year to the day later, on April 2, 1973, a U.S. executive was kidnapped on the outskirts of Buenos Aires. Anthony R. DaCruz, a technical operations manager for the Eastman Kodak Company, was taken from his car at gunpoint. This time the kidnappers, who identified themselves as members of a guerrilla organization without volunteering which one, ignored the question of jailed revolutionary comrades altogether. They demanded instead a then-record $1.5 million ransom. Kodak quickly agreed, and DaCruz was released unharmed on April 7.

It didn't take long for the lesson to sink in. On May 22, 1973, an attempt was made to kidnap Luis V. Giovanelli, an executive with the Ford Motor Company in Buenos Aires. Plant security guards intervened, and Giovanelli and another employee were seriously wounded in the ensuing exchange of gunfire. In an effort to recoup something from the fiasco, the ERP released a communique through a local newspaper which announced that the victims were shot because they had resisted. They then demanded that Ford pay them a million dollars in protection money to avoid repetition of such an attempt. That money wasn't paid, but the terrorists were sure they were on to something anyway.

The same day the communique was released, May 23, the ERP kidnapped an Argentine executive, Aaron Bellinson, from his home in Buenos Aires and demanded a ransom of one million dollars "to help finance the revolutionary struggle." Bellinson's company paid what was believed to be the equivalent of a million dollars and he was released unharmed on June 3. Just three days later, the ERP struck again. This time, the victim was an executive of an Argentine affiliate of Britain's Acrow Steel Company, Charles Lockwood, and the ransom demanded was two million dollars. On July 30, Lockwood was released, after payment of a sum estimated to have been very close to two million dollars. The revolutionary terrorist business clearly was turning out to be very profitable, at least in Argentina.

Given the relative vulnerability of businessmen in Argentina, and the spiraling ransom demands that were being paid, it would have been surprising if the kidnappings had stopped. On June 18, 1973, while negotiations were still going on for the release of Charles Lockwood, the ERP abducted John R. Thompson, the American president of Firestone's Argentine operations. Although Firestone officials refused to comment, the media reported that the ransom demand this time was for three million dollars. Negotiations took place over the next two weeks or so, and an undisclosed figure was agreed upon. Whatever the final amount, it was reported that huge piles of five-hundred-peso notes were delivered in an armored car, which the terrorists thoughtfully provided. Thompson was released unhurt three days later, on July 6.

## WORLDWIDE APPLICATION

There are numerous other examples, but we think the point is made. The shift in focus from Guevara to Marighella meant a shift in political violence from the countryside to the cities, and the birth of what came to be known as modern terrorism. The taking of hostages proved successful for several groups in Latin America, and the idea spread from country to country. By the early 1970s there were hostage incidents occurring in other parts of the Western Hemisphere, even where there had been no previous tradition of rurally based guerrilla warfare.

For example, two incidents occurred in Canada in October 1970, just five days apart. On October 5, James R. Cross, the British Trade Commissioner in Quebec, was abducted from his home in Montreal by members of the *Front de Liberation du Quebec* (FLQ). In exchange for his safe return, the group demanded the release of thirteen of its members from prison, a ransom of $500,000 in gold, publication of an FLQ manifesto, reinstatement of jobs to recently dismissed postal workers, and the name of an informant against whom the group wanted revenge. Canadian authorities rejected these demands outright.

The group then kidnapped Pierre LaPorte, Minister of Labor in the Quebec government, and announced that it would kill both men unless its terms were met. The government again refused, but offered the terrorists safe conduct out of Canada if Cross and LaPorte were set free. On October 18, LaPorte's body was found in the trunk of a car in Montreal. The government responded with a massive manhunt, culminating in the arrest of more than four hundred FLQ members and sympathizers. Agreement was reached for the safe return of Cross, and on

December 3, 1970, he was released. In return, the kidnappers were flown to Cuba on a Canadian military aircraft. Two FLQ members ultimately were arrested and convicted of LaPorte's murder, but it was clear that the tactics of modern "urban guerrilla warfare" were not going to remain confined to the countries of Latin America.

Within just a few years, the fever spread and the stakes increased. On January 23, 1973, the U.S. ambassador to Haiti, Clinton Knox, was briefly taken hostage, along with his consul general, Ward Christensen. The kidnappers originally demanded the release of thirty prisoners and the payment of one million dollars. They settled for twelve prisoners (which were all of the thirty that Haitian authorities were holding) and seventy thousand dollars. The money, which was all that could be raised within the terrorists' four-hour deadline, was paid, and the twelve released prisoners were flown to Mexico. Knox and Christensen were then freed, on January 24. This was the second incident involving a U.S. ambassador, and the first to result in concessions.

Only a few weeks later, on March 1, 1973, the U.S. ambassador to the Sudan, Cleo A. Noel, Jr., was taken hostage by members of the Black September group. Also captured were his deputy chief of mission, G. Curtis Moore, and Belgian *Chargé d'Affaires* Guy Eid, and a number of other diplomats from various countries. The terrorists barricaded themselves in the Saudi Arabian Embassy (where the kidnapping took place during a diplomatic reception) and demanded the release of sixty Palestinian guerrillas plus freedom for Sirhan Sirhan, the assassin of Robert Kennedy. When these terms were refused, they murdered the three diplomats. After the terrorists surrendered to Sudanese authorities, they were granted safe passage out of the country.

It is not unreasonable to suppose that the successes of terrorist groups in Latin America had a significant influence on groups in Canada, Haiti, and the Sudan. Applying the new revolutionary theories of Carlos Marighella, they consistently had won freedom for many of their imprisoned comrades, to say nothing of the huge ransom payments some had achieved. Once the strategy had been shown to work, it was natural that it should be copied by other would-be revolutionaries. The taking of hostages for the accomplishment of political objectives, once limited mainly to soldiers and royal families, was extended to private citizens, and the modern era of terrorism was under way.

This is not the complete answer, however. The shift in focus among Latin American guerrillas, and their early successes with political kidnapping, provide part of the explanation of this phenomenon. But other, seemingly unrelated events were taking place in another part of the world at just about the same time. In 1967, the loss of a war in the Middle East—many miles distant from the cities of Latin America and light years away in political terms—would combine with the new guerrilla theories to visit a plague of terrorism and hostage-taking on the modern world.

# Chapter 3
# NO ONE A NEUTRAL

The history of the past forty years in the Middle East is sufficiently familiar for us not to recapitulate it in detail, and sufficiently controversial for us not to want to. The main elements of the problem are not in dispute, though, and will be well known to most readers. In 1947, the United Nations voted to partition Palestine (then under British mandate) into two states—one Arab and one Israeli. In 1948, the British withdrew and war immediately broke out between Israel and the surrounding Arab states. To escape the violence, many Palestinians whose homes were now in the new State of Israel left or were forced out (this point is in dispute). Whatever their reason for leaving, most Palestinians expected to return quickly on the heels of the Arab armies' victory.

Israel was not defeated, however, and the nations of the Arab world committed themselves to the ultimate destruction of this enemy—enveloping the Middle East in what became a permanent state of war. The Palestinians, many of them displaced into "temporary" refugee camps, continued to believe that they would be returned to their homes once the defeat of Israel had been accomplished. Twenty years passed in this manner and an entirely new—and more radical—generation of Palestinians grew up in what they considered exile.

This situation could continue only so long as the destruction of Israel was considered inevitable, and that could not go on forever. When war came in June 1967, the issue had to be resolved one way or the other. The Arab countries were decisively defeated in just six days, and Israel significantly increased its territory. Palestinian aspirations had been dealt a terrible blow. The fiction of the inevitability of an Arab military victory in the region had been discredited, and the Palestinians realized that they could no longer rely upon this option for their eventual return.

## THE NEXT STEPS

If direct military confrontation wasn't the answer, and a diplomatic solution was for the moment out of the question, then guerrilla warfare was the next logical option. Small Palestinian commando groups—known as *fedayeen*—had been formed and Palestinian strategists believed that they could operate effectively in this type of environment. *Fatah*, the largest of the Palestinian nationalist groups, issued pamphlets full of information on making bombs, organizing boycotts, sabotage, and so forth. Like Ché Guevara and Carlos Marighella before them, they specifically looked to the examples of Algeria and Vietnam.

In reality, however, very little happened. Although the occupied West Bank superficially resembled the classic guerrilla landscape, in which small groups of dedicated commandos could move among their own people, the simple truth is that it just did not work. The Israelis kept their interference in the daily lives of the people of the West Bank to a minimum in order not to antagonize them any more than necessary.[1] They concentrated their efforts instead on cracking down on the *fedayeen*, capturing about a thousand of them by the end of 1967. When the *fedayeen* punished residents who cooperated with the Israeli authorities more than they thought was necessary, they only succeeded in further eroding their own popular support. The residents distanced themselves from the guerrillas, and the Vietnam/Algeria analogy quietly disappeared.

Following the teachings of Carlos Marighella (consciously or not), the *fedayeen* then attempted a campaign of urban terrorism based in Gaza in 1968 and 1969. Unlike the pattern in Latin America, however, this effort did not meet with much

---

[1]Contrast this approach with what happened later. As the Israelis allowed (and encouraged) the development of new Israeli settlements on the West Bank, they were forced increasingly to become involved in daily affairs. When the *intifada* and its attendant violence broke out in the late 1980s, this involvement drastically increased. Yet, conditions continued out of control and no amount of military or police effort was able to resolve the rebellion.

success. The Israelis transferred the refugees in Gaza to new camps and the campaign died out. Thus, as the 1960s were drawing to a close, the Palestinian guerrilla groups were more frustrated than ever and they desperately cast about for some new strategy that might work.

## INTERNATIONALIZATION

The problem, in terms of the theory propounded among the terrorist groups of Latin America, was that the *fedayeen* did not have the active support of the masses living on the West Bank. What they did have, though, was the political and financial support of most of the Arab world, which included some of the wealthiest and most influential oil producers in the world. This combination of assets and liabilities led George Habash, leader of the Popular Front for the Liberation of Palestine (PFLP) and a student of the theories of Mao tse-Tung, to develop the doctrine of international terrorism.

Habash's idea essentially was to take the battle beyond the arena of Israel or the West Bank and to internationalize it. Operations were to be carried out against ''the forces of imperialism and reaction'' as part of a worldwide revolutionary struggle. Israel was still to be the main target, but the battleground was now the entire world—which in practice meant mainly Western Europe and the Middle East. This strategy was largely born of necessity, of course, but it also incorporated elements of the prevailing anti-imperialism of the day.

In many ways, Habash's internationalization of the guerrilla theories of Guevara and Marighella was analogous to Lenin's adaptation of Marxist theory to Tsarist Russia. Marx had taught that every society had perforce to develop from a feudal structure through a capitalist system before it could experience a socialist revolution. While he believed the socialist revolution to be inevitable (the byproduct of the very logic of capitalism), he thought that it could only happen in the most economically advanced capitalist bastions, such as England and

Germany. Lenin's application of this theory to a basically feudal country like Russia in 1917 required some serious ideological recalculation.

The Russian revolutionary solved the problem by arguing that capitalism was not a national phenomenon, but had to be seen as an international system. As such it would break, like a chain, at its weakest link. In Lenin's view, the weakest link was Russia. Therefore, the socialist revolution could begin in the Russian feudal economy because it really was the beginning of a revolution against international capitalism. Whether this was mere sophistry or a legitimate re-working of Marxist theory is beside the point—it became the basis for the Bolshevik approach to the governance of the Soviet Union.

Fifty years later, George Habash put forth a very similar argument for the theory of modern guerrilla warfare. Israel was the manifestation of the much larger problem of "imperialist oppression" and, as such, was the focal point of "world revolution." Just as capitalism could be attacked by a revolution in pre-capitalist Russia, so imperialism and colonialism could be attacked by a wave of terrorist assaults in Western Europe and the Middle East. Again, the sophistry or sincerity of the approach doesn't matter—it was the basis of a huge and violent upsurge of terrorism in the early 1970s.

Habash's theory had two important elements: (1) nearly anything or anyone could be a target, and (2) any revolutionary or terrorist group could be enlisted for action in anyone else's cause. No longer would the activities of the Eritrean Liberation Front, for example, be limited to targets in Eritrea, or the work of the *fedayeen* take place solely in Israel. Now, as *Time* magazine put it, "an action could be planned by Palestinian Arabs in Germany, executed in Israel by terrorists hired in Japan, with weapons acquired in Italy . . . purchased . . . with Libyan money." This was exactly what Habash had in mind.

The result was a coalition of terrorist organizations, each with their own particular grievance and target, but willing to come together for the furtherance of "world revolution." Besides the Palestinian guerrilla/terrorist groups—Habash's PFLP,

*Fatah's* Black September, and Ahmed Jibril's PFLP-General Command, to name a few—there was participation by the West German Baader-Meinhof gang (and its successor, the Red Army Faction [RAF]), the Irish Republican Army (IRA), the Eritrean Liberation Front, the Dutch "Red Help", the Liberation Front of Oman, the Japanese Red Army (JRA), several Turkish and Latin American groups, and various others. These groups helped each other out with money, training, weapons, and documents. Occasionally they participated in joint operations.

What distinguished the Palestinian approach, then, was its willingness to make common cause with other, seemingly unrelated terrorist groups and its intention to use the whole world as its battleground. But there was another distinction as well: the Palestinians' cause, though popular in the Arab world, was little known or understood anywhere else. To be effective, they had to concern themselves not so much with prisoner releases or monetary ransoms (although these were important also), but with the need to capture and influence world public opinion. The PFLP and its allies therefore cast about for the most spectacular, attention-grabbing acts they could think of, and the term "skyjacking" entered the language.

## THE WORLD AS A STAGE

Any terrorist operation is going to gain a certain amount of publicity. Arson, bombing, assassinations, and so forth will all make the news. But, as we have suggested, there is something especially dramatic inherent in a hostage situation. We learn of the other things only after they have happened, when they cannot be prevented. A hostage/barricade situation, on the other hand, can drag on for many days, and the outcome remains in doubt. There is suspense and danger, and the whole affair is an almost sure-fire attention-getter for as long as it lasts. When there are dozens of hostages, and when they are ordinary people engaged in a common experience like airline travel, the theatrical appeal is irresistible.

Airplane hijacking was, in fact, nothing new. The first one took place way back in February 1931, on a domestic flight in Peru. By the time the Palestinians hijacked their first plane, on July 22, 1968, there had already been some ninety-five skyjackings in various countries around the world. Nonetheless, the PFLP was the first group to tie it in with a "foreign policy goal"—the kidnapping of an entire plane and the people on board as part of a strategy of world revolution. The spectacular nature of the attack, its international quality (as opposed to the mainly local attacks of the Latin American kidnappers), and the stakes for which the Palestinians were playing guaranteed a large and spellbound audience for the duration of the incident.

The first aircraft to be hijacked by Palestinian terrorists was, appropriately and not surprisingly, a Boeing 707 commercial flight of El Al, the Israeli national carrier. The plane, with thirty-eight passengers and a crew of ten, was en route from Rome to Tel Aviv when it was taken over by three members of the PFLP. The pilot was wounded, and the hijackers took over the controls and flew the plane to Dar Al-Bayda Airport, in Algeria, where they demanded the release of a number of Arab prisoners from Israeli jails. All non-Israeli passengers were freed, and the remainder were held hostage while the PFLP's demands were negotiated. The incident lasted almost six weeks, with Israel eventually agreeing in the end to release sixteen prisoners in exchange for the hostages.

In the year that followed, there were approximately seventy more skyjackings, but none involved Palestinians and few caught the popular imagination (or, what largely is the same thing, the sustained attention of the media). While skyjackings in other parts of the world were reported, they lacked the peculiar excitement produced by the combination of Middle Eastern politics and high-altitude terror. To offer but one example, on August 29, 1969, two unrelated skyjackings took place in different parts of the world. A U.S.-flag National Airlines flight on its way from Miami to New Orleans was taken over by a man named Jorge Carballe Delgado, who was flown to Cuba and quickly (by the world at-large) forgotten.

On the other hand, that same day found TWA Flight 840, en route from Rome to Athens, hijacked to Damascus by two members of the PFLP. One of the terrorists was the infamous Leila Khaled, not only a Palestinian terrorist but a young, attractive woman. (If public attention is what a group is after, this is arguably a very effective way to get it.) Khaled and her partner, Salim Essawi, ordered all the passengers off the plane and blew up the cockpit. Once again, all the passengers were freed except for six Israelis, who were held pending the release of prisoners in Israeli jails. The situation dragged on until December 5—more than three months—when the hostages finally were returned in exchange for the release of seventy-one prisoners from Israeli jails.

This incident had everything: an exotic locale, an explosion, a beautiful and dedicated terrorist, six Israeli hostages in fear of their lives, and the romance of self-styled Palestinian freedom-fighters. If it really wasn't that way, that hardly mattered. It was the stuff of drama, it sold newspapers, and it achieved not only the release of some prisoners, but something much more valuable—international publicity. The ideas of George Habash, like those of Carlos Marighella in Latin America, were beginning to bear fruit.

To continue the success of the campaign the PFLP had begun, the Palestinian groups recognized that it was essential to maintain the fascination of the world-at-large. Every action had to capture the public's imagination in order for it to yield the maximum political value. Since the public had very little intrinsic interest in either the Palestinians or Middle East politics in general, it would be necessary to carefully vary the pattern and plan. Popular attention is easily diverted, and public interest wanes with repetition, so the Palestinian strategists took care that each incident would be spectacular and that there would be enough variety to hold the spectators' attention.

Toward that end, the next major incident took place on *terra firma*. On June 7, 1970, sixty hostages were seized by the PFLP at the Intercontinental and Philadelphia Hotels in Amman, Jordan. The captives were innocent civilians from a number of countries, including the U.S., Britain, Canada, and West Germany. After a few days, a cease-fire was arranged between the Jordanian Army and the Palestinians, and, on June 12, the hostages were released. The terrorists were granted safe passage to Beirut under the aegis of the International Committee of the Red Cross.

Six weeks later, on July 22, Palestinian terrorism was back in the airline flight paths. This time, the target was an Olympic Airways 727 on its way from Beirut to Athens. The Greek plane, with forty-seven passengers aboard, was hijacked by five members of the Palestinian Popular Struggle Front. The demand was for the release of seven *fedayeen* who were being held in Greek prisons. The International Red Cross once again acted as intermediary, and the Greek Government capitulated. The seven prisoners were released on August 12, and the Palestinian terrorists had another victory. The new tactic was working very well!

All this was in a sense mere prelude, however, to what came next. On September 6, the PFLP coordinated attacks on four separate international flights, intending to hijack them all to Dawson's Field (a former British Air Force desert landing strip) in Zerka, Jordan, and to negotiate from there. One of the attacks failed and another did not work out exactly as planned, but the PFLP still accomplished the hijacking of the other two aircraft to the Jordanian landing strip.

The successful skyjackings occurred aboard a TWA 707 en route from Frankfurt, West Germany to New York, and a Swissair DC-8 on its way from Zurich to New York. These hijackings were carried out by just four PFLP members, two on each plane. Both aircraft were diverted to Jordan and forced to land at Dawson's Field. There the two sets of crews and passengers began four hellish days as hostages under the broiling desert sun.

Meanwhile, another two members of the PFLP were supposed to hijack an El Al flight from Amsterdam, but they were not allowed to board the plane. Instead, they boarded—and hijacked—a Pan Am 747 en route to New York. Apparently, they were not entirely certain what to do once they had taken control of the plane, so they ordered the pilot to fly to Beirut for refueling. In Beirut, they were joined by seven more terrorists. The plane eventually was flown to Cairo, where it was blown up on September 7.

While all this was going on, yet another plane, an El Al flight from Tel Aviv to New York, was the target of a hijacking attempt by Leila Khaled and a Nicaraguan accomplice, Patricio Arguello. An armed guard shot and killed Arguello, however, and Khaled was overpowered and subdued by several passengers. The plane then flew to London, where the now famous female terrorist was imprisoned. This appearance of a Nicaraguan Sandinista in a Palestinian scenario seems to mark the first example of George Habash's doctrine of cooperation among revolutionary guerrilla and/or terrorist groups from entirely different parts of the world.[2]

With the two planeloads of hostages sitting in the Jordanian desert and Leila Khaled being held in a British jail, the PFLP struck again. On September 9, three Palestinian terrorists hijacked a British Overseas Aircraft Corporation VC-10 en route from Bombay to London, diverting it to join the other hostages at Dawson's Field. The PFLP then announced that it wanted the release of seven of its own comrades—three from West German jails, three from prison in Switzerland, and Leila Khaled in Britain. They also demanded the release of *fedayeen* from jail in Israel, and announced that all three planes would be blown up if these terms were not met.

The Israelis flatly refused, but the other three nations agreed, and the seven terrorists were freed. Most of the passengers were then released. About forty others were moved from Dawson's Field and imprisoned in a refugee camp, and on September 12, the three aircraft were destroyed by Palestinian

---

[2]This event has an honored place in the mythology of the Sandinista National Liberation Front (FSLN), which waged a long campaign culminating in its taking power in Nicaragua. The death of Patricio Arguello is cited as an example of international revolutionary solidarity.

explosives experts. The immediate result was a final rupture between Jordan's King Hussein and the Palestinian leadership. The next few weeks saw the Jordanian military attack the Palestinian camps and bases, freeing the remaining hostages and driving the Palestinian guerrillas out of Jordan once and for all. This action was to have a great many consequences for both the Middle East and the world-at-large—not the least of which was the formation of a new terrorist group, "Black September."

The next eighteen months were a relatively quiet time for the Palestinian promotion of "world revolution," but neither skyjacking nor terrorism abated in other parts of the world. There were eight more skyjackings in September 1970 alone, and close to thirty more by the end of the year. Another sixty occurred during 1971. There were also several major hostage-taking incidents on the ground—including the seizure of a consulate (in Sweden), the kidnapping of a British ambassador (Sir Geoffrey Jackson, in Uruguay), and the kidnap/murder of an Israeli diplomat (in Turkey). But none of these involved Palestinian groups, many of whom spent this period embroiled in a cycle of internecine warfare. By early 1972, George Habash was acutely aware that his group(s) needed some spectacular incident to recapture public attention.

The various Palestinian terrorist groups now fully understood the publicity value of their actions. More attention was being paid to the situation of the Palestinian refugees in the early 1970s than at any time since the end of the 1948 war. But the public was becoming jaded with repetition; skyjacking threatened to become *passé*. On February 22, 1972, five Palestinians hijacked a West German-flag Lufthansa 747 in flight from New Delhi to Athens. Diverting it to Aden, South Yemen, they released the passengers, then demanded a five million dollar ransom for the return of the sixteen crew members. The West German government paid the money, and the hijackers surrendered to South Yemeni authorities. They were released a few days later.

Then, on May 8, four members of Black September—two men and two women—hijacked a Belgian Sabena flight and diverted it to Lod Airport, outside of Tel Aviv. This time they demanded the release of 317 imprisoned *fedayeen*. Israeli security forces attacked the plane, killing the male hijackers and capturing the females (who were sentenced to life imprisonment). Neither event really fired the imagination of the world—which, after all, had been the central purpose of the operations—and the Sabena hijacking in fact had been a victory for the Israelis. The Palestinians desperately needed to capture the world's attention, and the result, a few weeks later, was the bloodiest and most terrible the world had seen up to that point.


## TARGETS OF OPPORTUNITY

While the terrorist groups of Latin America concentrated their operations on diplomats and business executives, people who were seen to be in some way allied with the "forces of repression" and were, therefore, "appropriate" targets for guerrilla or terrorist operations, Habash and his allies took a broader view. The PFLP leader was quoted as saying in 1970 that "he who takes no interest in politics gives his blessing to the prevailing order, that of the ruling classes and exploiting forces." This condemnation of apathy was, in Habash's "revolutionary" view, sufficient justification for the mass murder of random victims.

The massacre at Lod Airport on May 30, 1972, was not an incident involving hostages, nor was it intended to be. We mention it here because it contained all the elements of George Habash's theory of revolution: cooperation with other, seemingly uninvolved terrorist groups; an attack on Israel as the focus; and commission of a spectacular crime intended to shock the public's sensibilities (and sense of security) as profoundly as possible. The assault, code-named "Operation Patricio Arguello" in honor of the Nicaraguan hijacker killed during the Dawson's Field operation, took place in the arrival hall of Lod Airport.

For this attack, Habash had arranged the cooperation of the Japanese Red Army (*Rengo Sekugin*, [JRA]), a rather bizarre collection of self-styled socialist revolutionaries with anti-social tendencies. The two groups had met through the making of a film in 1970, and the three Japanese terrorists responsible for the Lod attack had trained with the PFLP in Lebanon. The JRA had very little in common with the aims of the PFLP, but they evidently accepted the "world revolution" rhetoric of George Habash. After the massacre, the leader of the JRA, Fusako Shigenobu, declared that they had participated in order to "consolidate the international revolutionary alliance against the imperialists of the world." The incident itself took less than a minute. Opening fire and hurling grenades at a crowded room of arriving airline passengers, the three terrorists killed twenty-four people and wounded seventy-eight others. Most of the dead were Catholic pilgrims to the Holy Land from Puerto Rico. The world was shocked and outraged, but Habash had accomplished what he set out to do: Palestinian demands were back in the headlines. And more was to come.

## MUNICH

With world attention once again focused on the cause, the leaders of the guerrilla and terrorist groups were anxious to establish the legitimacy of the Palestinian people as a "nation in exile." While the terrorist operations had been extremely successful in gaining publicity, the Palestinians also wanted to be taken seriously as a political entity. As it happened, the 1972 Summer Olympic Games were scheduled for Munich, West Germany. This was an opportunity for the Palestinians to represent themselves as members of the world community, on an equal footing with every other participating nation, before literally hundreds of millions of spectators worldwide.

Two letters were sent to the International Olympic Committee requesting that a team of athletes be allowed to participate in the 1972 Games under the name of Palestine. The letters, according to Abu Iyad of the Black September Organization, were never answered. So Black September decided that it would use the Olympics to accomplish its purposes in a different way. By taking members of the Israeli team hostage, Black September could avenge the Olympic Committee's slight, obtain fantastic publicity for their cause, and negotiate the release of a number of their imprisoned compatriots.

At four o'clock in the morning of September 5, 1972, eight members of Black September scaled the fence surrounding the Olympic Village and made their way to the apartments housing the Israeli athletes. Within an hour, they managed to locate their targets, kill two team members who resisted, and take nine others hostage. Two Israelis managed to escape, and the terrorists somehow failed to locate eight others.

Holding their nine hostages in the Olympic Village, the Black September *fedayeen* issued their demands—typewritten in English. They wanted the release of 234 prisoners from Israeli jails, plus freedom for several prisoners being held in West Germany. Among these were Andreas Baader and Ulrike Meinhof, the leaders of the Baader-Meinhof gang.[3] They further demanded that three planes be made available to take them to a safe destination once their other demands had been met. And all of this was to be accomplished by 9:00 a.m., or the hostages would be executed.

The situation was a nightmare, and it was being played out on live television before the largest audience imaginable. The West German authorities were anxious to bring it to an end, and offered to release Baader and Meinhof. The Israelis, however, took a hard-line position. In a brief telephone conversation with West German Chancellor Willy Brandt, Israel's Prime Minister Golda Meir made her country's position clear. There would be no deal, under any circumstances, with terrorists.

---

[3]Now known as the Red Army Faction, the Baader-Meinhof gang grew out of West Berlin's student protests during the late 1960s. Meinhof was the group's theoretician and set its anarchist, anti-American agenda. Both committed suicide following several unsuccessful attempts by the RAF and the PFLP to force their release.

The first deadline passed, and was extended throughout the day to nine o'clock that evening. Long hours of negotiation had reduced the terrorists' demands to one plane, to take them and their nine hostages to Cairo. Once there, they said, the Israeli government would have to release the people whose names were on their list or the athletes would be summarily executed. The West Germans had no intention of allowing the terrorists to leave the country, but they played along to buy time while a rescue effort was organized.

The terrorists and their hostages were transferred by Volkswagen bus to two helicopters, and at about 10:20 p.m. they left the Olympic Village for the Munich Airport. After a fifteen-minute flight, the helicopters landed at the airport, a short distance from the plane that was supposedly to take them to Cairo. Four of the hostages were in one helicopter, five in the other. Four of the Black September group got out to inspect the plane.

Having ruled out any sort of deal, the Israelis had agreed to a West German rescue effort, however risky. This was the best chance the Germans were likely to get and five German sharpshooters opened fire.[4] Despite the darkness and the distance, some of the *fedayeen* were hit. An exchange of gunfire ensued, with the nine Israeli hostages bound and blindfolded in the two helicopters.

The battle raged for about an hour and a quarter without a clear-cut result. At this point, the hostages were still alive, the terrorists were pinned down but unwilling to surrender, and the German marksmen were unable to take out the Palestinians without endangering the Israelis—as the Arab terrorists had taken refuge under the helicopters, badly limiting the Germans' options. Around midnight, the authorities tried to break the deadlock with an assault. The terrorists almost immediately

---

[4]Some have suggested that the terrorists would have been more vulnerable on their way to the helicopters at the Olympic Village, but this will never be known for sure.

killed their hostages by throwing a grenade into one helicopter and machine gunning the victims in the other.

The fight continued for a while longer, but it finally ended around 1:30 a.m. Five of the terrorists were killed and three were taken into custody. After some discussion, the Olympics continued. The Israeli government objected, but it was decided that to do otherwise would be a capitulation to terrorism. Chancellor Brandt had ordered that the flags of all competing nations be flown at half-mast, but ten Arab nations protested, and their flags were restored. Black September had achieved the release of no prisoners, and all eight of its operatives were killed or captured, yet, in one sense, they had won their biggest victory to date. The efficacy of George Habash's doctrine of aiming for maximum publicity through sensational international incidents had once again been demonstrated.

Black September remained active throughout the next year, although hardly anything it might have done at that point could have matched the impact of the Olympics massacre. In an ugly postscript to the Munich incident, on October 29, 1972, two members of the group hijacked a Lufthansa flight en route from Beirut to Munich and demanded the release of the three terrorists who had been captured on September 6. The West German government, which had been ready to make concessions at the time of the original incident, quickly agreed, and the three prisoners were freed. They were flown to Zagreb, Yugoslavia, where the hijacked plane picked them up. The plane then went to Libya, where the hostages were released.

Two months later, on December 28, four Black September members assaulted the Israeli embassy in Bangkok, Thailand, took twelve people hostage, and demanded that Israel release thirty-six of their comrades. Israel once again refused to make any sort of deal, but the Thai authorities—with the help of the Egyptian ambassador—got the Palestinians to agree to release the hostages in return for safe passage to Cairo. Shortly after that, in March 1973, came the kidnapping and murder of the U.S. ambassador, his deputy, and the Belgian *Chargé d'Affaires* in Khartoum, Sudan. By the middle of 1973, the Palestinian terrorist groups were meeting with less and less operational success, even as they were achieving their larger goal of publicizing and "legitimizing" the Palestinian cause.


## THE RESULT

An important element in the political success of the Palestinians was their ability to keep the terrorist groups distinctly separate in the public mind from the responsible political leadership. Terrorist and guerrilla groups splintered and operated under different names with different, but often overlapping, memberships. Among the most active were the Popular Front for the Liberation of Palestine-General Command (PFLP-GC), the Popular Front for the Liberation of Palestine-Special Command (PFLP-SC), the Popular Democratic Front for the Liberation of Palestine (PDFLP), Black September (the terrorist arm of *Fatah*), and Black June (the original name for Abu Nidal's group). But there were many others. A few, like the Eagles of the Palestinian Revolution (one of the names of *As Saiqa*, the Thunderbolt) were heard from once and then disappeared from the world scene. Many of these groups were rivals—or worse—and the effect was to divorce them from Yassir Arafat and the mainstream of the Palestine Liberation Organization, the umbrella political group seeking to speak for the Palestinian people.

The result was a growing public awareness of both the PLO and the Palestinian people. The publicity generated by the actions of the previous four years bore political fruit. By mid-1974, ninety states recognized the PLO as the legitimate representative of the Palestinian people. No fewer than sixty-three states petitioned to have the "Question of Palestine" placed on the agenda of the twenty-ninth session of the United Nations General Assembly. Seventy-two states proposed that the PLO be invited to speak at the General Assembly when the matter was debated. And on November 13, 1974, Yassir Arafat—over the protestations of the Israeli and other governments—appeared before that body.

We do not intend to take a position on the political issues of the Middle East. Rather, we merely wish to suggest that such an appearance would have been unthinkable only half a decade earlier. The doctrine of George Habash did not lead to the "world revolution" he envisioned, but his emphasis on the importance of publicity brought about a major change in the status of the PLO. His methods were morally reprehensible, and often unsuccessful in the short-term, but the long-term goal was well served. So much so that the 1970s and 1980s would see them copied and adapted by dozens of disparate groups (and a few individuals) from radically varying backgrounds all over the globe.

We began this discussion in an effort to address the question of why hostage-taking had become so much more frequent, and why the definition of a legitimate target had been so greatly broadened since the 1960s. We have suggested that the shift took place in part because of the urbanization of guerrilla revolutionary movements in Latin America (the writings of Carlos Marighella), and in part because of the doctrine of "world revolution" of the radical Palestinian groups (the teachings of George Habash). Both of these movements have a common thread, however: the quest for publicity. Beyond the operational goals of prisoner releases or huge money ransoms, the aim of both was always to capture—and hold hostage—the public consciousness.

This simply would not be possible without the media. It is the media which determines to a large extent what we will think about and how we will think about it. It is the media which conditions much of our response to political violence and to the demands of competing groups. And it is from the media that other would-be hostage-takers have taken their ideas, tactics, and role models. Sometimes unwittingly—and always unwillingly—the media has become a central part of modern terrorist strategies. The role of the media in this modern epidemic of hostage-taking is so important that it deserves examination in some detail.

# Chapter 4
# PRIME TIME

To understand the influence of the media in the modern world, we need only look at the political upheavals of the late 1980s. Signs waved by protesters in the Soviet Union read "Long Live Complete Freedom of Georgia;" in China, they proclaimed "We no longer trust dirty public servants;" in West Germany, the slogan was "New Lance is Nonsense." Graffiti scrawled on a wall in the West Bank announces that "the uprising will continue until we get our right." And all of these sentiments were written in English—**regardless of the native language of those writing them**. If it is safe to assume that Chinese students normally do not carry on their political discussions with each other in English, and that Soviet Georgians usually do not express their grievances to Moscow in that language, then there can only be one explanation: people seeking political change have become acutely aware of the need to get their message to the international media—especially television. The audience is a great deal larger than just those public officials being petitioned.

This point was grasped early by the terrorist groups of the late 1960s and 1970s. The organizations which heavily involved themselves in skyjacking and hostage-taking were anxious to make their existence known to the public, and to fix their purposes and demands firmly in the public mind. The Palestinians met with considerable success, as we have seen, and it was not long before other, more obscure groups realized the tremendous potential heavy media coverage of a hostage incident could have for them.

Few people had heard of the South Moluccans before December 1975, when they took forty-seven hostages at the Indonesian consulate in Amsterdam and hijacked a passenger train in another part of Holland. Few knew who the Croatians were until six of them hijacked a TWA 727 in September 1976, holding eighty-six passengers hostage until their propaganda leaflets were distributed and their communique was published in a major newspaper. The Croatian group was very straightforward about its intentions. Their demand was for publicity and, once they got it, they surrendered. Rarely has the influence of the media on hostage-taking been so nakedly demonstrated. As incidents of this type proliferated, and as more and more groups got into the act, many questions arose about the impact—and the responsibility—of the media in this whole area.

The word most often used to describe the relationship between terrorism and the media is symbiosis. The people who take hostages—or commit any other type of terrorist act, for that matter—are absolutely dependent on media coverage. Whatever the amounts of ransom collected, or comrades freed from prison, there would be far fewer incidents if the perpetrators couldn't count on massive, worldwide publicity. This is absolutely central to the planners of such operations.

The media, for its part, can hardly ignore the kinds of events which we have been describing. It would be an overstatement to say that the media needs terrorism to the same degree or in the same way that terrorists need the media, but the relationship is there. In the first place, news is news. Journalists and broadcasters have an obligation to report on the world as it is, rather than on the way they wish it to be. Some pretty bad lapses of judgment have been committed in the name of the public's "right to know," but there is no denying that this right exists or that the media has an obligation to satisfy it. Secondly, news reporting is a competitive business, and prolonged, dramatic hostage situations sell newspapers and draw viewers. It is unreasonable to think that journalists and broadcasters might willingly ignore a ready-made piece of political theater in the absence of an extremely compelling reason to do so.

The result is an inherent tension between the demands of a hostage situation and the needs of those reporting on it. The problem actually has two components. One is the larger question of the value of publicity to those who take hostages. Newsworthy incidents must be reported, yet, were it not for the expectation of that reportage, many incidents would never occur in the first place. The other component of the problem is practical rather than philosophical, but even more serious. Coverage of an incident while it is in progress can influence the outcome of the incident itself by impeding the efforts of law enforcement and government officials, and by creating problems which otherwise would not have existed. In a society that values free speech, the media must find a way to address both of these concerns while still doing its job and remaining in business.

## THE INFLUENCE OF PUBLICITY

Unlike the state-controlled media of a totalitarian society, a free press cannot tell us what to think. It does, however, tell us what to think about. The average member of the public pays little attention to most foreign policy issues. If they are not thrust before him in the form of newspaper headlines and news briefs on radio and television, he is not likely to seek them out—or even in some cases to know of their existence. It is only when he gets the message, through repeated media stories, that he should care about a specific issue, that he begins to see this as a matter about which he should have an opinion.

Research suggests that the media does not play a very important role in changing people's opinions. This largely is due to the phenomenon of selective perception—most readers, listeners, and viewers expose themselves as far as possible only to those sources which agree with the opinions they already hold. This enables them to screen out any dissonance and to be comfortable with a fairly consistent, if simple, view of the world. Media sources do, however, play a major role in the shaping of new opinions. In a situation about which little of the information previously existed, media coverage can have a very large effect on the formation of public opinion.

A good example of this process concerns the longstanding grievance of the Armenian community against Turkey. In the winter of 1915–16, about a million Armenians died as the result of a variety of factors. The Armenian community alleged that this was the result of a consciously adopted policy on the part of the Turkish government, and therefore constituted genocide. Turkish authorities responded that this was not the case, that the Armenian deaths were part of the larger tragedy of the First World War. For the next fifty years, the international Armenian community demanded an apology and redress, and the Turkish government steadfastly refused.

Whatever the truth of the case, the entire tragedy was so obscure outside of Turkey and of the international Armenian community that Adolph Hitler alluded to it when he advocated the destruction of the Jews in the early 1940s. Warned that his proposed "Final Solution"—the total annihilation of the Jewish people—would inflame world opinion, Hitler answered that no one remembered the Armenians. Despite the commitment of the Armenian people themselves, the average Westerner knew virtually nothing about the matter and showed little inclination to learn.

Then, in the middle 1970s, two new terrorist groups burst upon the world scene—the Armenian Secret Army for the Liberation of Armenia (ASALA) and the Justice Commandos for the Armenian Genocide (JCAG). They began a series of spectacular incidents, including assassinations of Turkish diplomats around the world, hostage-takings, bombings, and a slaughter at the Turkish airport of Esenboga. The media covered all of these in vivid detail, and suddenly Armenia and the question of the 1915–16 deaths became a contemporary issue. In reporting on what ASALA and JCAG were doing, the media also had to report on why they were doing it, and the Armenian question received a degree of publicity it had never been able to approach in the previous sixty years. Thus, the public was given something new to think about—Armenian claims against Turkey—which it would almost surely have never considered without the prodding of the newspapers and TV. Yet the media never would have paid that kind of attention to this issue in the first place had it not been for the spectacular nature of the terrorist attacks.

There are numerous similar examples of aggrieved groups seeking to exploit the publicity value of hostage incidents. The Palestinians and the Armenians are perhaps the most successful cases, but many other organizations have gained their fifteen minutes of fame via attacks on innocent victims. The coverage provided by the media—most particularly, television—provides even the most inarticulate and dysfunctional terrorist with a platform from which to expound his views. The continuing drama of a hostage situation, the visual image of a few armed individuals holding the lives of innocent people in their hands, guarantees that millions will hear what the hostage-takers have to say. In what other way could such individuals ever hope to command such an audience?

As well as providing a platform for terrorist groups, or perhaps because of that, extensive media coverage of hostage incidents has had a contagious effect. Since the early 1970s, innumerable groups (and not a few individuals) have sprung up, espousing a staggering variety of causes and imitating the actions of their better-known predecessors. The spotlight played on previously unknown causes has led any number of similarly aggrieved groups to copy their methods in the hope of achieving some of that same publicity for their own concerns. Hostages have been taken by Basque separatists, Italian radicals, Central American revolutionaries, Muslem heretics, Turkish dissidents, outraged students, people who were refused jobs, people who wanted to impress other people, a man who objected to a pizza chain's advertising, another who wanted the moon turned off, and still another who wanted all white people to get off the earth within seven days. It seems safe to suggest that many of these incidents would not have occurred had it not been for the massive publicity given to the earlier incidents of kidnapping, skyjacking, and hostage-taking.

But media attention has done more than just spread the idea of taking hostages. Many news reports have gone a long way toward popularizing the tactics and techniques required as well. Not only can disaffected groups and individuals come to see terrorism as an option; some people who ordinarily would have no idea how to carry out a kidnapping can learn about the subject from the media. Indeed, some reports have gone into such detail that they furnished a virtual blueprint for anyone else who might be interested in hijacking a plane or negotiating a ransom.

Some of this is inevitable. Dramatic stories are going to be reported, and such reportage is going to have to satisfy the reader's or viewer's curiosity. Good journalism requires the *how* as well as the *who, what, when, where,* and *why.* But some of it is irresponsible: the details of a hostage-taking may spice up a media report, but reporting them can cause a dangerous situation farther down the road. It is hard to draw a precise line between what merely is the unfortunate byproduct of good journalism and what is irresponsible and dangerous. But one thing is certain: the more details that make their way to the public on what works and what doesn't, and on who is vulnerable and who is not, the greater the difficulty in handling future hostage situations.

Finally, there is a less tangible, but nonetheless real, aspect of the media's influence. A good deal of research suggests that exposure to violence tends to lower the average person's inhibitions regarding violent acts (a fundamental criticism of movies and television, as well as other popular media). The argument goes that the constant portrayal of violence hardens the audience, inuring it to the very real and ugly consequences, and ultimately makes us all more tolerant of acts we normally would consider atrocious.

This is an even greater problem in the case of news reporting, because the violence is real, not simulated. What was once considered unthinkable—holding a planeload of hostages in a desert for days on end, for example—becomes merely a topic of current discussion. The media does not give the terrorists their moral approbation, of course. On the contrary, it often strongly condemns the action. But the very fact that such actions are being taken, that they are the subject of extensive media attention, that they have become the subject of editorial debate and cocktail party conversation, makes them less remote. A violent solution to one's problems may seem like a more plausible option when the media is awash with stories of others who are following such a path.

All of this is a structural problem in a free society, a problem of the philosophy of democracy. The media will report newsworthy events, and the taking of hostages is newsworthy. These reports, no matter how carefully they are prepared, will publicize terrorist platforms, spread information about techniques, and offer encouragement to others to consider terrorist activity as a means of advancing their cause. Some believe that this is the price of a free society and that a certain level of terrorism must therefore be tolerated; that censoring the media would be a cure worse than the disease. Others believe that the danger is great enough to justify curtailing some traditional press freedoms in order to protect lives and property. A democratic society must find a balance between these conflicting demands, and accept the reality that no solution is going to be either perfect or complete.

On a less theoretical level, however, there is a different sort of problem. Ideally, the media are to play the role of uninvolved bystander, reporting dispassionately on events as they unfold. But as a hostage situation drags on, and as journalists and cameramen jockey with each other for the most recent information or the best camera angle, they actually can become a part of the story themselves. When they do so, they may hinder the activities of law enforcement officers and political decision-makers, complicate negotiations, and endanger lives. This is a more practical side of the problem, and it should have more practical solutions.

## MEDIA ENTANGLEMENT

In reporting on the vast majority of news stories, representatives of the media have little difficulty dissociating themselves from the events they are covering. The peculiar nature of a hostage situation—whether terrorist or not—makes it unique. Given the prolonged nature of an incident, the need to keep tight control of the information flow, the volatile nature of the hostage-taker, possible political sensitivities, and the pressure on decision-makers, there are any number of ways for the reporters on the scene to thrust themselves unwelcomely into the process. Not all these considerations will be present in any given situation, but at least some of them will be there in all cases. Furthermore, for problems to occur, it is not necessary that journalists act with reckless disregard of the complexities of the situation. Some have done so, but most are highly responsible professionals who never deliberately endanger a hostage's life or impede the actions of the authorities. The problem is that responsible journalists, competing with each other for the best story and operating according to the ethics of their profession, can still inadvertently do a great deal of harm to the process of hostage negotiation and rescue.

This is particularly true in the case of the electronic media— radio and television. During a hostage situation, there are almost always certain pieces of information best kept by the authorities to themselves. Tactical matters (such as the need to stall for time, the decision whether to attempt an assault, the timing of such an assault, placement of personnel, and so forth) are things that obviously must be kept secret. Terrorists often have access to a radio or a television set, and they may almost instantly learn of anything that affects their situation. A report that snipers are being moved into position, for example, or that an assault seems imminent, can have disastrous consequences for the people being held hostage.

A well-known example of this sort of thing occurred during the October 13, 1977 hijacking of a Lufthansa plane en route from Majorca to Frankfurt. The plane was taken over by four terrorists and directed to fly, after a number of refueling stops, to Mogadishu, Somalia. During the three days or so that the plane was ordered from stop to stop, the pilot was able to pass information to the authorities without the hijackers being aware of it. Unfortunately, the media got wind of this and broadcast it on commercial radio. The terrorists, who presumably would otherwise have known nothing about it, heard the news on the radio and killed the pilot. Thus the media contributed directly to the murder of a hostage.

Several examples of this type of media interference came out of the Hanafi Muslim takeover of the B'nai B'rith building in Washington, D.C., in March 1977, though thankfully without similar consequences. The group was holding its hostages together on the building's eighth floor, but it had somehow missed a few people who had managed to barricade themselves in a room on the fifth floor. These people were trapped there (gunmen were patrolling the lower floors), but at least they were safe as long as their presence was unknown. A television reporter spotted a basket being lifted up to the room by rope, however, and immediately broadcast that fact. Fortunately, nothing happened, but it is easy to see how terrible the consequences might have been. Accepting the media's usual defense of the public's "right to know," it is very difficult to see why the public needed to know such a thing in the middle of a life-threatening crisis.

In another hostage incident, at the Washington, D.C. courthouse in 1974, the media managed to create problems for the authorities by broadcasting the fact that the police were able to watch the scene through a two-way mirror. Hearing the broadcast, the hostage-takers immediately taped newspaper over the glass. What should have been a relatively easy situation to handle, since the police were able to operate with complete knowledge of the hostages' location and their captors' movements, was vastly complicated by the thoughtlessness of a reporter.

Members of the media also have occasionally done a great deal of harm by contacting hostage-takers directly during an incident. Such interviews are no doubt great theater and generate considerable interest among the listening and viewing public, but they can do untold damage. At the most abstract level, giving the hostage-taker the chance to be heard directly feeds his desire for publicity, romanticizes the individual or group, and can seem to confer legitimacy on what is fundamentally a criminal and dangerous act. It is the kind of thing which can encourage others—especially if they are not too well balanced to begin with—to copy the actions of the person being interviewed. Beyond that, there also can be practical repercussions.

A reporter conducting an interview on the telephone with a man holding hostages is primarily interested in a good story. While few journalists purposely would do anything to exacerbate the situation, neither is anything they say likely to defuse it. The interviewee has the opportunity to put across his side of the story, to expound upon his sense of aggrievement and injustice. In a situation where people's lives depend upon keeping the hostage-taker calm, a telephone interview can have the opposite effect. Reporters normally are not trained in the intricacies of hostage negotiation, so the possibilities of saying the wrong thing at the wrong time are ever-present.

In one such incident, the subject actually had been talked into giving up and was preparing to release his hostages. At that point, a reporter called, looking for an interview. Naturally, the first question was about the reason why the hostages had been taken in the first place, and in answering, the hostage-taker got himself worked up all over again and decided not to come out after all. It was hours before he was finally brought around again.

Two more examples of a reporter saying exactly the wrong thing during a hostage/barricade incident came from the 1974 Hanafi Muslim takeover. One interviewer, in a live telephone conversation with the group's leader, actually asked whether he had set a deadline. One of the biggest headaches in hostage negotiation is the setting of deadlines, since they put tremendous pressure on the people trying to resolve the incident. They also tend to destabilize the hostage-takers as the selected hour approaches. When, for one reason or another, demands are made with no deadlines established, it is a good sign, and something for which to be grateful. Hostage-takers should never be reminded how to make things more difficult for everyone else.

The other example from the same situation illustrates how unstable a hostage-taker may be, and how easy it is for an untrained interloper to say the wrong thing. One reporter referred to the Hanafi leader, Hamaas Khaalis, as a Black Muslim. Since it was the Black Muslims who had killed his family, Khaalis flew into a rage at the "insult" and threatened to kill one of the hostages in retaliation. Peace was restored when the reporter issued an apology, but the results obviously could have been disastrous. Hostage negotiation is a very delicate art, and it should not be learned on the job—least of all by someone in the media whose first priority necessarily must be to get something newsworthy out of an interview.

The presence of the media also has a potentially damaging effect because it can place undue pressure on those responsible for making decisions. What to do about deadlines, how to respond to specific demands, whether to use force, and if so, when and how, are all critical decisions which have to be made—usually with little time to ponder and always with lives hanging in the balance. There is pressure aplenty and little leeway for mistakes. The media's mere presence, and all the public attention it brings, adds to this pressure and makes the job that much harder. When there are also constant demands for statements and progress reports (in time for reporters' deadlines), it is even worse. The danger exists that a decision will be taken prematurely, merely because patient waiting may look too much like doing nothing. The media, by its very nature, wants action, and decision-makers can sometimes find it difficult to resist that pressure.[1]

The media also can be a problem in dealing with the friends and relatives of hostages. While most journalists are decent men and women, some have been remarkably insensitive in their haste to get newsworthy interviews or scoops. The tears or rage of a concerned family member at the height of a hos-

---

[1] A fuller examination of this phenomenon and techniques which decision-makers can use to satisfy journalists while retaining control over events can be found in the chapter on "Crisis Communications" in *The Handbook for Effective Emergency and Crisis Management* (Mayer Nudell and Norman Antokol, Lexington Books, 1988). The book also contains considerable information on dealing with victims and their families and friends.

tage crisis undoubtedly makes for a dramatic thirty seconds on
television, but it hardly seems worth it in human terms. Friends
and relatives are upset enough at a time like that, without having cameras and microphones shoved at them from all direc-
tions, accompanied by the shouting of a lot of inane questions.


## CONCLUSION

Some of the specific abuses we have been describing can be
eliminated by a little more care on the part of the media. A
greater awareness of the intricacies of hostage negotiation, and
greater sensitivity to the problems that can arise, would go a
long way toward redressing the problem. The evidence suggests
that newspaper reporters and television people have become
more sensitive in recent years, as they have gained more experience with the multiplication of hostage incidents. It is still a
problem, and the potential for disaster is unfortunately always
present, but the question is not one that defies resolution.
Decision-makers must be responsive to the needs of the media,
and reporters have to understand the sensitivities of the situation. Fortunately, this seems to be the direction in which things
are moving.

The theoretical question, however, of the long-term influence
of the media on terrorism and hostage-taking is another matter.
Terrorists will continue to take hostages if they believe it will
help to publicize their demands. The copycat effect will continue to operate so long as the taking of hostages is given big
media play. And the publicity given to such incidents will continue to lower our threshold for political violence. The only apparent answer is some type of censorship—at least in terms of
delaying the publication and/or broadcast of certain types of information—and this opens up serious questions about the role
and rights of a free press in a democracy. It is not a problem
which can be easily solved; but it is one of which we must
remain constantly aware.

Certainly it is related to the question we posed as to the reason for the emergence of hostage-taking as a political phenomenon at the end of the 1960s. Along with the shift from rural to urban guerrilla warfare, the theories of Marighella and Habash, and the introduction of the concept of "world revolution," the influence of the media must be taken as a major contributor to the upsurge of political hostage-taking. What followed, as we shall see in the next chapter, was an epidemic of political violence which was global in scope and virtually unprecedented in human history.

# Chapter 5
# COMING TO GRIPS

Once the potential for hostage-taking had been established—vast sums of ransom money in Latin America, enormous publicity in the Middle East—the floodgates were open. After only a half-dozen such incidents in 1968–69, a new era began in 1970 with no fewer than forty-five kidnappings or hostage/barricade situations. (Skyjackings also greatly increased during this period, but many of these were the result of personal rather than political motivation. Nonetheless, they were a definite feature of the political landscape in the 1970s.) Except for 1972, between 1970 and 1978 there were at least twenty-five politically motivated hostage incidents each year, with a high of sixty-three in 1975.

In the early 1980s a shift occurred. Takeovers of embassies and similar facilities became less common and kidnappings also decreased considerably. In 1983 there were just nine incidents, the lowest count since 1969. The numbers started back up again in 1984, with the emergence of hostage-taking as a major operational tool of terrorist groups in Lebanon. While there have been many, many hostages taken since 1982, the bulk of the incidents have taken place in only a few countries—most notably Lebanon. In general, the incidents of the first dozen years or so, 1970–82, were both more numerous and more spectacular.

Terrorism in general was unquestionably a growth industry in the 1970s. Counting all types of terrorism—bombing, arson, assassination, and so forth, as well as those involving the taking of hostages— there were over 3300 incidents worldwide. Of these, approximately ten percent were either kidnappings (259) or hostage/barricade situations (73). The hostage/barricade situations typically received the most media coverage, but kidnappings were far more common for several reasons: they are somewhat easier to engineer; they are less risky for the terrorists; they have a higher probability of success; and they generally have been more profitable than embassy takeovers or similar operations. On the other hand, hostage/barricade situations usually are inherently more dramatic and, consequently, result in much higher levels of publicity. For the decade (if we count politically motivated hijackings) there were more than 425 hostage-taking incidents, involving close to eight hundred kidnapping victims and another two thousand or so in hostage/barricade situations. These were spread over more than forty countries, in every part of the world.

Geographically, the bulk of the kidnappings took place in Latin America. This is not surprising, since it was there that Carlos Marighella developed his theories and that urban guerrilla groups had their first successes. Of the 259 politically motivated kidnappings involving international terrorist groups in the 1970s, 140 (55 percent) took place in Latin America. In no other part of the world was the scope of this problem as great during this period. There were forty kidnappings (15.5 percent) in sub-Saharan Africa, thirty-four (13 percent) in the Middle East and North Africa, twenty-five (9.5 percent) in Western Europe, and fifteen (5.8 percent) in Asia.[1]

Hostage/barricade situations were more evenly divided. Of the total of seventy-three for the decade, nineteen (26 percent) took place in Latin America. This was the same number as occurred in the Middle East/North Africa and somewhat fewer than the twenty-four (33 percent) in Western Europe. Many of the incidents in Europe, however, involved groups from outside the region which usually were based somewhere in the Middle East. The remaining nine took place in North America (six) and Asia (three).

---

[1]The other five were accounted for by North America (3) and Oceania (2). Interestingly, there was not a single known kidnapping or hostage/barricade situation in either the Soviet Union or Eastern Europe during this period, suggesting that terrorism can be decreased greatly if one is only willing to do away with freedom of movement, civil protections under the law, and all the other trappings of a free society.

## PREFERRED TARGETS

It is also worth noting that throughout the 1970s, American citizens and property were the favored targets of terrorist attacks. Overall, Americans accounted for forty percent of the victims of terrorism from 1970 through 1979. The figure was slightly lower for kidnappings (37 percent) and significantly lower for hostage/barricade situations (22 percent). Apparently, U.S. facilities have been sufficiently well guarded in most countries to discourage takeovers. (Unfortunately, this was not equally true for bombing and arson attacks.) Kidnappers, however, often liked to target Americans: their numbers were plentiful abroad, the U.S. was an easy (if inaccurate) symbol of imperialism, and many represented enough money (as in the case of expatriate executives of U.S. companies) to hold out the promise of highly lucrative ransom payments.

Expressed as a percentage of the total, Americans were most vulnerable in the Middle East. Of the thirty-four kidnappings in that part of the world in the 1970s, no fewer than twenty (59 percent) involved U.S. citizens as victims. Similarly, of nineteen hostage/barricade incidents in the region, eight (42 percent) had Americans as their target. Contrast this with the nineteen hostage/barricade situations in Latin America during the decade, of which only three involved U.S. citizens or facilities. Latin American kidnappers, on the other hand, had no such qualms, as fifty-seven of their 140 victims (41 percent) were Americans.

In Western Europe, despite considerable terrorist activity, the number of American hostages was negligible. Of twenty-five kidnappings, only one had an American victim. And while Europe was the site of more hostage/barricade situations than any other geographic area (twenty-four), only one involved an American target. Few of the rest of the incidents worldwide involved U.S. citizens or property, although a surprising 35 percent of the kidnappings in sub-Saharan Africa had American victims (fourteen of forty). Few of the incidents in Asia were aimed at Americans.

In all, hostages were taken and concessions demanded of more than fifty countries and more than forty private companies and organizations. The most frequent victims, after Americans, were British, French, and West German. Diplomats and official government representatives accounted for about half of the hostages, and business executives comprised another twenty-five percent.

As the world struggled to come to grips with this frightening new phenomenon, it was clear that the initiative largely lay with the terrorists. Kidnappers escaped with their victims nearly eighty percent of the time, and collected ransoms in almost seventy percent of the cases in which that was one of their demands. In hostage/barricade situations, the perpetrators achieved at least some of their demands three-quarters of the time, and were granted safe passage in close to half of the incidents.

## A SELF-PERPETUATING CYCLE

This degree of success, plus all the attendant publicity, served to encourage a wide spectrum of terrorist (and more than a few criminal) groups. The result was a continuing increase in the number of incidents throughout the middle 1970s. The Latin American and Palestinian groups discussed earlier continued to successfully operate, and now they were joined by a number of others who could hardly help but be impressed by their achievements. Many governments and companies—too many, in our view—responded by making concessions, and the cycle of hostage-taking fed on itself.

1974 provided several good examples of this trend. In February, the Popular Front for the Liberation of Palestine (PFLP) took hostages in the Japanese embassy in Kuwait and demanded that four terrorists imprisoned in Singapore (two members of the PFLP and two from the Japanese Red Army) be released and flown to Kuwait. The governments of Japan and Singapore both accepted the demand. The prisoners were given their freedom in return for the safe release of the hostages, and the terrorists were given safe passage to South Yemen.

In April a group calling itself the Armed Forces of the Chadian Revolution attacked a research center in Chad and took several French and German citizens hostage. Their demands fluctuated during the course of the incident, but the West German government ultimately agreed to pay a ransom of more than a million dollars, and to broadcast the group's manifesto. The French government also agreed to pay a ransom of close to a million dollars. The concern of these governments for the lives of their citizens was admirable, but the results were encouraging to terrorists and revolutionaries everywhere. The incidence of hostage-taking predictably continued to increase.

The following September, for example, four members of the Japanese Red Army (JRA) seized the French Embassy in the Netherlands, taking the French ambassador and ten others hostage. They demanded a ransom of one million dollars, the release of one of their members being held in a French prison,[2] and safe passage to the Middle East. Negotiations were complex, because of the need to involve the governments of both France and the Netherlands, and they dragged on for several days. The major problem centered around the hard line taken by the French, versus the Dutch conviction that concessions would have to be made.

Although the French objected to the prisoner's release, they eventually agreed to fly him to Amsterdam, where he remained for a time under the guard of French security officers. The ransom was negotiated down from one million to three hundred thousand dollars. The question of safe passage was a major sticking point, because the French government was not willing to endanger a French flight crew (who could themselves easily become hostages). The point was resolved with the provision of a volunteer Dutch crew. After more than four days of negotiations, two hostages were released, three were left behind at the

---

[2] Yutaka Furuya, who was in a Paris jail for possession of false papers and counterfeit money.

embassy, and the other six (which included the French ambassador) were taken to the plane.

These last hostages were released just before take-off, five in exchange for the JRA prisoner and the sixth (the ambassador) a few minutes later. The plane bearing the terrorists, their comrade Furuya, and the Dutch crew departed for the Middle East, ultimately landing in Syria. The Dutch Prime Minister, pleased that no one had been killed or injured, expressed his satisfaction. Undoubtedly, the JRA—which had freed their comrade from another country's prison, received a large sum of money, and escaped scot-free—was satisfied too.

Less than two weeks later, in an unrelated incident, members of the January 12 Liberation Movement of the Dominican Republic seized the Venezuelan embassy in Santo Domingo. Although their demands for a one million dollar ransom and the release of thirty-eight prisoners were not met, they still received safe passage to Panama in exchange for the freedom of their hostages. Even in an incident such as this, where the terrorists essentially were thwarted, they still held eight people hostage for almost two weeks (September 27-October 9) and walked away scot-free.

## THE TREND PEAKS

The trend continued, and in fact reached its apogee, in 1975. Interestingly, while 1975 was the peak year for kidnapping and hostage/barricade situations, this was not the case for other types of terrorism. Incendiary bombing, for example, of which there had been fifty-three incidents in 1970 (and which would climb to ninety-one in 1976), occurred only twenty times in 1975. Likewise, the year saw 169 incidents of explosive bombing, down by seventy from 1974. Letter bombs, which had been a major tool of terrorists in the early 1970s (ninety-two in 1972 alone), were only sent three times in all of 1975.

Terrorist tactics have always tended to be somewhat cyclical, so it is dangerous to make generalizations. Nonetheless, it is clear that the middle years of the 1970s were marked by a sharp increase in hostage-taking and a corresponding drop in some other forms of terrorist activity. It seems reasonable to suggest that this was due at least in part to the successes of the early part of the decade. In a huge percentage of cases, large ransoms were being paid, demands were being met, and terrorists were escaping unpunished. Political hostage-taking was having an effect, and both governments and private organizations seemed unsure how to deal with it. Under such circumstances, it is hardly surprising that widely disparate groups appeared to be reaching the same conclusion.

The trend largely continued through 1975. In May, four students were kidnapped from a research center in Tanzania by members of the Zaire People's Revolutionary Party. The group's demands included a ransom of half a million dollars, arms, ammunition, and the release of two of their members imprisoned in Tanzania. The Tanzanian government refused the demands and the situation dragged on for over a month. Three hostages were finally released in late June and the last one was held until almost the end of July, following payment of a reduced ransom by their families. Even though most of their demands were not met, this result demonstrated yet again that hostage-taking was a profitable, low-risk endeavor.

Not long after, on August 4, the JRA struck again, this time in Kuala Lumpur. They took over the consular sections of the embassies of both the United States and Sweden—fifty-two hostages in all—and demanded the release of five of their comrades imprisoned in Japan. The Japanese government acquiesced, and the five were released and flown to Libya. The JRA members holding the hostages in Malaysia were also flown to Libya, giving the group another clear victory.

A few weeks later, on September 15, the Black September Organization announced its opposition to the agreement concluded between Israel and Egypt over the Sinai. They did this in characteristic fashion, by seizing the Egyptian Embassy in Madrid and threatening to kill the ambassador if the Egyptian government refused to repudiate the agreement. This was a rather silly demand to make, when one thinks about it, since there was no way to ensure that such a repudiation would remain in effect once the incident was over. This point seems to have eluded Black September, however, and so the Egyptian ambassador, joined by the ambassadors of Algeria, Iraq, Jordan, and Kuwait—who were all there assisting with the negotiations—duly signed a piece of paper "denouncing" the agreement. The terrorists were then flown to Algeria, where they released the hostages, and the Sinai "repudiation" promptly was itself rejected. Still, terrorists had once again threatened the lives of innocent people and walked away unpunished.

If 1975 was the apogee of the hostage-taking epidemic of the 1970s, that year's own peak came in December. On the twenty-first of that month, six terrorists, from four different countries, attacked an OPEC conference in Vienna. Among the six were two Palestinians, two West Germans, a Lebanese, and Ilich Ramirez Sanchez—the internationally known and deservedly infamous "Carlos the Jackal" of Venezuela. The gang took eighty-one hostages (including eleven OPEC oil ministers), killing two Arab staff members and an Austrian policeman in the process. Seven others were wounded.

The group then issued a communique demanding that OPEC refuse to sell any oil whatever to Western countries, and that the OPEC member countries declare immediate war against Israel. This document also condemned Egyptian President Anwar Sadat as a traitor for signing the Sinai agreement with Israel and denounced the Shah of Iran as an imperialist tool. As in the case of the Madrid incident in September, these were the kinds of demands which would be impossible to enforce once the incident was over and the hostages freed. Yet the lives of eighty-one people were in danger, and some sort of solution was required.

This was not the kind of incident that could be allowed to drag on, considering the presence of the eleven oil ministers. By the next day, Austrian Chancellor Kreisky and Algerian Foreign Minister Bouteflika had worked out an arrangement whereby the forty-one Austrian hostages would be released immediately, while the rest would "voluntarily" agree to accompany their captors to Algeria. An Austrian airliner flew the terrorists and their remaining hostages to Algeria and Libya under safe conduct. During the Algiers stopover, the hostages were released and the six terrorists surrendered to Algerian authorities. Despite their having killed three people, wounded seven others, and endangered the lives of dozens more, they were held only briefly in Algeria, then restored to freedom.

However, this was the high-water mark. The number of hostage-taking incidents thereafter declined fairly sharply, especially in the case of barricade situations. Although the numbers continued to fluctuate, the levels of the 1973–75 period were not reached again. It is difficult to pinpoint precisely why this occurred, but it seems likely that it was in large part due to a change in the nature of the response that hostage situations were starting to elicit.

## EFFECTIVE RESPONSE

When political kidnappings, embassy takeovers, and airplane seizures first began in large numbers, everyone naturally was caught unprepared. There was little in the way of a methodology of hostage negotiation, and little experience in the field of hostage rescue missions. The psychology of the terrorist and the nature of hostage situations were both largely *terra incognita.*

Governments therefore responded by treating terrorism essentially as an aberration, and taking the path that would be least likely to cost lives. On the assumption that the lives of innocent hostages were worth more than money or political concessions, governments and companies tended to look at each incident as separate from all the others. That is to say, if lives could be saved by making concessions in a specific incident, perhaps that would be the end of it. This turned out to have been wishful thinking, but it is understandable in the context of those times.

What happened, unfortunately, was that concessions encouraged more acts of terrorism and larger demands. Hostage-taking quickly came to be seen as a successful tactic: an effective way to publicize an otherwise unpopular or obscure cause, a means of gaining freedom for imprisoned comrades, or a road to quick riches. The willingness of governments and companies to meet these demands was taken as an admission of weakness. While each did what it concluded was necessary to save lives, and hoped to avoid future incidents, such decisions ensured that future incidents would occur in ever-growing numbers.

By the mid-1970s, it was becoming obvious that a tougher stand was going to be necessary. Concessions encouraged more terrorism, and the rare refusal to negotiate often led to the murder of hostages. Governments began to think in terms of rescuing hostages, and capabilities began to be built for this purpose. This necessarily meant a harder line on dealing with terrorists, and this contributed to a drop in the incidence of hostage-taking. Some of the operations discussed below were extremely successful, and have become justly famous. Others were less so, and innocent people died. Ultimately, this harder line contributed to the decrease, and the saving of many lives. But the decision in each incident was difficult and the results were sometimes painful.

## RESCUE OPERATIONS

### MA'ALOT

One of the earliest examples of this new trend took place in May 1974, and it provides a clear case of both the refusal to make concessions and the terrible consequences that can result. On May 14, three members of the Popular Democratic Front for the Liberation of Palestine (PDFLP) slipped into Israel through an unguarded part of the country's northern border and made their way to the town of Ma'alot. They forced their way into an apartment building, killing two and wounding two. They then managed to take control of a nearby school, rounded up more than ninety children, and presented their demands to Israeli authorities. These included the release of twenty terrorists from Israeli prisons and safe passage to Syria.

The three terrorists imposed a deadline of 6:00 p.m. that evening, and demanded that the French and Romanian ambassadors act as intermediaries. Their plan was for the Israelis to fly their twenty comrades to Syria first, whereupon a pre-arranged code word would be passed to the terrorists at the Ma'alot school. They promised to release the school children once they knew their friends were safe. This may indeed have been their plan, but the Israelis didn't believe them. Nor did Israeli authorities have any wish to soften their posture toward terrorists and thereby demonstrate the success of a hostage/barricade operation on their own soil.

The problem was, of course, that this wasn't exactly the usual sort of hostage/barricade situation. The hostages were ninety or so terrified school children in the hands of men who already had demonstrated their willingness to shed innocent blood. The horror of the situation was made worse by the group's portable loudspeaker, which the terrorists made sure carried the children's pleading to everyone within earshot. So desperate was the case that the Israeli government, meeting in emergency session, reversed its standing position on concessions and accepted the PDFLP's demands.

Nonetheless, the twenty prisoners were not released, and the afternoon wore on with the terrorists vainly waiting for a code word that had never been sent. The Israelis requested an extension of the deadline, as they no longer had any hope of meeting the stated terms by 6:00 p.m., but the terrorists refused. This left no option but a rescue attempt, which had been the Army's recommendation all along. The danger to the children was frightful, but the alternative was worse: the Israelis believed that the PDFLP would carry out its threat.

Half an hour before the deadline was to elapse, a military assault was launched on the school building in Ma'alot. The odds were not good, of course, and neither were the results. One of the terrorists was shot while trying to detonate an explosive, but the other two opened fire on the children with automatic weapons, killing sixteen and wounding sixty-five before they were themselves killed. Five of the wounded children died later, bringing the total to twenty-one dead. This result certainly was better than what might have come from waiting for the deadline to expire without either a concession or an assault, and it marked a break from the pattern of concessions in other incidents, but only at a fearful cost.

It is not entirely clear just why the Israeli government, having once decided to accept the terrorists' demands, did not carry through and actually release the prisoners. It may be that they really did not accept the word of the PDFLP that the hostages would be released. Or it may be simply that they could not bring themselves to take the steps that would mean capitulating to terrorism, even if that was what they felt the situation required. Certainly there is no point in criticizing the Israeli government for any choice it might have made under such circumstances. Whatever the reason, and whatever the outcome, the Ma'alot incident marked a clear-cut, highly publicized incident in which concessions were rejected and terrorists died. Despite the tragedy at Ma'alot, many began to think that the error might not be in the concept of rescue operations, but only in the execution. Although still a couple of years away, a new era of response to hostage situations was about to begin.

For the next couple of years, however, hostage rescue operations were not common and the incidence of hostage-taking, as we have seen, continued to increase. There were a few notable failures for terrorists during this period—as in April 1975, when the Red Army Faction (RAF) seized twelve hostages at the West German Embassy in Stockholm. Their demands, for a twenty thousand dollar ransom and the release of twenty-six terrorists from West German jails, were refused, and one hostage was murdered. Nonetheless, the Swedish police were able to capture the RAF members as they fled the embassy following an explosion in the building. Two terrorists were killed in

the explosion and the surviving RAF members were extradited
to West Germany and sentenced to life imprisonment.

This outcome was the exception rather than the rule in 1975,
however, and it was not until the following year that hostage
rescue operations began to come into their own. The most famous episode, one which even became the subject of a movie,
was the Israeli raid at Entebbe on July 4, 1976. Before that,
though, there was an often overlooked but highly successful
operation in Djibouti. While it didn't get the publicity the Entebbe raid received, it was a very skillful and dramatic rescue
which set the stage for much that was to come later.

DJIBOUTI

The Djibouti incident began early on February 3, 1976,
when four members of the Front for the Liberation of the Coast
of Somalia (FLCS) hijacked a school bus carrying thirty children of French Air Force personnel. The bus was moved close
to the Somalian border, where two other terrorists joined the
original hijackers. The usual demands were made for the release of prisoners, and the FLCS made it clear that it would
kill the children if its demands were not met.

Ten members of the *Groupement D'Intervention de la Gen-
darmerie National* (GIGN), France's elite paramilitary unit,
were flown in to see what could be done. Although the bus was
parked in an open, outlying area, snipers were positioned in
what cover there was, about two hundred yards or so away.
Nothing could be done until all of the terrorists were simultaneously covered by the snipers, as anything less would lead to
the immediate murder of the children. Four of the six were always on the bus.

After a dramatic ten-hour wait, the opportunity at last presented itself, and the four FLCS members on the bus were simultaneously shot and killed. Even so, a gun battle erupted
between the other two terrorists and the GIGN unit. One child
was killed during this shootout, but the possibilities for the use

of a highly trained hostage rescue team had been effectively demonstrated. This lesson was reinforced a few months later at Entebbe.

## ENTEBBE

It began on June 27, 1976, when a Palestinian commando unit, in conjunction with members of the West German Baader-Meinhof group (later to become the Red Army Faction), hijacked an Air France plane and its 254 passengers and crew to Entebbe Airport outside Uganda's capital city, Kampala. The demand this time was for the release of fifty-three terrorists from prisons in several different countries. The Government of Israel, by now implacably opposed to making concessions, immediately began planning for some sort of rescue attempt. The magnitude of the problem, which can hardly be overstated, was reduced somewhat when the terrorists decided to keep only the Jewish hostages and to let the others go. This not only reduced the number of hostages; it also provided Israeli planners with valuable information which would prove vital to the success of the rescue mission.

Despite that small advantage, the Israelis nevertheless faced a truly daunting task: the rescue of a group of hostages from overtly hostile territory (Idi Amin's Uganda) thousands of miles away. More than one hundred Israeli troops had to be air-lifted into the area, land secretly, take out heavily armed terrorists supported by Ugandan troops, collect the hostages, and get away—all in as little time as possible, lest Amin's army have the opportunity to bring in reinforcements.

Israeli planners did have several things in their favor, however. One important advantage was that Entebbe Airport had been designed and built by an Israeli firm. They thus had access to blueprints and were able to make their plans with the aid of an accurate scale model. Added to the intelligence developed as a result of the release of the non-Jewish hostages, this simplified their task immeasurably. The hostility of neighboring Kenya to Idi Amin's government also contributed to the mission's success. Not only were the Kenyans not going to warn Uganda of the Israelis' arrival, but they also were willing to allow the Israeli aircraft to refuel at Nairobi Airport.[3]

Probably the most important thing the Israelis had going for them, however, was the element of surprise. Nothing of this scope had ever been attempted before, and it is unlikely that either the terrorists or the Ugandans gave much thought to this possibility in July 1976. As impressive as this rescue mission was, it is unlikely that it could have succeeded if the hostage-takers had seriously prepared for such an assault. In rescuing the hostages at Entebbe, Israel showed the world that it could be done. Unfortunately, this was also demonstrated to future terrorists.

The assault itself was a model of efficiency. Three planes flew into Entebbe, informing the tower that they were carrying released Palestinians. After landing, one plane taxied close to the terminal (where the hostages were being held), and let out a black Mercedes which had been customized to resemble Idi Amin's personal limousine. As the army guards, who lived in mortal terror of the Ugandan dictator, snapped to attention, they were machine-gunned by Israeli forces dressed as Palestinians.

The Israelis then rushed the terminal, firing on the terrorists while shouting for the hostages to stay down. (In the confusion, three hostages stood up and were killed.) Simultaneously, a second Israeli team attacked the control tower, while a third set up a roadblock in order to keep the alarm from being spread or reinforcements from arriving. All the terrorists were killed and the hostages were hustled onto one of the aircraft. A number of Ugandan planes were destroyed to eliminate the possibility of pursuit, and one of the greatest hostage rescue missions

---

[3]In fact, the Israeli plan provided for the seizure of Nairobi's airport had the Kenyans been unwilling to cooperate.

of all time was over. The entire operation took just fifty-three minutes.[4]

Hostage-taking didn't disappear as a political tactic after this, of course, but the Entebbe raid does seem to have marked something of a turning point. Hostage situations sharply declined after the Entebbe rescue, to the relatively low number of thirty-six in 1976 (from a high of sixty-three in 1975). Equally important, the message was received by other countries who had been suffering from terrorist attacks that rescue missions were a possibility which might offer a superior option to making concessions.

## HOLLAND'S TURN

Nowhere was this more dramatically demonstrated than in the attack by South Moluccan terrorists in the Netherlands early the following year. This group had been using terrorist tactics for years in an effort to gain independence for the South Moluccan Islands (formerly a Dutch colony and now part of Indonesia), and apparently was convinced that the Dutch would not resort to force no matter what the provocation. So, on May 23, 1977, they hijacked a passenger train with fifty-one people on board between Groningen and Assen, and simultaneously took 110 hostages at a nearby school. The Dutch responded by opening negotiations, but after almost three weeks no progress had been made and the situation was deteriorating.

The problem was particularly tricky, partly because a rescue at one location could trigger a massacre at the other, and partly because of the nature of a hijacked train. Unlike an airplane, a train has its passengers spread out over a considerable distance—essentially sealed off from each other into smaller-

---

[4]One Israeli soldier, the mission's commander, was killed and one elderly hostage, a woman who had been taken to a hospital shortly prior to the Israelis' arrival, was later murdered by the Ugandans.

compartments (cars). While the Dutch at least had the advantage of dealing with the situation on their own territory, they faced the enormously difficult task of coordinating two separate rescue efforts and getting to the terrorists before any harm could be done to the hostages in either locale. In the assault on the train, they would have to eliminate the terrorists over the entire length of the train without killing or causing the deaths of the hostages.

The situation was made a little easier when most of the children at the captured school developed gastro-enteritis and were released. There were still four teachers being held there, however, so the fundamental problems remained. The Royal Dutch Marines, aided by special heat-detection devices (to help pinpoint the terrorists' locations) and six fighter aircraft, were up to the task.

Before sunrise on the morning of June 11, the six planes repeatedly buzzed the train, distracting the terrorists and increasing the likelihood that the hostages would stay down. Sharpshooters then began firing at the parts of the train where they believed the terrorists to be, immediately followed by a ground assault. As at Entebbe, the rescuers rushed onto the train simultaneously firing and shouting for the hostages to remain on the floor. (And, as at Entebbe, two hostages stood up, and lost their lives.) At the same time, another assault team crashed through the wall of the school, catching the South Moluccans by surprise and rescuing the four remaining hostages. Once again, notice had been served, this time from an unexpected quarter, that future hostage-takers might have to face a different kind of response from that which they had come to expect.

## MOGADISHU

Another indication of this trend came a few months later, when a Lufthansa flight was hijacked while en route from Palma de Mallorca to Frankfurt. The aircraft, with eighty-six passengers and a crew of five, was seized by four terrorists from the "Martyr Halimeh Commando" on October 13, 1977. After being diverted through a series of refueling stops, the plane finally was brought to rest four days later in Mogadishu, Somalia. The hijackers then announced their demands, which included the release of eleven prisoners in West Germany and two Palestinians in Turkey, plus a ransom of fifteen million dollars and an extra one hundred thousand Deutschmarks for each of the released German terrorists. There was no chance that such a set of demands would be met, so a rescue mission was mounted.

Approximately thirty members of the West German counter-terrorist unit *Grenzschutzgruppe 9* (GSG-9) were flown to Mogadishu, where they found a highly cooperative attitude on the part of the Somalian government. This gave them a considerable advantage over what the Israelis had encountered in Uganda—although they still faced a formidable task. It also, parenthetically, gave them a considerable advantage over what the French had faced in the Djibouti incident, when Somalian forces had actively supported the terrorists. Rescue forces had another advantage for a while, in that the Lufthansa pilot, Jurgen Schumann, was able to pass important information from inside the plane. This advantage disappeared when the terrorists learned of his efforts and killed him. (As mentioned earlier, they would not have known of it except for a press report—an example of how media irresponsibility can lead to the loss of lives in a hostage situation.)

The rescue itself was one of the smoothest on record. Negotiators were able to buy a little time by convincing the terrorists that their imprisoned comrades had been freed and were on their way to Mogadishu. This provided the necessary breathing space for the sniper and assault teams to move into position. Shortly before midnight on October 17, with everyone in position, the Somalians ignited a fire about a hundred yards in front of the aircraft. As hoped, the terrorists moved up to the front of the plane to see what was going on, and the assault teams launched their attack from the rear. Going in with stun grenades and handguns, the GSG-9 teams took out the hijackers and freed the hostages without the loss of a single life. (Three of the hostages were wounded, but none killed—making the Mogadishu rescue in that sense even more successful than those of Entebbe, Djibouti, or the Netherlands.)

## IRAN

Although the trend of the late 1970s was in the right direction, with governments starting to stand up to the demands of terrorists and rescue missions showing greater success, no discussion of the period would be complete without mentioning the events that followed the fall of the Shah in Iran. The Shah, who reportedly had taken a staggering amount of personal wealth out of the country, was looking for some place to resettle while the new regime in Tehran was doing everything it could to force him back home to stand trial. On May 2, 1979, Iranian Foreign Minister Ibrahim Yazdi announced that his government had requested that the United States freeze the assets of the Pahlavi Foundation and agree not to allow the Shah to enter the U.S. Despite indications from the Carter Administration that the Shah would not be welcome in the U.S.,[5] there were influential voices (Henry Kissinger and David Rockefeller among them) who felt the nation owed the fallen leader a debt of gratitude for his friendship of the past thirty-seven years.

Despite the implacable hostility of the Khomeini Government and the deep Iranian suspicion of American intentions, the Shah ultimately was allowed to enter the United States for emergency medical treatment. On October 22, he arrived in New York from Mexico City to begin treatment at the Cornell Medical Center. The Department of State announced that the decision had been made on humanitarian grounds.

The Iranian government officially protested this decision on October 26, October 30, October 31, and November 1, and

---

[5]In fact, the Shah had not even applied for a U.S. visa.

raised it again with National Security Adviser Zbigniew Brzez-
inski at a meeting in Algiers on November 1. Iranian officials
refused to accept the "humanitarian" justification but stated that
the U.S. Embassy in Tehran (which had already been temporarily overrun on the previous February 14 and was thought to
be in some danger again) would be protected. Three days later,
on November 4, 1979, the Embassy was taken over by armed
"students" and the entire staff was held hostage against the extradition of the Shah—an odyssey which would last for 444 days.

By accepted diplomatic practice, it is the responsibility of
every government to see to the safety of accredited diplomats
within its territory. It quickly became apparent, however, that
this was a new—and dangerous—situation. The Iranian government was not about to denounce the actions of the hostage-
takers, nor was it about to take any steps to rescue the staff of
the U.S. Embassy. Nonetheless, in keeping with the decision
not to accede to terrorists' demands, the U.S. announced on
November 6 its unwillingness to comply.

On the same day that the U.S. refused to meet the terrorists'
demands, Abolhassan Bani-Sadr (who spoke for Ayatollah
Khomeini on matters of foreign policy) issued a public statement, saying:

> This occupation is certainly positive because it shows that the
> youth of Iran remain loyal to the ideal of national independence
> and . . . has gone into action without bothering about the polit-
> ical consequences which their initiative would have.

In other words, the U.S. could expect no help from the Iranian
authorities, who fully supported the actions of the so-called
"students." Khomeini himself was even less encouraging. The
*New York Times* quoted him as saying:

> In the name of God the Merciful, death to your plots, U.S.A.
> The blood of our martyrs is dripping from your claws. The
> United States is the main enemy of mankind and of the Iranian
> people. Under the pretext that the Shah is ill they shelter him.

The 1970s drew to a close, then, with hostage-taking on the decline, but with America facing its most serious terrorist challenge to date. Fifty-two hostages were being held inside Iran, and there appeared to be little that U.S. authorities could do about it. It would take more than a year before those hostages would be freed, and the American self-image would suffer considerably. It seemed strange to many that the U.S. could appear so powerless at just the time when hostage negotiation and rescue operations were coming into their own as responses to terrorism. The fact is, however the media chose to describe it, the events in Iran did not constitute a hostage/barricade situation. At least, not a negotiable one.

In Chapter 7, we will discuss some of the preconditions that hostage negotiations require. Among these are: containment of the situation, a clearly identified decision-maker for the hostage-takers, and a credible threat of force. In fact, very little of this was present in the Iranian situation. It was unclear whether the Khomeini government had known in advance of the "students' " plans, and what degree of control (if any) the government had over them. Faces kept changing, and no one was ever quite sure just who was in charge or who was empowered to speak for the hostage-takers. The location of the hostages and their captors was not known with any accuracy, and the option of using force was therefore so remote as to be nearly non-existent. Hostage rescue tactics had come a long way by the beginning of 1980, but not so far that they could be employed without knowledge of the hostages' location. Furthermore, negotiation can never be effective when you don't know with whom you are supposed to be negotiating.

So the 1980s began on a paradoxical note. Things generally were improving, but the United States was locked in the worst hostage crisis in its history. Security, rescue, and negotiation were all becoming more exact sciences, yet terrorism was coming to be seen as a productive tactic by more groups than ever before. The Iranian hostage crisis would continue, and others would come along as well. The 1980s would be a decade of profound challenge to the civilized world.

# Chapter 6
# A FACT OF LIFE

The beginning of a new decade is really never more than an arbitrary calendar division, and the start of the 1980s marked no change whatever in the hostage-taking situation. Americans were still being held in Iran—where, in fact, they would spend all of the next year. Hostage seizures remained at about the same level as in the previous few years, down from the 1973–75 peak, but still depressingly high for a world that wanted to think of itself as civilized. Indeed, the new decade was less than forty-eight hours old when the first hostage incidents occurred.

On January 2, 1980, the Afghan embassies in both India and West Germany were seized by mobs of Afghan students to protest the invasion of their homeland by Soviet troops. About a hundred students held three diplomats and a businessman for six hours in the embassy in New Delhi. The embassy in Bonn, seized by a crowd of around thirty, was vacated after about an hour. A few days later, on January 6, another forty Afghan students and workers captured the Afghan Embassy in (of all places) Iran, where they held thirteen hostages for approximately four hours.

While Afghan students around the world expressed their displeasure by these unconventional (for them) means, the pattern of hostage-taking elsewhere was business as usual. On January 5, 1980, while the decade was still less than a week old, members of the Camilo Torres Front of the National Liberation Army (ELN) kidnapped a British-Colombian woman and her sixteen-year-old son from their ranch in northern Colombia. The two were held until the following August, finally being released after payment of a $300,000 ransom by the family. A similar incident took place on January 9, when the wife and two daughters of a local bank manager were kidnapped by the Irish National Liberation Army (INLA). They were released the next day, on payment of a $60,000 ransom. (Despite their "liberation" rhetoric, these groups were not above a straight profit deal.)

The first really major hostage incident of the new decade, involving demands for political concessions, occurred on January 11 in El Salvador. A large contingent of the February 28 Popular League (LP-28) seized the Panamanian embassy in San Salvador, the capital city. Among the dozen or so captives were the Panamanian and Costa Rican ambassadors. A number of demands were issued, the most important of which was for the release of seven prisoners who had been arrested during a recent labor dispute. After three days of negotiations, during which a considerable number of interviews were granted by the terrorists to representatives of the press, the incident ended with the release of the seven prisoners and safe passage for the hostage-takers. The LP-28 had accomplished everything it had hoped to—both in concessions and publicity. The 1980s were not starting off well.

The early eighties showed a couple of marked trends, however, not all of which were negative. While international hostage-taking remained at about the same level as the late 1970s, along with the figures for other types of kidnapping, the composition of the statistics began to change. Governments were becoming more adept at dealing with these types of situations, and more and more incidents were ending with either a rescue or, at worst, the freeing of hostages in exchange for only minor concessions. Terrorism continued in the forms of arson, assassination, bombing, etc., but the attractiveness of hostages for political gain began to decline.[1]

---

[1]This is particularly true of hostage incidents with an international aspect—i.e., those in which either the terrorists or their captives were not citizens of the country in which the incident took place. Such events averaged about forty per year from 1976 through 1981, fell to thirty in 1982, then to just nine in 1983 and nineteen in 1984. International skyjackings, which we are treating separately here, also fell dramatically after 1981, from eighteen in that year to just five each in 1982 and 1983. Although the numbers started upward again in the middle of the decade, this was due almost entirely to events in Lebanon and Colombia.

## EMBASSY TAKEOVER IN COLOMBIA

Nonetheless, there were still a few spectacular attacks. On February 27, 1980, sixteen members of the Colombian terrorist group April 19 Movement (*Movimiento de 19 Abril*, [M-19]) attacked the embassy of the Dominican Republic in Bogota during its National Day party and took fifty-four hostages. Because of the local diplomatic community's attendance at the party, the M-19 netted a number of prize captives—including the ambassadors of Austria, Brazil, the Dominican Republic, Mexico, Uruguay, Switzerland, Costa Rica, Guatemala, Haiti, Bolivia, Egypt, Israel, the Vatican, and the United States. There were also numerous Colombian officials present, along with lesser diplomatic lights from a number of other countries. The terrorists narrowly missed capturing the ambassadors of the Soviet Union and three other East European countries, who had left only minutes before the attack.[2] They also missed the Salvadoran and British ambassadors, who arrived late and managed to get away before being captured. All in all, a very rich harvest for the M-19.

Once they had secured the embassy and identified their captives, the terrorists announced their demands. These included the release of 311 prisoners, two hundred of whom were M-19 members, a ransom of fifty million dollars, and publication of a manifesto. In other words, the classic triumvirate of terrorist demands—political concessions, money, and publicity. The $50 million ransom was an unusually large demand, even by the inflated standards of South American kidnappers, but it was predicated on the assumption that each government would pay a sizable sum for the return of its nationals.

The incident dragged on through March, with the M-19's demands gradually being negotiated down to the release of twenty

---

[2]Those who believe the Soviet Union orchestrates an international terrorist network have suggested that these four ambassadors knew the exact time of the attack. We know of no convincing evidence of this.

prisoners and a ransom of "only" ten million dollars. Mexico, Costa Rica, Panama, and Venezuela offered asylum to the terrorists, but Colombian President Turbay Ayala felt that all four of these were too close to his country and refused to grant safe passage. He offered instead safe passage to Algeria, Syria, or Libya, but none of these was acceptable to the terrorists. Turbay Ayala also ruled out any prisoner releases or ransom, but indicated that he would do nothing to prevent other governments from doing as they saw fit.

Throughout the two months this situation lasted, the terrorists slowly released the majority of the hostages they had taken. Twenty-three remained by the time the incident ended on April 27. While some of these hostage releases may have reflected good-faith negotiating by the M-19, undoubtedly it is true that fifty-four hostages must have been something of an administrative nightmare for their captors. Certainly, most of the more prestigious individuals were held to the very end.

Finally, concessions were made, though the governments involved put as good a face on it as they could. The Colombians continued to insist that no prisoners would be released, but nine leftists were freed on April 18 when authorities decided that there was "no basis" to hold them. Reportedly, a $2,500,000 ransom was paid by private sources. Other reports suggested that a few of the involved governments cut private deals with the terrorists. In any event, on April 27, the M-19 released a few more hostages and boarded a Cubana Airlines plane for Havana. With them were Ambassadors Diego Asencio of the United States, Virgilio Lovera of Mexico, Geraldo Eulalio do Nascimento de Silva of Brazil, Jean Bourgeois of Switzerland, Aquiles Pinto Flores of Guatemala, and Leonard Pierre-Louis of Haiti, Papal Nuncio Msgr. Angelo Acerbi, and a number of other diplomats. Also accompanying the group, though presumably not as hostages, were the Cuban ambassador and a representative of the International Committee of the Red Cross. Once safely in Havana, the remaining hostages were freed and the terrorists were granted asylum.

Kidnapping in Latin America apparently was as profitable as ever.

## PRINCES GATE

Just three days after the two-month Colombian ordeal ended, another major embassy takeover occurred—ironically at the expense of Iran. On April 30, 1980, as the captivity of the Americans in Tehran was beginning its seventh month, six Iranian Arabs seized twenty-six hostages in the Iranian embassy in the Princes Gate section of London. They demanded autonomy for their region (Kuzestan, the population center of the Arab minority in Iran), release of ninety-one prisoners from Iranian jails, and safe passage for themselves and the freed prisoners. The demand for prisoner release was dropped after two days, but the British authorities refused to agree to the demand for safe passage. Predictably, the government of Iran saw no similarity between the events in London and the seemingly interminable hostage situation in Tehran. The London crisis, said the Iranian authorities, was the work of the British, the Iraqis, the Israelis, and, of course, the Great Satan, America. Iran would have nothing to do with any negotiations.

The terrorists, variously identified as belonging to the Arab People's Movement, the Arab People's Political Organization, the Arab Masses Movement, and a half-dozen or so others of similar nomenclature, announced their intention to blow up the embassy if their demands were not met and began setting deadlines. However, the deadlines passed without concessions being made or threats being carried out. Over the next five days, in fact, a number of hostages were released for a variety of reasons. It began to appear that the incident might be peacefully resolved.

On the evening of May 5, however, the terrorists announced that they had executed two hostages and would begin shooting one hostage every thirty minutes if their demands weren't met. At first this was thought to be a bluff, but half-an-hour later, the body of twenty-five year-old press counselor Abbas Lavasani was dumped onto the sidewalk in front of the Embassy.[3] The military attaché apparently had been murdered also. Time had run out.

At 7:30 p.m., members of the British Special Air Service (SAS) launched a rescue operation. Entering the embassy behind a volley of "flash-bang" (stun) grenades, they killed five of the six terrorists and rescued all nineteen remaining hostages. Three Iranian hostages were wounded in the shooting. The surviving terrorist was captured, tried, and sentenced to life imprisonment. It was an impressive performance by the SAS, and a victory of sorts over the forces of terrorism, but it had no effect on the Iranian government. The American hostage situation went on as before, and the Iranians continued to reject any parallels between their own behavior and the tragedy that had just taken place at Princes Gate.

## HOSTAGES IN IRAN

The hostage situation in Tehran continued despite the best efforts of the United States and others. The Carter Administration had made it clear from the outset that the Shah would not be returned to Iran under any circumstances, and the followers of the Ayatollah Khomeini turned a deaf ear to assertions concerning the guaranteed inviolability of diplomats. Several steps had been taken by U.S. authorities, but none had borne fruit.

Within days of the seizure of the its embassy, the United States government announced that it was suspending the shipment of more than three hundred million dollars worth of military spare parts to Iran until the hostages were released. These parts already had been paid for. The day following this announce

---

[3]Lavasani apparently was chosen for death because of his penchant for arguing with his captors. He was an articulate and persuasive speaker, easily capable of scoring debating points off his less-educated captors. Unfortunately, their response to his oratorical skills was not conversion, but hostility. When they decided that the time had come to sacrifice a hostage, he became their logical choice. See Chapter 7 for a discussion of the dangers of this sort of behavior by hostages.

ment, November 9, 1979, a U.S.-requested session of the United Na-tions Security Council was held to address the problem. That body urged the release of the hostages "in the strongest terms," but chose not to interfere in the "internal" affairs of any country(!).

The following day, November 10, U.S. President Jimmy Carter ordered that the visas of all Iranians in the United States be examined, and that any Iranians found without valid documents be deported. These actions were invalidated by a federal judge in Washington, D.C., but were upheld by the federal appeals court on December 27. More than fifty-four thousand Iranian students were interviewed, many of whom turned out to have been in the country longer than their visas allowed. Only a handful were actually deported, however.

On November 12, President Carter ordered an embargo on Iranian oil, estimated to represent between seven and eight percent of total U.S. oil imports. Iran responded that it had decided to stop selling oil to the United States in any event. (Indeed, it is difficult to see how business could have proceeded as usual under the circumstances.) Two days later, the U.S. announced that, under a 1977 International Emergency Economic Powers Act, it was freezing "all property and interests in the property of the Government of Iran . . . and the Central Bank of Iran which are or become subject to the jurisdiction of the United States." Estimates of the value of these assets varied at the time from one billion dollars (claimed by Iran) to six billion (the U.S. estimate). Iran responded with some tough talk, declaring that it would no longer accept the U.S. dollar in payment for its oil and renouncing its obligation to honor Iran's foreign debt, estimated at about $15 billion.[4]

---

[4]This crisis offers an excellent example of how a hostage situation can profoundly influence world politics. European economic experts feared that other OPEC countries might reject the dollar, causing severe exchange rate fluctuations and ultimately leading to a decrease in oil production. On December 10, the Swiss government issued a warning that the pressure generated against the dollar by Iran's reaction to U.S. efforts to achieve the hostages' release could actually threaten the stability of the world monetary system.

There were some forces within the Iranian government who were hoping to find some fairly reasonable solution to the crisis (notably President Bani-Sadr and Foreign Minister Qotbzadeh), but hardliners like Ayatollah Mohammed Hossein Beheshti made this impossible. Beheshti and his Islamic Republican Party continued to insist that the U.S. return the Shah to stand trial in Iran—a rather unreasonable demand once the Shah had left the United States for Panama in mid-December. Islamic right-wingers refused to accept that there were any limits to what the U.S. could do where the Shah was concerned, a stance which made compromise virtually impossible.

The situation took a turn for the worse in late March, when the Shah left Panama for Egypt (just one day before the Iranians were to formally request his extradition). Some Iranian hardliners wanted to put the American hostages on trial in his place, making it imperative that the U.S. immediately take some kind of action. On April 7, President Carter announced a new round of sanctions, including: the breaking of diplomatic relations; expulsion of all Iranian diplomats; closing of all diplomatic and consular offices; an end to all exports to Iran (food and medicine were exempted); an inventory of frozen Iranian assets, preparatory to possible confiscation; and invalidation of all visas issued to Iranians for future entry into the United States.[5]

When these new measures had no apparent effect, the president went further. On April 17, he announced a ban on travel to Iran, prohibition of imports of Iranian goods, and a crackdown on financial dealings between U.S. citizens and Iran. He warned that, "If this additional set of sanctions . . . is not successful then the only step available that I can see would be some sort of military action, which is the prerogative and the

---

[5]In reality, these sanctions were likely not to have much effect. Trade between the U.S. and Iran already had been reduced to almost nothing, normal diplomatic relations between the two had ceased to exist when the hostages were first taken, and Iranian representation in the U.S. had long since been drastically reduced. The new measures had no effect on Iranian diplomats assigned to the United Nations in New York.

right of the United States under these circumstances." This was indeed the only step left, and—just seven days after these latest sanctions were announced—the U.S. attempted a military resolution. Unfortunately, it worked no better than any of the other options which had so far been tried.


DESERT ONE

Given that the American hostages were being held thousands of miles away in a hostile environment, and that many things were not known for certain about the conditions of their captivity at that point, the chances for success were never propitious. Nonetheless, by mid-April the president had decided that the steps already taken were not going to be enough. On April 22, six Hercules aircraft were flown to Egypt carrying weapons, helicopter fuel, and commandos. Two days later, they took off for "Desert One,"[6] where they were to rendezvous with eight Sikorsky RH-53D helicopters which had taken off from the USS Nimitz in the Arabian Sea.

Even had the rendezvous gone smoothly, the team would still have faced tremendous obstacles, considering how far they were from Tehran and how limited were the resources available to them. As it was, the mission never got beyond Desert One. One of the helicopters lost the use of its gyroscope as the result of a sandstorm and two others developed hydraulic problems. Because a minimum of six helicopters was required for the operation, the decision was reluctantly made to abandon the mission and withdraw from Iran. President Carter gave the order himself, at 2:30 a.m., Iranian time.

Then, what had been merely a failure turned into a nightmare. One of the helicopters, flying a short distance in total

---

[6]An area of the Dasht e Kavir desert between Tabas and Yazd, about 300 miles from Tehran. Ironically, U.S. personnel were familiar with this area as a result of having been involved in an earthquake relief operation there in 1978.

darkness to fill its tanks, flew too close to one of the Hercules and sliced into the plane's fuselage. Both aircraft immediately burst into flames, killing everyone in the helicopter and five crewmen inside the Hercules. The surviving members of the team could not remove the bodies and, at 4:00 a.m. local time, they withdrew—leaving behind the dead plus all four remaining operational helicopters (which, it was feared, might have been damaged by flying shrapnel from the collision).

The next couple of months were a very bad time for the United States, as world attention focused on the disposition of the remains of the men left behind at Desert One. The Iranian government put the bodies on public display, an act that President Carter denounced on April 29 as "ghoulish" and a "horrible exhibition of inhumanity." Iranian authorities called the failed rescue attempt an act of war, fantastically denouncing it as part of an "international plot between imperialism and Zionism." Although things improved slightly in July, when Iran released one hostage for health reasons[7], the situation remained as far from resolution as ever.

Even the death of the former Shah of Iran had no effect on the situation. Mohammed Reza Pahlevi, who had been Shah from September 1941 until his ouster in 1979, passed away in a Cairo hospital on July 27, 1980, at the age of sixty. His death was greeted in Iran with the announcement that "the bloodsucker of the century is dead." Despite the fact that the hostage crisis had originally begun over the demand for the return of the Shah to stand trial, Iranian authorities insisted that his death now made no difference. The fate of the hostages was linked to the return of the assets frozen in the United States.

While negotiations continued for the release of the Americans being held in Tehran, the rest of the world was hardly quiescent. 1980 was a busy time for terrorists, although statis-

---

[7]Richard Queen, a 28-year-old vice consul, who was diagnosed as suffering from multiple sclerosis, was released on July 10. He had been transferred to a hospital in Tehran at first, but medical facilities there were not sufficient to treat him.

tics indicate that it was not particularly atypical in that regard. There were no fewer than 843 assassinations worldwide in 1980, more than a thousand bombings, and 124 kidnappings. The year came to a close with a number of major incidents, including the kidnapping of a Ministry of Justice official in Rome by the Red Brigades and the hijacking of a Colombian plane carrying 127 passengers by the M-19.

1981 started out a bit more quietly, at least as far as hostage-taking was concerned. The early weeks of the new year were wracked by terrorist shootings and bombings, but no kidnapping incident occurred until January 19. On that day, a splinter group of the Colombian M-19 abducted an American bible translator, Chester Bitterman. The terrorists demanded that the Summer Institute of Linguistics, for which Bitterman had been working (and which the group predictably claimed was a CIA front), leave Colombia; and that their twenty-one page manifesto be published by a number of major newspapers, including the *Washington Post* and the *New York Times*. The Colombian government refused to negotiate, as did the company which ran the Summer Institute of Linguistics, and Bitterman's body was found wrapped in an M-19 flag and surrounded by propaganda pamphlets on March 7, 1981.

The day following Bitterman's abduction ironically was a joyous one for Americans—marking both the inauguration of a new president and the long-awaited end of the hostage crisis in Iran. It is difficult to say how long the incident might have continued under other circumstances, but the outbreak of hostilities between Iran and Iraq in September 1980 forced the Iranian government to seek some sort of resolution. Mediation by Algeria provided a way out of the impasse, and an agreement was finally concluded on January 19, 1981, the last full day of the Carter presidency.

By the terms of the agreement, the hostages were to be released from their captivity. In exchange, the U.S. agreed not to interfere in the internal affairs of Iran; to freeze the assets of the late Shah, pending the outcome of future court decisions; to end all trade sanctions against Iran; and—the most controversial provision—to restore to Iran all assets which had been frozen on November 14, 1979.[8] In addition, the two sides agreed to the establishment of an international tribunal to decide any claims that the citizens of either country might bring against the other. In a final spiteful slap at outgoing President Carter, the Iranian government held off releasing the hostages until just a few minutes after the inauguration of President Ronald Reagan. The 444-day ordeal was over.

## LEBANON

The next major incident was something of a watershed, though hardly discernible as such at the time. The kidnapping of Jordanian *Chargé d'Affaires* Hisham Muheisen from his home in Lebanon was the first such event of its kind there. There had been numerous assassinations, rocket attacks, and terrorist bombings in Lebanon since 1975. Indeed, the country was something of a political basket case, well on its way to becoming "merely a geographical expression," as Metternich once described nineteenth century Italy. The abduction of Muheisen, however, marks the first time a group attempted to achieve its political ends in Lebanon by taking a hostage. The tactic was to be repeated many times throughout the eighties.

The Jordanian diplomat was kidnapped by twenty gunmen, members of a group whose identity remains in some doubt. The attack was attributed variously to the Arab National Organization, the Eagles of the Revolution, and even the Palestine Liberation Organization. Multiple and somewhat conflicting demands were made in exchange for his safe return, and he was variously reported to have been taken to Damascus for medical

---

[8]Some critics saw this provision as the payment of a ransom—something explicitly prohibited by U.S. policy. The U.S. government's position held that this was the return of Iran's own property in exchange for the return of the hostages. There remains considerable disagreement on the subject.

treatment, incarcerated in the town of Laboue (fifty miles from Beirut), held in a Palestinian office in the Shatila refugee camp, and released by the National Confrontation Front.[9]

While Lebanon was to become the focal point of hostage concerns by the end of the decade, it was not yet so in 1981. Latin America was the area of greatest activity in the early eighties, at least insofar as kidnapping was concerned. Most of the incidents there were essentially local rather than international, and their motivation likely was as to be criminal as political, so they generally received less attention in the world press. Nonetheless, it was the Latin American groups who accounted for most of the kidnappings that took place prior to 1986, and a very large percentage of those afterward. In 1980, ninety-eight of the 124 kidnappings committed worldwide took place in Latin America (79%); in 1981, sixty-five of ninety-five (68.4%); in 1982, seventy-nine of 102 (77.5%); and in 1983, ninety-three of 119 (78%).

## THE DOZIER KIDNAPPING

The big story of 1981 for Americans (at least, the biggest since the release of the hostages from Iran in January) was the kidnapping of Brigadier General James L. Dozier by the Red Brigades on December 17. Dozier was the senior U.S. officer at NATO's southern Europe ground forces base in Verona—a very big prize for the Italian terrorist group. In fact, this was the first time the Red Brigades, whose previous actions included the 1978 kidnapping and murder of former Prime Minister Aldo Moro, had targeted a foreigner.

---

[9]This confusing scenario became the hallmark of terrorist hostage-taking in Lebanon. Groups have come and gone with bewildering speed and complexity. Several groups might claim responsibility for one kidnapping, while no group might assert its claim for another. Some organizations are heard of only once. The location of a hostage, even the country in which he is being held, can be almost impossible to determine. Fixing responsibility for a kidnapping with any degree of certainty is sometimes out of the question.

Two days after the kidnapping, a six-page document was received which called for war against NATO and condemned U.S. military forces in Europe as an "occupation army." The document also called for cooperation among "European revolutionary forces," particularly among the Red Brigades of Italy, the Red Army Faction of West Germany, and the Irish Republican Army of Northern Ireland. "War against imperialist war," the paper asserted, "is an essential passage for the transition to communism." It is interesting to note the similarity between this and the doctrine enunciated by George Habash in the early 1970s. We suggested earlier that Habash's doctrine owed something to Lenin's description of the assault on capitalism. Here, the Red Brigades seemed to be closing the circle, arguing for a concerted terrorist offensive to advance the cause of communism.

No demands were forthcoming, but on December 27 another communique was received, stating that Dozier's "trial" had begun. This was accompanied by a photo of the general and a 188-page "strategic resolution."[10] A massive manhunt was underway throughout Italy and the next month saw numerous arrests and interrogations of suspected members and confederates of the Red Brigades. The methods adopted by the Italian police were sometimes harsh (there were allegations of torture) but their results were impressive. On January 28, 1982, the forty-second day of Dozier's captivity, a special police rescue squad burst into the Padua apartment where he was being held. One man, who was holding a gun to the general's head, was knocked to the ground, and the other four terrorists in the room surrendered. The entire rescue, which ended three days of surveillance of the apartment, took just ninety seconds. It was the first time the Italian police had successfully located and freed a prisoner of the Red Brigades.

Despite the group's formidable reputation, General Dozier described them as "rather amateurish." They had made no ef-

---

[10]The package was bound in a yellow ribbon. One wonders whether the symbolism was intentional.

fort to interrogate him during the forty-two days, even though he was obviously a potential treasure-trove of information. They had never made very clear demands for his safe return. And ultimately they had been unable to elude the police. This incident proved to be a turning point in Italy's struggle against the Red Brigades, as captured terrorists began cooperating with the authorities and the police started to roll up their networks. Arrests led to more information, which in turn led to more arrests, and before long the back of Italian terrorism was largely broken. It did not disappear, but the outcome of the Dozier kidnapping was a major setback for the Red Brigades.

January 1982 was a bad month for hostage-takers. The Basque separatist group ETA/PM had kidnapped sixty-six-year-old Dr. Julio Iglesias Puga, father of the famous singer, the previous December 29 in Madrid. For his release, they had demanded a ransom of two million dollars, half in U.S. dollars and half in Spanish pesetas. On January 17, Spanish police raided their hideout in Trasmoz (in northeast Spain), successfully rescuing Dr. Iglesias and capturing four members of the ETA/PM. This was the first time a kidnapping by this group was foiled entirely by police action. For the moment, at least, both Italian and Spanish antiterrorist forces could feel very good about their operations.

## THE PACE QUICKENS

Despite this promising beginning, 1982 was a fairly active year for kidnappers and hostage-takers, as well as for bombers, hijackers, and assassins. The year saw more than one hundred kidnappings, most of which occurred in Latin America. In May, thirteen terrorists took over the Brazilian Embassy in Guatemala, holding the Brazilian ambassador and eight others hostage. They eventually were given political asylum in Mexico. In September, a dozen people were held hostage in the Polish Embassy in Switzerland by a group demanding an end to martial law in Poland and freedom for political prisoners. The incident ended after three days with a rescue by Swiss police. Two weeks later, 105 people were taken hostage at the Chamber of Commerce building in San Pedro Sula, Honduras, by members of *Los Cinchoneros*. The terrorists, who began by demanding the release of political prisoners, repeal of an antiterrorism law, and removal of foreign military advisers from the country, ultimately settled for asylum in Havana. But it was in Lebanon that the West was given its most serious indication of things to come.

On July 19, David Dodge, the acting rector of the American University in Beirut, was kidnapped from his campus. Dodge was spirited away by members of Islamic Jihad, the umbrella under which much Lebanese terrorism would be conducted in the future, and seemed to almost totally disappear. There was no lack of speculation as to his whereabouts, and more than a few rumors, but his fate remained a mystery for a full year. Finally, on July 21, 1983, he was released, reportedly from Iran via Damascus. Dodge was the first Westerner to be held hostage in Lebanon. Unfortunately, this was just the beginning.

1983 was a peculiar year in the modern history of political hostage-taking. While the total number of incidents was fairly high (119), only eleven had international aspects. Only eight hostage-taking incidents were recorded throughout the Middle East, and all of these were essentially local in nature. At the same time, ninety-three of the 119 kidnappings took place in Latin America. And of the eleven cases that had an international dimension, four took place in Colombia. Like the 1982 kidnapping of David Dodge, this was a portent of things to come.

On March 7, 1983, Kenneth Bishop, an American executive with the Texas Petroleum Company (TEXACO), was kidnapped while on his way to work outside Bogota. He was held for about five weeks by the People's Revolutionary Organization (ORP), finally being released on April 14. A ransom reportedly was paid for his release, part by members of his family and part by TEXACO, although the amount was never disclosed. During the time that Bishop was a prisoner of the ORP, another Colombian terrorist group, the Revolutionary Armed Forces of Colombia (FARC), kidnapped another American, Catherine

Wood Kirby. Following payment of a reportedly large ransom by her family, Kirby was released unharmed after slightly more than four months of captivity. About the same time that she was regaining her freedom, yet another Colombian terrorist group, the Army of National Liberation (ELN), kidnapped American rancher Martin Stendal. Stendal was held until January 1984, when, like the others, he was released after payment of a reportedly large ransom.

1984 was also a curious year for terrorism: assassinations, bombings, and hijackings were up substantially over 1983, yet the number of recorded kidnappings was cut almost in half (from 119 in 1983 to 61 in 1984). At the same time, a higher percentage of these terrorist kidnappings were international in nature. This is explained, however, by the fact that nearly all of these incidents took place in Lebanon. While hostage-taking was slowly phasing out in most of the world (owing mainly to improved security and rescue techniques), it was on its way to becoming a fact of political life in Lebanon.

## LEBANON

1983 had hardly been a quiet year for Lebanese terrorists. As the civil war's savagery continued, there were innumerable bombings and assassinations throughout the country, especially in Beirut. The most spectacular—and destructive—events by far were the bombing of the American Embassy in April and the murder of 241 U.S. Marines in October. But the year was surprisingly free of hostage-taking incidents. Early in 1984, however, the various groups operating within the country switched tactics.

On February 11, 1984, Frank Regier, an American professor at the American University of Beirut, was kidnapped off the street, apparently by Islamic Jihad.[11] Four days later, a French

---

[11]Although Islamic Jihad is an umbrella under which many groups operate, we have attributed activities to it as if it were a single entity. In the complex world of Lebanon, it is often impossible to be more specific.

citizen, Christian Joubert, was also abducted. The two were held for about two months, during which they were kept blindfolded the entire time. They were released together on April 15, without any explanation or demands. Meanwhile, on March 7, Islamic Jihad kidnapped Cable News Network bureau chief Jeremy Levin. Levin was held until he escaped (some believe he was allowed to escape) on February 15, 1985 and made his way to a Syrian Army position in Lebanon's Bekaa Valley and thence to safety.

Much worse was the fate of William Buckley, who was abducted outside his Beirut home on March 16, 1984. Buckley was held for over a year, during which he was interrogated, tortured, and "put on trial for world crimes perpetrated by U.S. intelligence." On October 4, 1985, his captors issued a statement that he had been "executed" for his "crimes." A picture of his corpse was released, but it was not at first accepted as incontrovertible proof of Buckley's death. Subsequent reports, however, most notably by journalist Jack Anderson, indicate that he had died a few months before the statement and photo were released, the victim of a heart attack brought on by prolonged torture.[12] It is also believed that during his captivity, Buckley was moved from Lebanon to Syria and finally to Iran.

Islamic Jihad and other groups had by now adopted kidnapping as a major political tactic. For the rest of the 1980s, Lebanon would dominate the political hostage-taking statistics. On May 8, the Reverend Benjamin Weir, an American, was abducted. He was released after fourteen months, this time to deliver Islamic Jihad's demands. These involved the release of seventeen terrorists being held in prison in Kuwait. If they were not released, Weir told the press, the group intended to kidnap more Americans and possibly to kill some of those already in captivity. Islamic Jihad had been active during the fourteen months Reverend Weir was their prisoner.

---

[12]This tactic of saving the announcement of the death or murder of a hostage for a propitious moment would be repeated four years later in the case of U.S. Marine Lt. Col. William Higgins (see Chapter 1).

A partial listing of the kidnappings which occurred in Lebanon during that period will give some idea of the extent of the phenomenon. On July 9, Libyan *Chargé d'Affaires* Muhammed Al-Faytuir and his bodyguard were abducted by a group calling itself the "Brigades of As-sad." They were released later the same day. On October 10, the Spanish Ambassador, Pedro Aristegui, was kidnapped outside his embassy by gunmen connected to two Shiite terrorists who had been arrested in Madrid. He also was released the same day. On November 8, American Peter Kilburn, librarian at the American University of Beirut, was kidnapped by a group calling itself the Arab Revolutionary Cells. His body was found on April 17, 1986, along with the bodies of two British hostages, Leigh Douglas and Philip Padfield. A note accompanying the bodies stated that they had been killed in revenge for the U.S. bombing of Libya earlier that month.

On January 3, 1985, Swiss *Chargé d'Affaires* Eric Wehrli was captured by relatives of a Lebanese terrorist who had been arrested in the Zurich airport carrying explosives. In a bizarre twist, he was rescued five days later by members of the Shiite Moslem *Amal* militia and released unharmed. On that same day (January 8), Father Lawrence Jenco, an American in charge of the Catholic Relief Services in Beirut, was kidnapped by Islamic Jihad. He was held almost a year and a half, finally being released on July 26, 1986 because of his deteriorating health.[13]

The list went on and on, dramatically accelerating in March 1985. On March 14, a British metallurgist, Geoffrey Nash, was kidnapped in front of his home. There was speculation that he may have been mistaken for an American (he worked in a building formerly occupied by the U.S. Embassy). Both Islamic Jihad and a group called the Khaybar Brigades-Lebanese Branch claimed responsibility. On the same day, Father Nicolas Kluiters, a Dutch priest, was abducted and

---

[13]According to his captors, in a statement published in Beirut. His release, said the terrorists, was a "goodwill gesture."

subsequently killed. His body was found on April 1, 1985. No group claimed responsibility.

On March 16, American journalist Terry Anderson was kidnapped. So was Abd Al-Basit Al-Tarabulsi, a member of the Libyan People's Bureau. On March 22, French vice consul Marcel Fontaine was taken hostage by Islamic Jihad "because he is an agent of French imperialism." The same day, French Chief of Protocol Marcel Carton and his daughter Danielle Perez were taken. Again both Islamic Jihad and the Khaybar Brigades claimed responsibility. Also on that day, Michel Seurat, a researcher at the French Cultural Center, was kidnapped, with the same two groups claiming responsibility.

Two days later, on March 24, Giles Peyrolles, Director of the French Cultural Center, was kidnapped by the Lebanese Armed Revolutionary Faction. The following day, Alec Collett, a British journalist working in Lebanon for the United Nations Relief and Works Agency (UNRWA), was kidnapped by a group calling itself the Revolutionary Organization of Socialist Moslems. He was accused of "working for British and Zionist aims in the Middle East," and reportedly was "executed for his crimes."

The Lebanese situation steadily worsened, and an already terrible month ended with five kidnappings in two days. Four prominent members of Beirut's Jewish community—Dr. Elie Hallak, Elie Youssef Sprour, Haim Halala Cohen, and Yitzhak Tarab— were abducted in three separate incidents on March 30, and Isaac Sasson, President of the Higher Council of the Jewish Community in Beirut, was taken the following day. Responsibility ultimately was claimed by the Organization of the Oppressed the following November, when the group demanded the release of prisoners in Israel in return for the five Jewish hostages. On December 25, 1985, Haim Halala Cohen was killed in retaliation for the Israeli bombardment of Shiite villages in south Lebanon. On January 1, 1986, the body of Yitzhak Tarab was found. On February 19, the kidnappers claimed to have executed Dr. Hallak, whom they accused of having been an Israeli spy.

Two French citizens were kidnapped on May 23, 1985, only one of whom survived. Jean-Paul Kauffman, a correspondent for *L'Evenement du Jeudi*, was held for three years by Islamic Jihad. He was finally released in May 1988, along with two other French hostages, Marcel Carton and Marcel Fontaine. The terms of release reportedly involved eventual normalization of relations between France and Iran, as well as payment of an outstanding loan made by the Shah's regime in 1974 for nuclear development in France. The other French hostage, Michel Seurat, taken at the same time as Jean-Paul Kauffman, was less fortunate. On March 10, 1986, Islamic Jihad released photos of Seurat's body, claiming to have "executed" him in retaliation for France's expulsion of two Iraqi dissidents (who were accused of being pro-Iranian). Ironically, the two dissidents who were deported to Baghdad, were ultimately pardoned by Iraq's President Hussein.

On May 28, 1985, David Jacobsen, an American working as an administrator at the American University Hospital, was kidnapped by Islamic Jihad. Two weeks later, on June 10, Professor Thomas Sutherland, another American on the American University faculty, was seized by the same group. On November 12, an open letter signed by four of the six Americans then being held hostage in Lebanon—Jacobsen, Sutherland, Terry Anderson, and Lawrence Jenco—was sent to both President Reagan and the Archbishop of Canterbury. The letter, which was authenticated by relatives of the hostages, asked that their release be quickly negotiated. The Archbishop of Canterbury responded by sending his personal envoy, Terry Waite, to Beirut. Waite met with the terrorists and pronounced himself satisfied that the four Americans were "alive and well." Jacobsen was released after seventeen months, on November 2, 1986. Jenco, as noted earlier, was released in July 1986. As of this writing, Anderson and Sutherland are still being held, more than four years later.

## TWA 847

The greatly accelerated pace of Lebanese hostage-taking exploded into the international media on Friday, June 14, 1985.

Two armed terrorists hijacked TWA Flight 847 shortly after its takeoff from Athens and demanded the release of 766 Shiites who had been arrested by Israeli forces in southern Lebanon and transferred to prisons in Israel. The hijackers ordered that the plane, most of whose 153 passengers and crew were American, be flown to Beirut. Once on the ground in Beirut, the terrorists demanded enough fuel to fly to Algiers. The pilot, John Testrake, informed the tower that the two gunmen were threatening to kill an American passenger if they did not receive the fuel "in three minutes."

Nineteen women and children were released by the terrorists in Beirut. The plane was refueled and flown to Algiers, where twenty-one more women and children were released. The hijackers then ordered that the plane be flown back to Beirut, where one of the gunmen announced that he was a member of *Hezbollah* (one of the Islamic Jihad groups) and asked for help from the larger Shiite Moslem organization, *Amal*. During the ensuing negotiations, the gunmen lost their composure—which resulted in the murder of Robert Stethem, a U.S. Navy diver who already had been tied up and badly beaten by the terrorists.

At dawn the next day, the pilot was forced to fly back to Algiers, where sixty-four more hostages were released. By Sunday, June 16, when the pilot was ordered to fly back to Beirut again, only the three-man crew and about forty passengers were still aboard. The following day, the hijackers decided to take all the remaining hostages off the plane, in order to make any rescue effort more difficult. The following week was filled with negotiations between the U.S. State Department, *Amal*, and Syria, along with hysterical demonstrations by *Hezbollah* supporters at the Beirut airport and some rather bizarre contacts with the media. The latter included an ABC interview with the captive pilot and crew, and a chaotic "news conference" with five of the hostages.

On June 25, President Reagan announced that he would impose an economic blockade on Lebanon and force the Beirut airport to close if the hostages were not released. *Amal* responded by freeing one hostage (who had become ill) and offering to transfer the rest to a Western European embassy in Lebanon or Syria. The U.S. decided at this point that all American hostages in Lebanon should be part of any deal made with *Amal* (a decision that did not sit well with some of the passengers and their families, who were anxious for an end to their own ordeal). This could not be arranged, but, after a U.S. guarantee not to retaliate against the terrorists once the hostages were freed, the final thirty-nine captives were taken by bus to Damascus and flown home. Not long after, Israel released the 766 detainees.[14]

## THE *ACHILLE LAURO*

While the media remained occupied with the aftermath of the TWA hijacking, it was largely business as usual for kidnappers through the remainder of 1985. There were approximately twenty more international kidnappings during the year, ten of which occurred in Lebanon. Victims included citizens of France, Kuwait, Canada, Italy, Egypt—even four Russians. There were also political kidnappings in places as diverse as Colombia, Mozambique, and the Philippines. But the incident that created the greatest media sensation—overshadowing even the TWA 847 affair—was the hijacking of the Italian cruise ship *Achille Lauro* on October 7, 1985, by four members of the Palestine Liberation Front at Alexandria, Egypt.

The *Achille Lauro* had begun its voyage at Genoa, Italy, with 750 passengers and a crew of 331, but only ninety-seven of the passengers were aboard at the time of the hijacking. The rest had gone ashore for an all-day tour of Alexandria, Giza, and

---

[14]One of the hijackers, Mohammed Ali Hammadi, was arrested at the airport in Frankfurt, West Germany, on January 13, 1987, with explosives in his luggage. He admitted his role in the TWA 847 incident, but claimed not to have been the one who shot Robert Stethem. He was tried and convicted of murder and air piracy in a West German court, and sentenced to life imprisonment.

Port Said. The gunmen ordered the ship to head for Syria, and instructed the captain to obtain permission to dock there. They also demanded to speak with the Italian and U.S. ambassadors[15] in order to make their terms known—release of some fifty Palestinians held in Israeli prisons.

No response was immediately given, so the terrorists decided to kill a hostage—apparently to demonstrate their seriousness. The unlucky victim, reportedly selected at random, was American Leon Klinghoffer. Klinghoffer, who was confined to a wheelchair, was shot in the head and chest during the afternoon of October 8, and his body was dumped overboard. The ship returned to Egyptian waters and direct negotiations between the hijackers and Egyptian officials began in earnest early the following morning.

Eventually, with the PLO playing a direct role in the talks, an agreement was reached.[16] The Egyptian government agreed to give the hijackers safe passage if they released the ship. This was supposedly based on the assurance of the ship's captain that no one aboard had been harmed, and Egyptian officials claimed not to have known at that point about Klinghoffer's murder. In any event, the hijackers were flown by the Egyptian government to Tunis, but the Tunisians refused to allow the plane to land. When the aircraft turned back for Egypt, it was intercepted by U.S. naval aircraft and forced to land in Sicily. After some tense moments between U.S. and Italian forces, the Palestinians were taken into custody by the Italian government. Despite the relatively happy ending in the *Achille Lauro* case, the deaths of Robert Stethem and Leon Klinghoffer, along with the continuing captivity of so many Americans in Lebanon, made 1985 a bad year for the United States in the Middle East.

---

[15]Twelve of the passengers who had remained aboard were American, and nearly all of the crew were Italian.

[16]PLO figures involved in the negotiations included Mohammed Abbas, a member of the PLO Executive Council and leader of the Palestine Liberation Front; Hani Hassan, an adviser to Yassir Arafat; and Zahdi Qourda, the PLO's official representative in Cairo.

If hostage-taking was more geographically limited in the 1980s
than it had been during the previous decade, it was certainly no
less difficult a problem.


## ENDING THE 80S

The years 1986 and 1987 continued the trends. Kidnapping
worldwide decreased slightly, to about seventy-five percent of
the rate for 1980-85, but the geographical distribution was now
very different. Out of 124 total kidnappings in 1980, for example, ninety-eight took place in Latin America and just seven in
the Middle East. Of ninety-five such incidents in 1981, sixty-
five occurred in Latin America and only seven in the Middle
East. In 1982, out of 102, the numbers were seventy-nine for
Latin America and a mere five for the Middle East. The shift is
even starker when one considers only international incidents.
Of seventy-eight such kidnappings in 1986–87, thirty-eight (almost half) occurred in Lebanon alone. All of the countries of
Latin America combined accounted for just sixteen such incidents during that period.

With the escalation of the drug wars in Colombia, this picture changed slightly in 1988. That year saw a huge jump in the
number of kidnapping incidents overall (120 versus only
seventy-three the previous year and seventy-nine in 1986), and
a return to a geographical distribution more like those of the
early years of the decade (sixty-eight in Latin America and just
sixteen in the Middle East). The majority of these seem to have
been local affairs. 1988 saw only twenty-three international kidnappings worldwide, down significantly from the forty-seven of
the previous year. Most telling, however, was the geographical
distribution of these international statistics: of the twenty-three
incidents in 1988, ten occurred in Colombia and eight in Lebanon. The rest of the world combined accounted for just five
such kidnappings!

To be sure, the day of the big media-capturing hostage incident has not completely ended. But it seems to have become

the preferred tactic of only marginal groups. On August 5, 1987, for example, a group of ten Kurdish workers took several hostages in a Lufthansa Airline office in downtown Copenhagen. Although they poured gasoline around the office and threatened to set the place afire, their demands were rather vague and they soon surrendered. Similarly, a month later, Iranian dissidents (opponents of the Khomeini regime) staged a "coordinated" attack against Iranian offices in Oslo, Frankfurt, and Paris. The group, members of the Organization of Iranian People's Fedayeen Guerrillas, took hostages in the Iranian embassy in Oslo, smashed furniture in the Iran Air office in Frankfurt, and broke windows in the Iran Air office in Paris. Ten men were arrested at the first location and nine at the second; the five window-breakers in Paris managed to run off before police could arrive. Needless to say, no concessions were made by the Iranian government. This was a far cry from the kinds of incidents that made headlines in the early 1970s.

The same groups were responsible for similar attacks in 1988. On November 30, seventeen Turkish Kurds held four employees hostage in the Turkish Airlines office in Paris for about six hours. Their single demand was to be allowed to explain their action to the media. They then announced that they were trying to publicize the cause of Kurdish prisoners in Turkish jails. After the press conference, all were arrested. Two weeks later, the Organization of Iranian People's Fedayeen Guerrillas struck again, with another series of "coordinated" attacks. This time, the targets were in Geneva, London, Hamburg, and Paris. Only in Geneva were hostages taken (at the Iranian consulate), and these were rescued by the police after about four hours. In London and Hamburg, the groups smashed equipment at Iran Air offices and an Iranian travel bureau, and in Paris they contented themselves with breaking another window and distributing leaflets.

Where the principal groups were still engaging in this type of activity, it generally was now for reasons very different from those of the 1970s. No longer in real need of media recognition, groups like *Fatah* now took hostages for reasons such as retribution. On March 7, 1988, for example, three *Fatah* members hijacked an Israeli commuter bus in southern Israel. Although Israeli police stormed the bus and killed the three gunmen, the terrorists were able to kill three passengers and injure eight others. *Fatah* announced that the attack had been in retaliation for the killing of three of their members in Cyprus in February, for which they blamed the Israeli *Mossad*.

Groups like *Fatah* have for the most part gone out of the hostage-taking business, however, at least for the present. The terrorist organizations that gave rise to the phenomenon in the late 1960s have met different fates. The PLO and its various factions—which, under the influence of Yassir Arafat and George Habash, used hostage-taking to force the world to pay attention to their cause—had largely achieved their ends. Today, their focus is on international diplomacy and support for the *intifada* in the Israeli-occupied territories. Some groups whose goals were nothing less than revolution and the overthrow of a national government, like the Red Brigades in Italy and the *Tupamaros* in Uruguay, were crushed by the authorities and ceased to be viable. And those whose major motive appears to have been profit, like the Latin American groups whose ransom demands became astronomical, seem to have found other avenues to wealth. Kidnapping continues in that part of the world, but now it appears to be more often an adjunct of the drug business.

The decline of political hostage-taking in most parts of the world, however, seems to be more than compensated for by events in Lebanon and Colombia. The 120 kidnapping incidents in 1988, in fact, was the second-highest annual total in the decade—surpassed only by the 124 recorded in 1980. Most of these were local affairs, though, and very few commanded the kind of attention that went to many of the incidents of the early 1970s. As of this writing, it would appear that experiences like those of the Munich Olympics, Lod Airport, and Dawson's Field are largely behind us. At the same time, numerous Western hostages are still being held in Lebanon and the outlook for their release any time soon is not bright. The chasm between the United States and Iran puts Americans (and others) at risk throughout the Middle East, as does the Palestinian question. The deteriorating political situation in Colombia is also likely to give rise to more and bigger problems of the type that have plagued that country since the onset of the drug crisis.

The trend line of political hostage-taking in the 1980s has been largely positive, even if the statistics don't reflect it. Fewer international incidents are occurring, and those which do are generally of a less serious nature. Many countries have learned to cope with the threat and have been able to neutralize their terrorist opposition. But for all that the geographic distribution of incidents has changed, the problem is no less serious. As Lebanon and Colombia continue to disintegrate, political hostage-taking is practically a way of life. Other countries with shaky political situations, such as the Philippines and Sri Lanka, also give indications of a rise in such activity. As the 1980s draw to a close, the most common goal of hostage-taking appears no longer to be either media attention or criminal profit. It is now geared to intimidation—in the hope of securing political victories which otherwise would not be attainable. In that regard, perhaps the phenomenon has gone full circle back to the theories of Carlos Marighella.

# Chapter 7
# HOSTAGE NEGOTIATION

The United States and many other countries have firm policies against making concessions to terrorists and, of course, there are a variety of laws intended to deny to criminals the fruits of their labor. Given this, the idea of negotiating with criminals or terrorists seems, at first glance, a contradictory endeavor. This is not the case upon closer examination.

What has come to be called hostage negotiation arose out of the recognition that barricade situations are different from traditional negotiations. They also differ from the type of negotiations which occur during a kidnapping. A traditional negotiation situation usually is characterized by two (or more) parties coming together in order to arrive at a mutually advantageous result. Of course, there are situations in which one party enjoys such an advantage that he can impose a solution (which is what kidnappers try to do by ensuring the secrecy of where they hold their victim), but even then, the other party can often influence the ultimate result. This is not the case during hostage/barricade situations. Hostage negotiations have a different and more limited purpose.

In a hostage/barricade situation, there are advantages to conducting a dialogue between the authorities and the hostage-taker. As the incident unfolds, these negotiations are the only alternative to capitulation or the immediate use of force. The authorities can engage in such a dialogue while employing delaying tactics to wear down the hostage-taker and induce his peaceful surrender. Should this prove impossible, the delay gains time for rescue forces to plan and conduct a successful assault.

Hostage-takers also have an interest in such negotiations. If the hostage-taker is a criminal, he will be concerned with saving his life and attempting to arrange any deal possible. If he is mentally ill, he may have taken hostages as an extreme form of seeking attention and/or help. If the hostage-taker is a terrorist, his political agenda will be better served by prolonging the incident and, of course, so will his chances of emerging alive. In addition, terrorists have an overwhelming likelihood of being able to negotiate their freedom and safe passage in such situations. The motivations of the criminal hostage-taker are straightforward and require no elaboration, and those of the mentally ill are too involved to briefly address here. However, the agenda of the terrorist is more complex and we will approach our discussion of hostage negotiations from this perspective.

The terrorist takes hostages because of his desire to reach an audience wider than the immediate victims and governmental authorities. This can only be done if his actions and demands are widely publicized. A prolonged incident and negotiation process offers terrorists a chance to accomplish this.

Thus, the interests of the terrorist and the governmental authorities temporarily converge to produce an opportunity to engage in hostage negotiation. Now, let us look at the hostage negotiation process itself.

## THE NEGOTIATOR

The first thing to remember about hostage negotiation is the maxim, "negotiators never command and commanders never negotiate." It is vital that the person in overall charge of the decision-making process **NOT** be the actual negotiator unless absolutely no alternative exists. Regardless of the size of the responding organization, there generally will be a central decision-making authority and an incident manager. The negotiator should be neither of these. If this vital distinction is ignored, many of the tactics discussed below become impossible and, indeed, the very delaying aspect of the negotiations process will be destroyed.

In many cases, a governmental representative will do the actual negotiating. There are private negotiators available for cases in which it is determined that governmental authorities are more effectively kept at arm's length. However, it is not impossible that an individual can find himself simply thrust into this position as a result of happening to answer a telephone or otherwise being in the right place at the wrong time. Indeed, this happened in 1975 to a junior U.S. diplomat when the Japanese Red Army attacked the U.S. Consulate in Kuala Lumpur, Malaysia.[1] If there is any choice in the matter, the person selected should be someone who is able to establish credibility with the terrorist(s) while having the obligation to refer decisions to a higher authority.

The negotiator must be able to project a neutral and calming aura and must be able to focus on the practical questions related to resolving the incident while avoiding as much as possible becoming involved in political or philosophical disputes. However, because of the intensity of the negotiating process, the negotiator must guard against losing objectivity as events unfold. His sole job is to keep the hostage-takers talking for as long as possible. If possible, the negotiator should have an assistant to "keep him honest" or to take over if necessary, but the principal negotiator should not be changed except in extreme conditions. It is not necessary that the negotiator be a psychologist or other mental health specialist as long as such specialized expertise is available to him.

During a hostage/barricade incident, it is vital that the negotiator move quickly to identify and establish rapport with the leader of the terrorists. A feeling of teamwork must develop between the two so that they can build mutual trust and understanding. This, in turn, will develop into a mutual commitment to resolve the situation. Later in this chapter, we will discuss a number of rapport-building tactics which hostages might employ during their captivity. These are equally valid tactics for the negotiator.

---

[1]The consulate was a separate building, so the first word of trouble received by the embassy came in the form of a telephone call from the terrorists. A junior embassy officer just happened to be the one answering the telephone and, once contact had been established, the terrorists refused to accept any other intermediary.

## PSYCHOLOGICAL TYPES OF HOSTAGE-TAKERS

Analysis of past terrorist incidents suggests that four basic psychological types are involved in hostage incidents, often in some combination. While the motivation of terrorists is heavily influenced by their ideological agendas, the tactics employed by the negotiator rely in large measure on an accurate appraisal of the psychological type with which he is dealing. At the risk of oversimplification, four basic types can be identified.

1. *Paranoid Schizophrenics.* This type of person is characterized by false mental perceptions and/or delusions of persecution. Such people can appear normal at some moments and psychotic at others. Their thought process is often loose and lacks internal consistency or logic. If a person acts "weird" or irrationally, he or she may fit this type. One experienced hostage negotiator considers this type of person a car with more than a full tank of gas.[2] It's ready to go and can head off in any direction. An explosion can be set off by a single incautious remark (just like a spark or a lighted match can ignite gasoline fumes) or the person can be rendered rational by helping him to ventilate (similar to allowing excess gas fumes to dissipate).

2. *Psychotic Depressives.* This type of individual displays feelings of extreme sadness, hopelessness, inadequacy, or worthlessness. Thought and speech may be slow, and indecisiveness may be apparent. The concentration span of such people is limited and they are prone to suicide. This type is unlikely to be in a position of authority among the terrorists, as most terrorists wish to survive.[3] If a negotiator encounters a "go away" response, he may be dealing with this type of individual.

---

[2]This analogy comes from Michael Guidry, President of Guidry and Associates, who has successfully negotiated hostage situations in the United States and other countries. Several of the analogies used in this section come from him.

[3]With the emergence upon the scene of significant amounts of Shiite terrorism, this assumption may need revision. It appears to remain true with regard to most terrorists, but fanatics such as are found among the Shiites are

3. *Antisocial Personalities.* This type is incapable of true loyalty and is often characterized by selfish, callous, and irresponsible behavior. Such people often become criminals. They feel no guilt and have a low frustration tolerance. They tend to blame others no matter what the circumstances and consequently they tend to be the most difficult personality type with which to deal. If a negotiator encounters a pragmatic, realistic response, he may be dealing with this type of person. Such an individual can be compared to a cat. Just as a cat generally will only fight when forced to, the criminal knows that cutting a deal will enable him to survive the incident without having to fight.

4. *Inadequate Personalities.* This type of individual is unable to respond effectively to emotional, social, intellectual, and physical demands. Such people rely on others to set their personal agendas; they are "joiners." They are often inept, show poor judgment and social instability, and they may lack physical and/or emotional stamina. If a negotiator encounters prolonged unreasonableness, he may be dealing with this type of individual.

## NEGOTIATIONS MANAGEMENT

Before we discuss the process of hostage negotiation, we need to briefly consider the preconditions which such negotiations require. Much of the pioneering work in this area has been done at the FBI's National Academy. Researchers there have concluded that successful hostage negotiations require eight preconditions. These are:

---

more likely to engage in suicidal acts of terrorism. Should this willingness to die become more widespread, one of the foundations upon which hostage negotiation is based would be called into question.

1. *A desire to live on the part of the hostage-taker.* The overwhelming majority of hostage-takers—whether they are terrorists, criminals, or mentally deranged—may be prepared to die, but would prefer to live through the incident. In some cases, most notably those involving Shiite terrorism, the reverse is true, but hostage-taking is only a small part of their operational repetoire. However, occasionally, terrorists' dedication to their cause can result in an intransigence which is predicated on the acceptance of death on a mission. The 1973 Khartoum incident, in which Black September murdered American and Belgian diplomats, was an instance in which the importance of the mission outweighed any personal considerations of the terrorists. The incident at Ma'alot in 1974, where many school children died along with Palestinian terrorists, may be another example.

2. *Sufficient force to threaten the life of the hostage-taker.* Negotiation depends upon leverage for success. If a hostage-taker does not take the authorities seriously, then none is possible. Force provides leverage for the authorities against the hostage-taker, just as the hostage provides his captor with leverage against the authorities. In 1977, during the train hijacking in Holland (described earlier), the terrorists never believed that the Dutch would employ force against them. Therefore, negotiations could never really begin—ensuring that force would have to be employed.

3. *Communication between the hostage-taker and a negotiator representing the outside force which threatens the hostage-taker.* Without communication, no negotiation is possible. This is generally easy to accomplish, since a primary objective of many hostage-takers is publicity and attention. However, in cases such as the holding of Western hostages in Lebanon during the 1980s, all communication has been one-sided, resembling a traditional kidnapping. In these cases, there can be little, if any, negotiation, because the authorities have no direct method of communicating with the hostage-takers. Hostage negotiation conducted through intermediaries is much more problematical, as evidenced by the deaths of at

least nine Western hostages held in Lebanon by Shiite terrorists.[4]

4. *A decision-maker for the hostage-taker(s).* The first purpose of hostage negotiation is to resolve the situation peacefully. This requires decisions to be made by the hostage-takers as well as by the authorities. If there is no accepted leader among the hostage-takers, this becomes impossible. This is frequently the case, as it was during the Iranian hostage incident of 1979–81. Real progress was made only when the Iranian government decided to assert itself over the terrorists holding the U.S. Embassy staff.

5. *One or more demands by the hostage-takers.* Negotiations of any kind require something to discuss. In the case of terrorists, demands are almost always present when hostages are taken. Ascertaining these demands is a high priority for the negotiator during the early stages of any incident.

6. *Containment of the situation which restricts the freedom of movement of the hostage-taker.* Just as force is required to foster negotiations, so is containment of the situation a further inducement to negotiate. During the Iranian hostage incident, there was no containment—unless one counts the fact that the terrorists never left Iran. The same is true of the Lebanese situation.

7. *Time to establish the necessary rapport between the hostage-taker and the negotiator, as well as between the hostage-taker and the hostages, if possible.* Time is an essential factor

---

[4]As of October 1, 1989, the following Western hostages died in captivity at the hands of Shiite terrorists in Lebanon: Lt. Col. William R. Higgins (U.S. commander of the U.N. Forces in Lebanon), Alec Collett (British consultant to the U.N. agency for Palestinian refugees), John Leigh Douglas (British professor at the American University in Beirut), Philip Padfield (British director of the International Language Center), Peter Kilburn (U.S. librarian at American University), Michel Seurat (French researcher at the French Center for Studies and Research of the Contemporary Middle East), William Buckley (U.S. station chief in Beirut), Denis Hill (British teacher at American University), and Father Nicolas Kluiters (Dutch priest).

for successful negotiations. With the passage of time the important psychological and physiological phenomena discussed later in this chapter can be brought into play. These are an important part of the negotiator's arsenal of techniques to induce the hostage-taker to surrender. As unpleasant as it is, the longer a hostage/barricade situation continues, the better the chances are that the hostages will be saved.

8. *A negotiator who can successfully represent the outside force's capability to harm the hostage-taker, but who can also demonstrate a credible willingness to help the hostage-taker.* Credibility on the part of the negotiator is essential. Once containment and force have induced the hostage-taker to negotiate, the negotiator must develop a bond of sorts with him. The hostility felt by Shiites toward the United States made it impossible for direct negotiations to occur during the Iranian and Lebanese hostage situations. In 1980, at Princes Gate in London (see Chapter 6), despite the cultural gap between the British and the anti-Khomeini terrorists, the negotiator was able to develop the kind of bond with the terrorists' leader which made it possible to prepare a successful rescue operation.

It is vital for the successful resolution of a hostage negotiation that the overall commander/decision-maker retain control over the situation. Indeed, that is the essential rationale for hostage negotiation: recapturing the initiative from the hostage-taker and retaining control of the situation until its conclusion. Full control over the physical scene, communications, and all the other elements of the situation are essential. Communications between the decision-maker, the negotiator, and the tactical incident commander must be frequent and unrestricted in order to assure the smooth coordination of the negotiating process. However, in order not to compromise the negotiator's position, tactical details related to the activities of the rescue forces should not be divulged to him.[5]

---

[5]Indeed, most experts caution against ever revealing such details to a negotiator. It is an unusual person who can ensure that prior knowledge of an upcoming assault might not affect his inflection, choice of words, or other-

During an incident, most things are negotiable. Among the negotiable items are: food, beverages, transportation, media access, and basic human needs (e.g., sanitation, air conditioning, heat, medication, etc.) There are, however, several things which are not. These include: alcohol, weapons, drugs, and usually the exchanging of hostages.

1. *Alcohol.* The effects of alcohol are at least as unpredictable during a barricade incident as they are in a social or business setting. The situation is already complicated and fraught with enough peril without the possibility that a terrorist might prove to be a hostile drunk or that a hostage might do something foolish under the influence of alcohol.

2. *Weapons.* Presumably the terrorists are already so sufficiently armed that they are able to retain control over the hostages and pose a threat to any rescue attempts. To allow them an increase in their arsenal would only worsen the situation.

3. *Drugs.* Just as the effects of alcohol are unpredictable, so are the effects of other drugs. Many hostage-takers already are mentally unstable, so why risk tipping them over the edge? In many cases (hijackings are a good example), terrorists already are using drugs to stay awake or for other reasons. This is an area which is not clear-cut. Some experts in the field believe that drugs can be used effectively under certain circumstances, for example, to disrupt biological processes. There are even some who suggest that certain types of drugs are worth giving to a hostage-taker in exchange for the release of hostages or

---

wise be signalled to the terrorists. After all, the negotiator has worked hard to establish a cooperative bond. The additional strain of knowing that he must remain in contact at the very moment of an assault is to be avoided whenever possible.

This is not to say that it is impossible for a negotiator to be intimately involved in the timing of an assault. During the 1980 Princes Gate episode, at the very moment the SAS was exploding stun grenades, the negotiator was saying, "What suspicious movements? Salim, there is no suspicious movement."

other concessions. (The damaging effects of withdrawal symp-
toms, for example, might have to be taken into account.)

4. *Exchanging hostages.* This generally is a bad idea, despite
what we see in movies. Two related reasons for this are that
(1) the new hostage(s) will be perceived as having greater importance than those exchanged and (2) such an exchange can
raise the emotional levels of everyone concerned. Since one of
the primary considerations of hostage negotiation is the calming effect of time and communication, rarely is such an exchange advisable.

The overwhelming majority of hostage/barricade incidents
are resolved through negotiation. Part of the purpose of hostage
negotiation is to stall for as much time as possible and this
process will occur under conditions of extreme stress. Therefore
an effective negotiator must structure the dialogue with the
hostage-taker in order to retain the maximum amount of control
over the process. There usually are three distinct phases in a
hostage situation. In many ways, these are like a chess game
and our terminology reflects this.

1. *The Opening Gambit.* This is the initial phase, which can
be measured in terms of hours at most. During this period, the
hostage-taker(s) will be extremely agitated and will demand the
moon. This obviously is a dangerous period for the hostages.
The negotiator's task will be to calm things down and to establish rapport with the decision-maker among the hostage-takers.
Once this is done, the serious negotiation can begin.

2. *Jockeying for Position.* In this phase, which will constitute
the bulk of the hostage/barricade incident, time and the discussion will usually result in a gradual reduction of the hostage-
taker's demands—first to realistic ones, finally to bottom-line,
face-saving ways of ending the standoff. The negotiator must
be patient and be prepared to exploit any openings provided by
the hostage-taker.

3. *Endgame.* When this stage is reached, things will begin to
move quickly. The hostage-taker(s) will want things to be done
NOW and the tension level will increase dramatically. Errors or
confusion can result in tragedy. This period is one of potential

danger for the hostages. The negotiator must remain calm and be alert to signs that agreements are unraveling. This is the time where all of the effort expended by the negotiator to create trust and credibility will maximize the likelihood that the outcome will be successful.

Another way of looking at the stages of a hostage situation is to liken it to an airplane flight. The opening phase is similar to the takeoff phase of the flight. It can be a period of extreme tension for passengers unused to flying. Once the plane is airborne, this tension is reduced and, for the bulk of the flight (jockeying for position), routine and **relative** calm ensue. The landing period, or our endgame phase, is once again a period of tension, when noises or other "startling" occurrences can provoke an unthinking reaction.

During each of these stages, the negotiator will employ different tactics. After an initial period in which the negotiator attempts to build rapport with the hostage-taker(s), it is important to remember that no concession should be made to them without receiving something in return. This develops a process in which the hostage-taker(s) begin to become conditioned to accepting suggestions and direction from the negotiator and increasingly places them in a frame of mind conducive to resolving the situation. Accordingly, food could be exchanged for hostages, fuel for being allowed to send medicine in to a hostage, media exposure for weapons, etc. The key here is to reduce the number of hostages at risk and/or the defensive capabilities of the hostage-takers. With this basic caveat in mind, the following types of tactics are among those which have been employed successfully in past incidents.

1. *Keeping the hostage-taker(s) in a detail-coping mode.* By being forced to concentrate on a myriad of minor problems, hostage-takers can be worn down and lose control over the flow of events. The negotiator used this technique with extreme effectiveness during the 1980 Princes Gate incident; one even covered the beginning of the rescue operation by diverting the terrorists' attention towards the discussion of the details of a bus they had demanded.

2. *Using open-ended questions, i.e., the type which cannot be answered with yes or no, but require a response and encourage continuing conversation.* This relates to the previous point regarding keeping the hostage-taker in a detail-coping mode. Again, the Princes Gate episode demonstrates the usefulness of this technique, not only for promoting negotiations, but also for buying time and covering the activities of rescue forces.

3. *Avoiding confrontations.* Hostage negotiations are about calming things down, not exacerbating them. One hostage, Abbas Lavasani, learned to his misfortune that confrontation can cost lives during the Princes Gate incident.

4. *Ignoring deadlines by trying to talk through them.* As the expiration of each ultimatum approaches, attention should be diverted from the deadline by introducing some new problem or aspect. This provides the hostage-taker with a plausible reason for allowing the deadline to pass without any action on his part. After the first deadline passes, subsequent ones will be easier to talk through. In a 1983 terrorist incident in the Sudan, the terrorists simply forgot that a deadline had passed. Allowing this to happen made it more difficult for them to stick to other deadlines during the incident and, not incidentally, saved the lives of five hostages.

5. *Ensuring control over who has access to the hostage-taker.* Every successful negotiation depends upon this factor. The movie *Dog Day Afternoon* is frequently cited by experts as a good example of what happens when this is not done. Based upon a true story, the movie depicts how public access to the scene resulted in the creation of a circus atmosphere—with the result that the authorities lost control of the situation.

6. *Seeking to have injured, women, children, or other categories of hostages released in groups.* During the opening stages of a hostage situation, hostage-takers (especially terrorists) tend to think of their captives as symbols or pawns. This makes them willing to consider them in categories and as commodities to be exchanged when advantageous. During the 1976 Entebbe incident, the terrorists decided to release all of the non-Jewish hostages. From their point of view, this simplified things; for the Israelis, it made the rescue operation easier. A

good negotiator will attempt to use this categorization to reduce the number of hostages at risk.

7. *Manipulating the environment of the hostage-takers.* Communications, electricity, water, and other factors can be manipulated to isolate the hostage-takers and wear down their resistance level. In March 1977, the Hanafi Muslim seizure of B'nai B'rith offices and other locations in Washington, D.C. (including the District Building) was resolved after over 40 hours in part because the leader of the terrorists, Hamaas Khaalis, could not tolerate performing his bodily functions in front of the hostages after authorities cut off all utility services to the building.

8. *Using terrorist rhetoric against them by appealing to humanitarian or other concerns.* Terrorists are very concerned with appearances. They generally couch their rhetoric in humanitarian or internationalist terms, using phrases such as "workers' rights," "anti-colonialism," "oppression," etc. These words—although only superficially relevant to terrorist actions—can sometimes be turned against them to gain the release of hostages. In many hijackings, the sick or injured, women, children, or other hostages have been released on "humanitarian" grounds. Negotiators can often employ the appeals of family members, religious leaders, and others to gauge the depth of terrorists' sincerity. Hostage-takers may choose to use such appeals as face-saving ways to make concessions.

9. *Avoiding negative responses.* Instead of saying no to a demand, the negotiator will stall, citing the need to refer to a higher authority. (Note the difficulty of a positive response, which might increase the hostage-taker's expectations.) Every professional in this field with whom we are familiar agrees on this point. Delay, not refusal, is the order of the day.[6]

10. *Being positive and upbeat.* The negotiator must always maintain the attitude that everything can be worked out and he must constantly reassure the hostage-taker(s) that this is the case. During the 1980 Princes Gate episode (surely one of the

---

[6]This and other points are covered in easily understood detail in Frank-Bolz's *Hostage Cop.*

best examples of the art of hostage negotiation), both police negotiators did this effectively.

11. *Seeking to downplay the importance of the hostages as a lever for the hostage-taker.* The hostage-taker must be persuaded to keep them alive, but he must not develop the idea that hostage safety will override all other considerations on the part of law enforcement authorities. During the 1980 incident at the Dominican Republic's embassy in Bogotá, Colombia, a group of Latin American terrorists were able to take as hostages a number of ambassadors and other diplomats. In this and similar incidents, the importance of these hostages was obvious—engendering delays and difficulties in the negotiations. However, in many other hostage incidents—hijackings, for example—the status of individual hostages is not immediately obvious to the terrorists.

12. *Keeping a record of deadlines, promises, actions, and other significant events so that nothing is overlooked and no surprises are encountered.* We have already mentioned the incident in the Sudan where terrorists simply forgot about their deadline. This can be advantageous for the authorities, but they must never allow themselves to fall into the same situation. During the Ma'alot incident in Israel, the Israelis were constantly aware of the terrorists' deadline, and structured their response accordingly.

13. *Forcing the hostage-taker(s) and hostages to cooperate in resolving problems.* One example of this is to provide food and drinks in bulk fashion, which requires a cooperative effort among the hostages and hostage-takers to produce the final meal. Doing so helps to promote important psychological bonding and enhances the positive effects of the Stockholm Syndrome (see below).

These and other tactics are dependent upon a trained evaluation of the situation and must be tailored to the circumstances of each incident. They are more easily prescribed than accomplished. Overall, the important thing for a hostage negotiator is to be flexible in approach and, if one tactic does not seem to work, to move smoothly to another.

If all goes well, the immediate problem is successfully resolved and the negotiator is, in effect, out of work. Having
talked himself out of a job, the negotiator should expect to experience a reaction to the stress and emotion of the situation.
This "letdown" will also apply to the other members of the
crisis team which dealt with the incident—and to the hostages
after their release. The recovery period for these people will
depend on the circumstances of the just-resolved situation, but
adjustments will be required on the part of supervisors, families, etc. to assist all concerned to return to normal.


## WHY IT WORKS

Numerous studies of the dynamics of hostage and barricade
situations have been made to identify their common characteristics. Out of this, experts have been able to isolate a number of
psychological aspects which appear to have been present. These
form the basis for the tactics of hostage negotiation. Some have
been mentioned above. We are fortunately giving nothing away
to the bad guys of the world, because many of the studies conducted reveal that **even where terrorists or other hostage-
takers are aware of the psychological aspects of hostage
negotiation, the techniques can still be employed successfully. Additionally, even where hostage-takers have attempted
to take countermeasures,[7] these psychological phenomena
manifest themselves anyway.** Some of these phenomena will
occur in any prolonged hostage/barricade or kidnapping incident;
others will occur only in particular cases. This is not to say that

---

[7]The case of Sir Geoffrey Jackson, British ambassador to Uruguay (discussed in Chapter 2), is a case in point. During his debriefings and in his
published memoirs, Sir Geoffrey noted that his guards were frequently rotated
and hooded and that his contacts with them were limited in an attempt to
prevent the development of any type of a relationship between them. Despite
this, a considerable amount of what would later be named the Stockholm
Syndrome was present by the time of his release.

terrorists and other thinking bad guys are not doing their homework on this subject. The average terrorist is a college graduate, young, intelligent, and innovative. These people critically study their subject matter and modify their tactics accordingly. Experts have noted changes in how the terrorists conduct their operations. These changes require that hostage negotiators constantly revise their techniques. There is a distinct possibility that the bad guys of the world may be improving their techniques faster than the good guys can react—suggesting that hostage negotiation may become vastly more complicated in the future.

Nonetheless, up to this point, the psychological aspects of hostage/barricade incidents have proven to be relatively constant and exploitable. During a negotiation, recognizing the manifestations of these phenomena is an important part of the negotiator's job.


## THE STOCKHOLM SYNDROME

The Stockholm Syndrome derives its name from a 1973 incident which occurred in the Swedish capital. After an attempted bank robbery was foiled by the rapid arrival of police, the hapless criminal retreated into the bank's vault with a number of the bank's employees and customers as hostages. During the ensuing six-day negotiations, which resulted in the would-be bank robber's surrender, a number of surprising developments occurred.

The criminal and the hostages established a cooperative relationship which complicated every action of the police. Hostages provided their captor with suggestions and acted as lookouts for him, even while he was asleep. When his surrender took place, the hostages formed a human wall around him out of fear that the police might shoot him. One of the hostages (a schoolteacher) even hugged and kissed him before he was taken away by police, professing her love for him. She married him while he was still in prison.

Puzzled by this, psychologists studied this case in considerable detail and ultimately determined that a type of transfer-

e, or bonding, took place between the hostage-taker and the
ages. Later cases have demonstrated that transference of
type can be encouraged by negotiators and can contribute
peaceful and successful resolution of hostage and/or barri-
situations.

his important phenomenon can be a two-edged sword. In
e critical ways it can complicate the resolution of an inci-
; at the same time, its manifestation is a key asset in secur-
the safe release of hostages. The Stockholm Syndrome has
e components, not all of which are always present. First,
e are positive feelings on the part of the hostage(s) toward
ir captor(s). Second, there are negative feelings on the part
he hostage(s) toward the police and other authorities. Third,
re are positive feelings on the part of the hostage-taker to-
rd his captive(s).

Jpon examination, none of these three factors is surprising.
sitive feelings about one's captors simply are a manifestation
dependence. After all, the hostage is completely dependent
on the hostage-taker for everything from food and the perfor-
nance of bodily functions to his very life. In such a case, it is
natural that the hostage will begin to seek ways to build an
alliance with his captor and to focus on the positive in doing
so. This is a form of bonding similar to that which occurs between an infant and his mother. The complete dependence of
the hostage promotes gratitude (for not being harmed) and a
positive affiliation with the captor in much the same way that
nursing promotes the development of love between a baby and
his mother. Because the infant-mother bond represents the most
basic form of security as well as dependence, some experts
have suggested that this facet of the Stockholm Syndrome represents a form of psychological regression by the hostage.[8]

The development of negative feelings toward the authorities
by a hostage is, in many ways, a logical extension of the first

---

[8]See, for example, "Hostage Negotiation: *Law Enforcement's Most Effective Non-Lethal Weapon,*" by FBI Supervisory Special Agent Clinton R. Van-
Zandt and David A. Soskis, MD, n.d.

component of the Stockholm Syndrome. As the positive affiliation with his captor occurs, the hostage comes to blame the
authorities for his predicament. After all, if the police would
just let the captor go, if the government would just agree to the
terrorist's demands, everyone could go home. When this is
coupled with a realization that the police may come through the
door shooting, the hostage comes to believe that the **real** danger to his life is the action of the authorities outside rather than
any threat from his captor inside.[9]

The last part of the Stockholm Syndrome, positive identification of the hostage-taker with the hostage, also has a readily
understandable basis. As an incident begins, the hostage has no
personality for the hostage-taker; hostages are merely leverage
to be used with the authorities during the negotiations process.
However, as events unfold, the close proximity between captor
and hostage as they share the crisis forces them to see each
other as human beings. In a terrorist setting, this changes the
hostage from an impersonal symbol to a living, breathing person. This makes it much harder for the terrorist (or any
hostage-taker) to harm the hostage.[10]

The hostage negotiator has no control over the development
of the first two components of the Stockholm Syndrome. However, he can and should do everything possible to encourage the
development of the third. In fact, a skilled negotiator may be

---

[9]It is interesting that a review of the deaths of 1001 hostages killed or
injured during incidents revealed that 781 of them resulted from police action. A second study, done by the FBI, found that during rescue operations,
12 percent of hostages were killed. Perhaps the danger sensed by hostages is
not completely a matter of psychological transference.

[10]The 1975 seizure by the South Moluccan Independence Movement of a
Dutch train provides an excellent example of this. During the 20-day incident,
the terrorists selected a hostage for killing in order to put pressure on the
Dutch authorities. The hostage, Gerard Vaders, was allowed to give another
hostage a message for his family. The terrorists listened to Vaders explain his
family situation and apologize for his lapses as a father and husband. They
then decided to select a different hostage for death. That person was instantly
killed, before anything could make them change their minds.

able to extend this third factor into a positive relationship between himself and the hostage-taker. Time is often a factor in this process, but the negotiator can assist by emphasizing the hostages' human qualities, by frequently inquiring about their well-being, and by creating tasks which the hostage-takers and the hostages must perform as a group (for example, the distribution of bulk foods and clothing).

The important thing to remember is that, while the development of the Stockholm Syndrome is a positive sign in terms of the ultimate resolution of an incident, the close identification between hostages and their captors must be kept in mind as the incident unfolds. This places an additional burden on the authorities during any rescue or surrender, as they cannot be certain of the extent to which this identification may prompt unexpected and dangerous actions by the hostages.


## GET RID OF THE JERK

Hostage-takers like things to go as they were planned. One of the reasons that violence commonly is used in the early moments of hostage incidents is to allow the hostage-taker to establish his dominance over his victims. If things do not develop as planned, hostage-takers can become agitated or upset. Losing face to or feeling outmaneuvered by a hostage can have unfortunate results. This gives rise to a potential for the unwary hostage to become his own worst enemy. In many ways, this is the reverse of the Stockholm Syndrome in that it causes the hostage-taker to dislike a particular hostage so intensely that, at the first opportunity, he harms or kills him. There are two ways in which this can be observed.

1. *The Wimp Effect.* It is frequently suggested that hostages cooperate with their captors in order to avoid unnecessary victimization during their ordeal. This is undoubtedly a good idea, but it is possible to overdo it. Terrorists often will select an overcompliant hostage if they decide a death or beating is necessary. During the preparations for the 1984 Summer Olympics

in Los Angeles, a simulation was staged in which this happened. Even trained FBI agents and other law enforcement personnel who participated in the simulation felt that one of the "hostages" was so cooperative with the "terrorists" that he was perceived as a wimp. In our conversations with them they reported that when the simulation reached the stage where the "terrorists" were considering killing a "hostage," they decided quite quickly to kill "the wimp." If trained and experienced peace officers can succumb to this phenomenon, consider what a terrorist might do.

2. *Lavasani's Mistake*. In 1980, during the seizure of the Iranian Embassy in London by anti-Khomeini terrorists, Abbas Lavasani persisted in debating the merits of the Islamic Revolution with the terrorists.[11] For what it is worth, he easily won the debate. His prize was death, for the terrorists disliked him so much that he became a symbol of all they despised about Ayatollah Khomeini and, when they wanted to demonstrate their resolve to the British government, guess who they decided to kill? This is the other extreme in undoing the beneficial effects of the Stockholm Syndrome.

## I'M STILL IN CHARGE

This phenomenon is rare, but it can be especially important in the case of a high-level corporate or governmental official being among the hostages. This occasionally means that more junior officials will be in charge of the incident response and will be making the type of decisions which normally would fall to the hostage himself. The case of Diego Asencio, U.S. ambassador to Colombia in the early 1980s, is a perfect example of this.

---

[11]In studies of the psychology of terrorists, one category of individual has been noted often. This is the incomplete problem-solver, someone who is not sufficiently articulate to debate the merits of his position and becomes frustrated when that position is challenged. In this instance, it appears that at least some of the terrorists fit this profile.

Taken hostage while attending a diplomatic function at the Dominican Republic's embassy in Bogotá, Ambassador Asencio concluded that the terrorists were inept and that their mishandling of negotiations with the Colombians risked provoking an assault in which everyone's life would be in jeopardy. Along with several of his fellow ambassadors, Asencio became an adviser to the terrorists, helping them formulate their negotiation strategy and respond to Colombian positions. To this day, Asencio maintains that his direct involvement in the negotiations was a major factor which ensured a non-violent resolution of the incident. Others, however, have suggested that his participation only complicated an already-difficult situation. Asencio not only advised the terrorists, but continued to perform his role as ambassador by telephone, giving instructions to the U.S. Embassy staff! In this case, he was involved on both sides of the situation, placing considerable pressure upon his deputy chief of mission, who was caught between Washington and the ambassador.

The Department of State has taken steps to reduce the likelihood of a recurrence of such a situation. Should an ambassador or other senior official be taken hostage or kidnapped, he would be immediately relieved of his authority for the duration of the incident. The normal chain of command provides an acting replacement, and orders received from the captured official are considered as suggestions of a person under duress. Corporations and other organizations would be well advised to establish a similar system in order to protect both potential victims and their staffs from an unnecessary source of complication and pressure.

## COMMON PHYSIOLOGICAL FACTORS

In addition to the psychological considerations we have discussed above, there are concrete physiological dimensions to a hostage situation. Manifestations of them may affect hostagetakers, hostages, and even the authorities attempting to resolve the situation. Just as the psychological factors repeatedly have been documented, so too have the physiological ones. In this field, too, the Federal Bureau of Investigation has been in the forefront of research. Specialists in the Special Operations and Research Section at the FBI Academy have identified at least seven physiological changes (and their associated disorders) which have occurred during hostage situations.

The first change involves the cardiovascular system. Cases are on record which document the occurrence of myocardial infarctions (heart attacks) and strokes, at one extreme, and fainting spells at the other. The stress of any type of involvement in a hostage situation can clearly induce these disorders.[12]

A second change involves the respiratory system. In this area, as in so many others, if a person is susceptible to a medical problem, the stress of a hostage situation may trigger its onset. Hyperventilation and asthma are common examples of the types of disorders which can occur. This change can also affect trained emergency response personnel. In one training simulation, a police officer who played the role of a hostage hyperventilated to the point that he could no longer talk.

The third type of physiological change which has been documented involves the gastrointestinal tract. Cases of diarrhea or loss of bladder control have been reported during hostage incidents. (Known among hostage negotiators as "the biologicals," these can be an important factor in the negotiation process.)

A frequent change—which many of us have experienced under less strenuous conditions—involves tension, with its associated disorders such as headaches. Given the life-threatening situation of a hostage/barricade situation, it is not a surprise that people involved in the matter experience this problem.

Adrenalin, that vital, often life-saving hormone which provides the human body with extra energy under stressful conditions, can also produce unwanted changes. Disorders such as

---

[12]When we turn shortly to a discussion of hostage conduct, we will stress the importance of maintaining physical fitness. This is important for crisis managers as well.

diabetes and shakes and tremors can be induced by too much adrenalin. A continuing hostage situation can result in the body's production of adrenalin over a prolonged period—a case of too much of a good thing.

Another change which can manifest itself involves the stomach. Ulcers are one example of a stress-induced disorder involving this part of the human anatomy.

Finally, and in some ways the result of the accumulation of many other changes, hypervigilance can result from the uncertainties of a hostage situation. Insomnia, for example, can result from the increased level of awareness which hostages often report or the combination of action and waiting on the part of crisis managers. Diego Asencio, whose case was discussed earlier in this chapter, reported that his increased level of awareness persisted for some time after he was freed.

## HOSTAGE CONDUCT

We have already discussed the hostage negotiator's objectives and some of the ways in which they can be accomplished. There are also techniques which have proven to be useful from the point of view of the hostage. We do not propose to provide the reader with an all-inclusive listing of sure-fire methods.[13] However, no discussion of the phenomenon of hostage-taking is complete without a look at things from the hostage's point of view.

To begin with, the Stockholm Syndrome and its manifestations have both positive and negative implications. The longer the duration of an incident, the more likely it is that these manifestations will occur. However, there is no particular time factor. One of us was involved in a situation which lasted 6½ hours in Managua, Nicaragua. Only an hour or two were nec-

---

[13]*The Handbook for Effective Emergency and Crisis Management, op. cit.,* contains some detailed suggestions for building rapport with captors and other important considerations of victimology.

essary for the beginnings of a relationship to develop which made the negotiations process much simpler.

The cases of Sir Geoffrey Jackson and a number of other hostage victims suggest that the beneficial effects of the Stockholm Syndrome can be induced if hostages exercise care. Remembering that there is a fine line between cooperation and over-compliance, consider how Sir Geoffrey's demonstration of quiet dignity may have impressed the *Tupamaro* terrorists to the point that he, not they, became the dominant influence. Remaining calm and in control of your emotions is a good idea at any time, but during a hostage-taking or kidnapping, it can be of crucial importance.

Another technique which experience shows to be worthwhile is for a hostage to keep himself occupied. Physical exercise may be possible in many cases; mental exercise is always possible. During the 444 days of captivity of the U.S. diplomatic staff in Tehran, despite constant confinement, many of the hostages engaged in physical fitness exercises and virtually all of them kept their minds occupied. Claude Fly, whose experience was recounted in Chapter 2, wrote his autobiography and developed a checklist to analyze the New Testament. A final example is the development of the game of Chinese Checkers, whose origins have been traced to an unnamed Irishman imprisoned by the British in the 1920s. Whatever the circumstances, mental and, where possible, physical fitness appear to contribute to lessening the effects—both psychological and physiological—of a hostage ordeal.

Avoiding provocative discussions is also important. We have mentioned the sad case of Abbas Lavasani in London. This is not to suggest that no conversation with captors could be productive. Gerard Vaders' discussion of his life with another hostage during a Dutch train hijacking ultimately saved him from death. As a situation evolves, there may be opportunities for many types of conversation between hostages and captors. Such contact is normally beneficial, but following the old adage of never discussing politics, sex, or religion, if they can be avoided, is a wise precaution.

Finally, those hostages who best survived their ordeal and were best able to resume their normal lives afterward unanimously advocate the importance of flexibility and adaptability to the circumstances of captivity. Eating what food is available, no matter how foul-tasting or unappealing, is one way of maintaining physical health. Eating also helps one pass a certain amount of time, as well as providing a mechanism to gauge the passage of time over prolonged periods (in most cultures, meals are taken at regular times). A sense of humor—as long as it doesn't offend captors—is an important asset. Keeping mentally active by noting details of surroundings and attempting to anticipate events can help to keep up morale and ward off despair and fear. The combination of keeping active and remaining flexible is the constant element reported by those who have endured captivity with the least amount of psychological damage.

## THE TERRORIST LEARNING CURVE

Earlier, we observed that the average terrorist is young, college educated, intelligent, and innovative. This combination of attributes suggests that, as in so many other areas, change is inevitable. As a result, considerable adaptation has been required to respond to new terrorist tactics.

In the February 1976 terrorist incident in Djibouti, tranquilizers were placed in food and sharpshooters waited for the proper moment to take out all of the terrorists simultaneously. As a result of the tranquilization-via-food tactic, hostage-takers have become suspicious and the technique has had to be adopted of sending in foodstuffs in their original **sealed** packages to assure that there has been no tampering. Of course, this dovetails nicely with the general goal of using meals to build a bond between hostage-takers and captives, but it has added a new, albeit small, problem to be overcome during the negotiations.

The more general fallout from the Djibouti incident is a problem for those charged with gathering intelligence and planning rescue operations. Since the Djibouti incident, hijackers of all types frequently have resorted to pulling down window shades or otherwise removing themselves from sight. During the 1980 Princes Gate incident, a technique used to try to overcome this was the passing of food, notes, etc. through a window via a box on a pole. However, this technique was only successful in identifying one terrorist.

Again, more related to rescue operations than to hostage negotiation itself, terrorists have also learned some of the techniques used in the past by elite units such as the SAS, GIGN, and GSG-9. These days, tactical intelligence units have discovered that hostages are moved within airplanes, stairwells are blocked, and other actions are taken which greatly complicate the mounting of a rescue operation.

In addition, the terrorists have learned the value of mobility itself—as the June 1985 hijacking of TWA Flight 847 demonstrated. Hijackers previously would order the captured airplane to a specific location and remain there. Once on the ground, many different ways were available to the authorities to keep it there. This allowed rescue forces to position themselves and begin their preparations.

The hijackers of TWA 847 thwarted this process by moving the plane several times between Algiers and Beirut, taking on additional confederates in Beirut, and, finally, moving the hostages off the plane and dispersing them throughout the city. Although the U.S. Delta Force was deployed, it could only chase the plane from location to location and watch helplessly as the terrorists retained the initiative. Additionally, all negotiations were conducted via the TWA pilot, which eliminated the possibility of any negotiator's building rapport with the terrorists.

Of equal concern to hostage negotiators are the examples in which terrorists have attempted to mitigate the development of the Stockholm Syndrome—principally by placing obstacles to the development of a bond between themselves and their captives. The *Tupamaros* recognized this psychological facet of hostage-taking even before the Stockholm Syndrome was named and unsuccessfully attempted to thwart it by frequently rotating Sir Geoffrey Jackson's guards. More recently, during the December 1981-February 1982 kidnapping of U.S. Brigadier General James Dozier in Italy, the Red Brigades kept the general in a tent which had its own toilet and a light. Dozier was kept chained to a cot inside and he took all of his meals alone therein. His guards never spoke to him and remained masked throughout the episode. There is no indication that any manifestation of the Stockholm Syndrome occurred. Over time, terrorists continue to employ new tactics designed to overcome the psychological tactics of the authorities. Staying one step ahead is increasingly difficult for the good guys.

A final example of how terrorists learn from experience deals with hijackings. During the early 1970s, hijackers tended to wear some sort of distinctive clothing or uniform during their operations. This may have been done out of a desire to set themselves apart as warriors in their self-proclaimed war of liberation, but it proved counterproductive. Such distinctive garb helped the authorities to identify them and, in at least one case, made it easier for sharpshooters to target them. This is no longer the case. There are even some cases of hostage-takers changing clothes with hostages and making them look out of windows carrying unloaded weapons—all in an effort to further confuse already confusing situations.

It is difficult to say just how long current hostage negotiation tactics will remain effective. There are indications of an increasing tendency for hijackers to remain mobile (e.g., TWA 847 and the *Achille Lauro*), a difficult problem for the authorities. What is certain is that current and future terrorists are learning from previous experiences just as surely as are the rest of us—at least we **hope** we are keeping up with them.

# Chapter 8
# THE DEMOCRATIC DILEMMA

In Chapter 1, we saw how hostage-taking has ebbed and flowed as a political tool over the years. This cyclical approach is particularly relevant in today's world, as the nation-state system which has characterized the past two hundred years shows signs of age. We have noted how the nation-state—political organization based upon national interests and goals—replaced feudal and dynastic government in the West and how, at the same time, hostage-taking changed from a political tool to a criminal one. In the late twentieth century, as the nation-state finds itself in competition with other international political actors—some of which are criminal—hostage-taking has again begun to assume a significant role in international politics.

The various terrorist groups we have discussed are essentially organizations of political criminality. For that reason, they are comfortable with the use of tactics such as hostage-taking.[1] Politically, this represents a reversion to tactics which

---

[1]The emergence of narcoterrorism demonstrates how the ultimate ramifications of terrorism can be unpredictable. In Colombia (the best example of how narcoterrorism can destabilize a country), the drug traffickers were a major target for kidnapping by the country's terrorist groups. Finally, in 1981, the M-19 group kidnapped Marta Ochoa, daughter of Fabio Ochoa, patriarch of a leading drug trafficking family. This proved to be the straw which broke the camel's back.

In response to this incident, Jorge Luis Ochoa, Marta's brother, called on the support of all the leading Colombian drug lords. The meeting they held to discuss how to end this threat once and for all is generally accepted as the beginning of what is now known as the Medellin cartel. Out of this meeting, the drug lords formed a joint strike force which immediately sought out and killed dozens of persons who were connected (however tenuously) to the M-19.

emphasize decision-making based upon personal or parochial considerations, as opposed to truly national ones. (Indeed, one could argue that the growth of media influence described earlier helps to "personalize" it.) In the Middle Ages, a kingdom could be crippled if its ruler was incapacitated or captured. Today, terrorist hostage-takers achieve the same result by abducting individual citizens. In countries such as Lebanon (and perhaps Colombia soon) where the breakdown of national political authority has become almost total, hostage-taking has become a way of life.

Different groups have used this tactic with varying degrees of success. They have done so because of their particular organizational dynamics and because of the responses of particular governments. This combination of needs and responses continues to be present in many parts of the world.

## ORGANIZATIONAL DEVELOPMENT

Just as civilizations pass through stages, so too do organizations of all types. Different techniques and objectives characterize organizations at particular periods of their development. Terrorist groups are no different.

Regardless of its ideology, each terrorist group passes through the same stages of development on its route to its hoped-for promised land of power.[2] They begin as a small band

---

The short-term result was the release of Marta Ochoa. The longer-term result was the realization on the part of both drug lords and terrorists that they had more in common than they previously had realized. Both groups liked the freedom of action which armed strength made possible and neither was interested in the Colombian government's reasserting its authority over the jungle areas where cocaine was grown and processed. And both groups enjoyed the immense revenues which their joint efforts generated.

[2]Few terrorist groups come even close to arriving there. The Nazis would qualify as one which did. Others might include the fascist government of Italy, various Communist regimes, and an assortment of others.

of like-thinking (they would claim, "right-thinking") individuals who are dissatisfied with the current state of affairs.

At first, these groups plot among themselves. They then move on to relatively simple propaganda activities. To finance themselves (in the absence of one or more donors), armed robberies of stores, banks, or other commercial operations are conducted. Once some financing is arranged, more weapons, explosives, and other equipment can be secured, along with safe houses, documents, and the other tools of the trade. By this time, an infrastructure and larger membership have been established, and experience has been gained.

At this point, the group may have established itself in the public's mind. (It certainly will have done so with the authorities!) Now, its immediate developmental and propaganda goals will have been met and the group will be ready for other activities. To keep the group motivated, more regular and more attention-getting activities will be required. This is the point at which hostage-taking becomes a viable tactic.

At this stage of the organization's development, the infrastructure exists to support a hostage-taking or a kidnapping. Trained operatives exist and are properly equipped, intelligence operations can be conducted, and planning can be perfected. Prior to this point, the organization has been too small and inexperienced to contemplate such activities. Now they are possible. The attention a hostage/barricade or prolonged kidnapping incident generates will serve the group well.

At a certain stage of the organization's development, such tactics are no longer useful. People and governments generally agree that hostage-taking is wrong and, once an organization achieves a more advanced level of development, it becomes counter-productive. An example of this is the Palestine Liberation Organization (PLO), the umbrella organization which is composed of a large number of groups, not all of which follow the direction of its leader, Yassir Arafat. Certain of the member groups have engaged in acts of terrorism. Among those which have is *Al-Fatah*, the largest component of the PLO and the basis of Arafat's power.

Over the years, Arafat adroitly has adjusted *Fatah* tactics to its political status. In the early 1970s, he authorized the formation of the group Black September, which acted as the terrorist arm of *Fatah*. Black September's purpose was to draw attention to the Palestinians' cause. By the 1980s, the PLO had been established as the representative of the Palestinian people. It had been granted observer status by the United Nations and it had offices around the world. In short, it had become accepted as a legitimate political actor. Terrorism—especially the hostage/barricade type in which Black September had engaged—had become a liability to Arafat (although he had carefully nurtured the myth that Black September was not an arm of *Fatah*). To continue the PLO's political advancement, he disbanded Black September (although many analysts contend that its infrastructure remains in place). As we write, the PLO has declared itself to be a government-in-exile with Arafat as its head. Some countries have recognized it as such and the organization enjoys a status of which it could only dream a decade before. In late December 1988, Arafat renounced the use of terrorism on behalf of the PLO and, as we write, no acts of terrorism have been attributed to any PLO group since then.

## WHY IT SPREADS

To this point, we have observed the cyclical nature of hostage-taking as an international political event. We also have noted that its employment is partly a function of the organizational development of the group using it. It remains for us to suggest why its geographical manifestations are sporadic; why, that is, it seems to move around the world in yet a different type of cycle.

In previous chapters, we have noted that political hostage-taking over the past several decades has moved from Latin America to Europe and the Middle East. Along the way, it showed up in various other areas and in different ways. This appears to be the case for two reasons. The first is commonly called the "copycat" effect. Simply put, this is the imitative result of example and it requires no further discussion.

The second reason is more complex, and it involves the question of organizational influence. We have suggested that, at different periods, different terrorist groups were role models for other terrorist groups. This was true not so much because of ideological purity or superiority, but rather because of the centrality of their cause in terms of world affairs. As different causes captured center stage, the groups pushing them were perceived by other terrorists as having identified successful tactics, which were then emulated. In some cases, the original role models either were eliminated by successful countermeasures or they moved on to different tactics more suited to their new stage of development and goals.

In the 1960s, Latin America held center stage in revolutionary circles. Castro had won his battle against Batista in Cuba and Ché Guevara was the darling of the revolutionary left. Most of Latin America was dominated by dictatorships of one sort or another. Ché's death in Bolivia in 1967 demonstrated that Castro's *foco* strategy would not work. In response, Carlos Marighella developed his theory of urban terrorism and published his *Minimanual of the Urban Guerrilla*, which became the bible of the *Tupamaros, Montoneros*, and other groups. For a time in the late 1960s and early 1970s, these Latin American groups held center stage, as they threatened to de-stabilize Argentina, Uruguay, and other South American countries. Part of their success can be laid to their use of kidnapping and hostage-taking. However, for a variety of reasons, by the mid-1970s all of these groups had overextended themselves and were either defunct or had retreated to Cuba.

At the same time, George Habash, leader of the Popular Front for the Liberation of Palestine (PFLP), was considering ways to attract attention to the plight of the Palestinians. Urban terrorism was ineffective for his purposes, and media attention was essential. Modifying Marighella's terrorist tactics of hostage-taking and other types of assaults, Habash and the PFLP institutionalized airplane hijacking as a political tool. Imitation being the sincerest form of flattery, once the viability of this tactic was demonstrated, other groups ranging from Croatians to the Japanese Red Army put it to use. The 1970s and early 1980s were a period of considerable activity in this regard. Countermeasures have made this tactic much more difficult (although, unhappily, not impossible).

Yet another variation of the hostage-taking tactic has replaced it. As the Palestinian cause achieved its goal of worldwide attention, another Middle Eastern group—the Shiites—have arrived on the scene, especially in Lebanon. Having as one goal the elimination of Western influence in the Middle East, the Shiites discovered that they could attract attention and bring enormous pressure on Western governments by taking captives and secreting them. Were it not for the public nature of this tactic, it would be more properly called kidnapping, due to the secrecy associated with the hostages' location (although this is less a safety factor than the result of the chaotic situation in Lebanon). The worst of this is that the tactic has a religious foundation and blessing, as Shiite leaders such as the late Ayatollah Khomeini of Iran and Sheik Mohammed Fadlallah, leader of the *Hezbollah* party in Lebanon, sanction such actions. It is safe to say that, as we write, the Shiites and their cause may share with the Palestinians the dubious honor of being the source of the world's most serious terrorist problems. Thus far, perhaps because of the unique melding of religious and political ideology and because the Shiites are not a particularly beloved group by others, their tactics have not been exported to any great degree.

As we have suggested, the re-introduction of hostage-taking into international political affairs is not an isolated phenomenon, even if its use is principally a Middle Eastern tactic. It parallels other, equally disturbing trends in the modern world. Today's hostage-taking reflects the convergence of political criminality with the decline of the nation-state as the dominant political actor.

## DIFFERING APPROACHES

We began this book with quotations from George Habash and David Gergen which, between them, reflect the state of affairs as we enter the 1990s. Terrorism is not going away. For the terrorists, no one is an innocent victim, no one is a neutral. To terrorists, human life is just another commodity which can be bartered for gain. Because of that attitude, political hostage-taking has been a problem for the past quarter-century and Americans and other Westerners have been held hostage almost continuously for the past 13 years.

The statistics we have provided in the preceding chapters and in Appendix B suggest that hostage-taking is only a small part of the terrorist problem confronting democratic societies. Yet, it has an impact completely out of proportion to its size. One of the cornerstones of democratic thought is the worth and rights of the individual. In this, the Free World is at a serious disadvantage in the struggle with terrorists. Democratic governments **are and must be concerned with individual lives**, whereas terrorists can treat them as pawns to be sacrificed.

How a democracy can best respond to this challenge is a continuing and highly controversial question. The arguments about "hard" and "soft" responses to terrorism are well-known. Unfortunately, the discussion has become polarized into only these alternatives. Very few observers of terrorist activities seem willing to consider a melding of the two into a third alternative. This is what we propose as a flexible approach. The reasons for such flexibility are compelling and justified by past events. Despite the attractions of an uncompromisingly "hard" response to terrorism, no country has ever been able to consistently employ it.[3]

---

[3]Abraham Maslow once wrote, "If your only tool is a hammer, you tend to see every problem as a nail."

## THE ISRAELI APPROACH

Perhaps the best example of a hard-line approach to terrorism is Israel. Understandably sensitive to the potential threat to its security, Israel has almost always been unwavering in its toughness. Yet there have been times when it has been forced to make compromises. The July 1989 abduction of Sheik Obeid from Lebanon is one example, as the Israelis announced their willingness to trade Obeid for captured Israeli soldiers and Western hostages—a demonstration that a pure hardline approach must often be moderated.

In some cases, Israel has successfully used an apparent willingness to compromise its policy to gain time for a rescue attempt, as was the case in Entebbe. However, on more than one occasion, Israel has released prisoners in the face of terrorist demands, as part of lopsided prisoner swaps to gain the release of captured Israelis, or to assist other countries (for example, in the wake of the 1985 TWA 847 incident).

Nonetheless, Israel's reputation for toughness and its unwillingness to make concessions routinely have stood it in good stead. Israelis are not often taken as hostages, for the terrorists know that Israel rarely deals on those terms. In fact, Israel would have little to gain from any other policy. Arab hostility is such that routine concessions certainly would invite further assaults.

## THE SOVIET APPROACH

Soviet policy toward terrorism has always been ambivalent. Soviet leaders long have recognized the disruptive value of terrorism and frequently have provided the means and training for terrorist groups to carry out their attacks. While evidence of direct Soviet involvement in acts of terrorism is sparse and even the intelligence community considers the evidence that exists to be arguable, there is no doubt that the disruptive effects of terrorism serve long-term Soviet political goals. However, when terrorism is practiced against Soviet interests, the response has been certain and swift.

One excellent example of this was the 1985 abduction of four Soviet diplomats in Lebanon. In addition to the normal diplomatic pressure, the Soviets engaged in some direct action. Once the hostage-takers were identified, the Soviets ferreted out one of the terrorists' relatives. To show they meant business, the Soviets sent the hostage-takers a piece of this individual—promising more if there was any delay in the release of the diplomats. The tactic worked, and three of the four diplomats were quickly released (one had already been killed).

Another example is the early 1980s hijacking of a Soviet airliner inside the Soviet Union. In that case, the Soviets wasted no time in staging an assault upon the aircraft. Despite the high casualties which resulted, the U.S.S.R. clearly established that it would not tolerate such activity.

Soviet authorities have considerable latitude in their actions because they do not have to account to their people for them. *Glasnost* aside, the Soviet Union is far from being a democratic country. There historically have been limits to the kind of internal criticism which is taken for granted in the Western world. Despite recent signs of the loosening of these restrictions, it is unclear how much this will change in the future. Yet even the Soviets have been known to occasionally compromise, as when they permitted several people to hijack a plane from Moscow to Israel in December 1988. The Israelis immediately returned both the plane and the hijackers in that case.

## THE U.S. APPROACH

The United States has approached the problem of countering terrorism cautiously. There has been considerable tough talk, but relatively little action. However, such action as has been taken has been decisive and effective. The problem for the U.S. is two-fold: a rigid public policy and an internal dynamic which all but precludes timely action when risk is involved.

President Carter allowed the Tehran hostage-taking to consume and paralyze his administration. The success of Camp David was overshadowed by the debacle at Desert One, and his re-election bid was defeated. President Reagan came into office proclaiming that terrorism would replace human rights as the most significant foreign policy issue of his administration and left office eight years later under the specter of the Iran-Contra scandal. As we write, President Bush has yet to fully define his position publicly, but his cautious combination of diplomatic pressure and veiled military muscle has won much praise in the early going.

Yet, despite this caution, the U.S. has dealt some effective blows against terrorists and hostage-takers. In 1985, in the wake of the *Achille Lauro* hijacking, the U.S. blocked the escape of the terrorists by intercepting the airplane on which they were fleeing and forcing it down in Italy—where the Italian government tried and convicted four of them.[4] And in April 1986, the U.S. staged a bombing raid on Libya which so intimidated Moammar Khadafi that his involvement in international terrorism decreased for several years.

Yet, each of these successes was met with mixed reviews within the U.S. Many decried perceived violations of international law and some alleged violations of U.S. laws such as the War Powers Act. In the case of the Libyan bombing, one U.S. plane was shot down and the crew killed—leading to criticism of the operation.[5] Despite these successes, the use of force by the United States against terrorists remained controversial throughout the 1980s, with the Secretary of State frequently calling for it and the Secretary of Defense resisting.

---

[4]The Italians unfortunately allowed the mastermind of the operation, Mohammed Abu Abbas, to leave Italy despite a U.S. request for his extradition.

[5]In a similar vein, in 1984, the U.S. sent two planes against terrorist targets in Lebanon's Bekka Valley. One plane was shot down, with one airman killed and one captured. Because it happened during the U.S. presidential election, much controversy and criticism ensued.

## THE FRENCH APPROACH

The French have a long tradition of providing political asylum and respecting the "right" of the downtrodden to resort to political violence to redress wrongs. This has led to a curious mixture of tolerance and firmness in French policy toward terrorism. The French have made deals with terrorist groups ranging from the Basque ETA to various Palestinian factions. These deals have given terrorists considerable latitude to use French soil as a safe haven to plan operations or recuperate from them—as long as French interests were free from attack. At the same time, the French GIGN ranks among the elite counterterrorist units in the world and it has forcefully performed on occasion, as in Djibouti in 1976.

In hostage situations, the French have been extremely pragmatic. Often, they have chosen to make accommodations with groups such as *Hezbollah* or with countries like Iran by paying ransoms, providing military arms, or releasing assets. Yet at the same time, the French responded to a bombing campaign by the Lebanese Armed Revolutionary Faction (to free its imprisoned leader Georges Ibrahim Abdullah) by intensifying security precautions and bringing him to trial. Even when French hostages were taken in Lebanon, French law enforcement officials held firm in the face of considerable pressure to release Abdullah.

The middle and late 1980s witnessed the breakdown of French efforts to maintain their accommodation with terrorist groups. A combination of terrorist violations of their understanding with France and pressure from foreign governments (notably Spain and the United States) induced the French to move away from such toleration, and France began to take more forceful action.[6]

---

[6]In the wake of the attack on the French and U.S. MNF facilities in Beirut on October 23, 1983, the French immediately retaliated by bombing areas of the Bekka valley.

## THE JAPANESE APPROACH

The Japanese have spent the last forty years creating one of the world's most formidable economic powers from the ashes of World War II. As a result, Japanese products and businesses have found markets in every corner of the world. Along with the expansion of economic influence has come targeting by terrorists.

The Japanese, however, have steadfastly resisted assuming a political role commensurate with their economic prowess. This has confined attacks on Japanese interests to low-level operations: extortion and kidnappings for ransom. In almost every case, the Japanese have proven willing to pay ransoms. While not enunciating a formal policy, it appears that the Japanese have elected to pay what amounts to protection money and/or ransoms where necessary. For them, this is just another cost of doing business in certain places.

## THE WEST GERMAN APPROACH

The West Germans also seem uncertain as to what policy they should follow with regard to terrorist hostage-taking. Even before the 1972 Munich Olympics, the West Germans frequently looked for the easy way out of terrorist incidents. In 1972, they pressured the Israelis to concede to the terrorists' demands and launched their assault only when Israel stood firm. Following that debacle, they developed one of the world's best counterterrorist forces, GSG-9, which was successfully used in incidents like the 1977 Mogadishu rescue.

Yet, when confronted with acts of terrorism, the West German government invariably comes under intense pressure to make concessions. This was the case as late as 1988, when the West Germans arrested Mohammed Ali Hammadi (involved in the 1985 TWA 847 hijacking) and announced that he would be tried. Immediately, several West German businessmen were abducted in Lebanon and a trade was offered. In that case, the West German government resisted considerable pressure to make the deal, and Hammadi was tried and convicted. It now appears that West Germany has come down on the side of resisting deals with terrorists, but this is not yet certain.

## THE THIRD OPTION: FLEXIBLE FIRMNESS

What then can a democratic country do in response to the threat of terrorism generally and hostage-taking specifically? Are there only two options, force or concession? Or can these two options be combined into a new alternative?

Experience has shown that neither force nor compromise is the best option in all cases. Democratic countries must recognize that either might be the most appropriate in any particular case and construct a policy accordingly. We are not suggesting an approach incorporating wholesale surrender to terrorist demands. Rather, there are times when compromise might be indicated. For example, granting media exposure to a terrorist group after it has released hostages gives them nothing which they would not get anyway. If economic assets have been similarly frozen in response to a terrorist incident, then freeing those assets as part of its resolution can be appropriate.

The freedoms which democratic countries enjoy also place their governments under extraordinary pressure during terrorist incidents—especially those of duration, such as hijackings and hostage-takings. The very openness of democratic societies (freedom of the press and expression, freedom to travel, independent legislative and judicial branches, etc.) can conspire to thwart realistic counterterrorist policies and programs. This dilemma must be confronted and resolved. Terrorism and hostage-taking will not disappear from the international political scene and democratic societies must grapple with the difficult decisions necessary to reduce their impact.

Flexible firmness must address six separate areas: negotiation, use of force, proactivity, media coverage, continuity of government, and individual responsibility. Each of these areas interacts with and depends upon the others. The decisions made in each area will create a public policy appropriate for the 1990s and beyond.


## NEGOTIATION

The question of negotiation is one which has confounded government officials in the United States and elsewhere for many years. U.S. public policy with regard to terrorism reflects its unwillingness to make concessions to terrorists, but does not directly address the question of negotiating with them. Negotiation and concession have become synonymous in this area, to the detriment of effective response. Even the U.S. takes an ambivalent view of the matter, depending upon whether an incident occurs overseas or within the country.

Negotiations and even the payment of ransoms have long been used effectively by law enforcement agencies to deal with domestic hostage and kidnapping situations. Within the U.S., the Federal Bureau of Investigation and other agencies firmly believe in the validity of such tactics. Frank Bolz, formerly with the New York City Police Department, peacefully and successfully resolved hundreds of hostage situations through negotiation. Many other police and private negotiators also have had great success in this area.

The politicization and militarization of counterterrorist policy has obscured the difference between negotiation and concession, between compromise and surrender. Yet this need not be the case. If one accepts the position that negotiation is simply an attempt to resolve a situation through discussion, then it is possible to do so without giving up anything. Beyond that, there are potential compromises which might be appropriate in particular situations.

The first decision to be made by a democratic society must be its willingess to discuss things under all circumstances. Then it must decide for itself which subjects are negotiable. Even if one accepts the idea that terrorism is another form of warfare, warring parties do sometimes come together to discuss their differences. This is not to suggest that negotiation is always desirable. In fact, it often is not. We agree with those who believe that example and precedent are very important in the terrorist arena. However, when incidents occur, they often catch governments at a disadvantage and, as we noted earlier, negotiation is a useful tactic to buy time and gain information. Furthermore, it is not impossible that some aggrieved group may have a valid complaint which should not be completely lost merely because it has resorted to an act of terrorism. Above all, negotiation must not be equated with cowardice if it is part of a comprehensive approach to counterterrorism. Equally important, it must not be allowed to preclude the use of force when necessary.

## USE OF FORCE

Force has always been seen by democratic governments as the option of last resort, and properly so. Unlike other potential responses, once it is used, damage cannot be undone. Yet, as we discussed in Chapter 7, credible force is required if there is to be any option beyond complete surrender. Furthermore, there are quite a few examples of the successful use of force in hostage situations.

The effective use of force requires the development of specialized units and capabilities. Even more important, it requires the political will to employ these capabilities. And it requires a long-term, continuing commitment to maintain these capabilities, along with periodic reaffirmation of the political will to employ them.

Force is usually equated with military action. However, there is a broader view—encompassing police action and economic and political sanctions, among others. Force is the power to influence, affect, or control. This could include the freezing of assets, arrests, diplomatic sanctions, and other non-military actions. In short, democratic societies have a wider variety of alternatives than are sometimes considered. This is a key point to remember, because proactive counterterrorism requires strength and political will to be effective.

Leaving aside the required checks, balances, and oversight which a democratic country must have, the political will to use force is a continuing problem for democratic societies. Resolving this issue will not be easy: there will always be those who reject it. However, in the counterterrorist area, as in many other areas, democracy must be preserved by force when necessary. And one of the preconditions for successful hostage negotiation is a credible threat of force on the part of the authorities.

## PROACTIVITY

The third component of flexible firmness is proactivity, a concept which is not widely understood. It is the process by which plans and capabilities are developed beforehand for foreseeable contingencies in order to ensure the most effective response to a situation. Proactivity includes the ability and willingness to act premptively where possible.

In 1987, the FBI successfully lured Fawaz Yunis, a suspected hijacker, into international waters and arrested him. In 1985, the U.S. Navy intercepted and forced down an airliner carrying the hijackers of the *Achille Lauro*, leading to their arrest by Italian authorities. And in 1989, the Israelis staged a commando raid into Lebanon, capturing a Shiite terrorist leader. These are a few examples of proactive tactics.

Other elements of proactivity include the development of capabilities to effectively employ force or negotiate, as appropriate. A comprehensive package of capabilities which use diplomatic, covert, law enforcement, military, and other assets in ever-changing combinations will keep terrorists of all types off balance and provide democratic societies with effective tools against them.

## MEDIA COVERAGE

One of the thorniest issues confronted by a democratic society is the question of freedom of the press. It is both a foundation of democratic society and a bane for democratic governments. It can keep government honest or it can cripple its effectiveness. Balancing society's need for a free press with the occasional governmental requirement for secrecy is a difficult job.

In the contemporary world, extensive and continuing media coverage of any terrorist incident—especially a hostage-taking—is a given. As a matter of fact, this can be a valuable adjunct to efforts to resolve an incident. Media coverage can be an important defusing component in hostage negotiation, **if it is confined to factual reporting**. Democratic governments generally have not been successful in establishing working relationships with the media which allow both government and journalists to do their jobs without jeopardizing the lives of hostages.

The media is responsible for its coverage of terrorist incidents, but it is not solely to blame for all the excesses which occur during such incidents. Officials who unnecessarily withhold information or selectively leak it for their own purposes contribute to an atmosphere of confusion and mistrust. In addition, when victims of terrorism or their family members believe that they are entitled to know more about what is being done or that more should be done for them, they naturally seek to publicize their views, hoping to influence events.

The result of this can be a circus-like atmosphere which places both government and the media at a disadvantage. Government must do a better job of protecting the **truly important** information while providing as much **accurate** material as is possible to the media. It must also do a better job of dealing with victims of terrorism and their families, so that they realize the limitations of the situation. Media, on the other hand, must indulge in less speculation—especially during the early phases of incidents—and engage in less exploitation of families and victims. Above all, true secrets must be protected and there must be a recognition on the part of the media that information delayed is not the same as information denied; not everything need be revealed at a particular momemt.


## CONTINUITY OF GOVERNMENT

Related to the question of media coverage is the pressure often felt by democratic governments to be seen as doing something. Very often the extent and nature of media coverage shapes a government's approach to resolving a particular terrorist incident. And often, a government's inability to rapidly conclude an incident can cripple it indefinitely, as was the case with President Jimmy Carter's last year in office.

One of the goals of terrorism is to destabilize democratic societies by demonstrating that governments are unable to provide basic security guarantees. Far too often, governments allow the terrorists this victory by default. Despite the undeniably human urge to demonstrate sensitivity and effective leadership in the face of a terrorist incident, there are many periods when nothing which is productive can be done. Effective leadership resides in ensuring that the many pressing issues of government continue to be addressed despite the on-going emergency. Presidents and Prime Ministers must reassert themselves and not feel that everything must be dropped for the duration of an incident. Of course, there will be times when the government will need to focus its entire attention on the matter, but these are few.

A terrorist incident, whether it is a hijacking, a hostage-taking, or an assassination, must not be allowed to monopolize governmental attention. With today's technological and communications advances, a government official need not return to his office to deal effectively with such a situation. We strongly believe that senior government leaders should proceed in the opposite manner. After being briefed on the situation, they should issue the appropriate statement, provide the appropriate agencies with instructions, and go back to doing whatever they had planned before the incident occurred.[7]


## INDIVIDUAL RESPONSIBILITY

This is perhaps the most controversial and difficult area of flexible firmness. It is a basic responsibility of government to ensure the safety of people and property within its jurisdiction. Over time, Western governments have come to be expected to do this internationally as well. There are many treaties and other international mechanisms which are intended to help accomplish this objective, but their effectiveness is far from even. The time has come for democratic societies to relieve their governments of this burden or allow them to have more control over the travel of their citizens.

The United States, for example, has no legal mechanism by which its government can require American citizens to leave an area which has become unsafe. This has resulted in many dangerous situations. Americans in Libya during the mid-1980s remained there despite U.S. government warnings that they might be in danger. Americans also remain in Lebanon despite U.S. government appeals for their departure. Doing so is their right (the Supreme Court has confirmed this) and the U.S. government can do nothing about it.

If a democracy prizes freedom of international movement without governmental restriction that highly, then it must place

---

[7]This is along the lines of what President George Bush did in July-August 1989, when Shiite terrorists threatened the lives of a number of American hostages as the result of the Israeli abduction of Sheik Obeid (see Chapter 1). Although he felt the need to return to Washington from a domestic trip and deal personally with the problem in its initial stages, after a few days he no longer scheduled daily meetings with his senior advisors in this area. President Bush did not allow a public image to develop of his grappling with the problem over a long period to the exclusion of all other matters—unlike President Carter ten years earlier.

a greater measure of responsibility upon individuals. As painful a decision as it might be, if a government cannot order its nationals out of a particular area, its obligation to them if they are taken hostage, for example, should be limited. This is not a prescription to relieve government from its obligation toward its citizens; rather, it is a more appropriate balancing of governmental obligations and citizen rights. Government must still be responsible for determining the danger level to its people—exerting every appropriate effort to help them. However, if someone ignores his government's directive to leave an area, then he must accept much greater individual responsibility for his own safety. He must recognize that his government may be unable to help him should he become a hostage or otherwise fall victim to terrorist attack. The holding of hostages must not be allowed to provide terrorists with the leverage to bring a nation to heel.

These six areas comprise the essentials of our third option: flexible firmness. The decisions are difficult ones, but they are necessary if Western democratic governments are to begin to master the terrorist threat. Hostage-taking will continue to be a fact, as terrorists test the mettle of democratic governments. Even as we write in the fall of 1989, Shiite terrorists are threatening to kill American hostages if the French government becomes militarily involved in Lebanon. *Plus ça change, plus c'est la même chose*—the more things change, the more they remain the same.

As the 1990s begin, political hostage-taking continues to pose a critical challenge to the democratic nations of the world. The open wound that Lebanon has become shows how serious the problem is. In an odd way, George Habash was correct: in the struggle against terrorism, no one is a neutral. This is the challenge for the 1990s and beyond.

# APPENDIX A
# FOREIGN HOSTAGES IN LEBANON*

| NAME/ NATIONALITY/ PROFESSION | DATE/PLACE ABDUCTED | ABDUCTORS | STATUS (10/89) |
|---|---|---|---|
| David Dodge/U.S./ Rector, Am. Univ. | 7/19/82 Beirut | Islamic Jihad | Released 7/21/83 |
| Christian Joubert/ French/Traveler | 2/15/84 Beirut | Islamic Jihad | Released 7/21/83 |
| Jeremy Levin/U.S./ Journalist | 3/7/84 Beirut | Islamic Jihad | Escaped 2/14/85 |
| William Buckley/U.S./ CIA station chief | 3/16/84 Beirut | Islamic Jihad | **Died in captivity** |
| Rev. Benjamin Weir/ U.S./Clergyman | 5/8/84 Beirut | Islamic Jihad | Released 9/14/85 |
| Muhammed Al-Faytuir/ Libya/Diplomat | 7/9/84 Beirut | Brigades of As-Sad | Released 7/9/84 |
| Pedro Aristegui/Spanish/ Diplomat | 10/10/84 Beirut | Uncertain** | Released 10/10/84 |
| Peter Kilburn/U.S./ Librarian, Am. Univ. | 11/30/84 Beirut | Arab Revolu- tionary Cells | **Body found 4/17/86** |
| Eric Wehrli/Swiss/ Diplomat | 1/3/85 Beirut | Uncertain | Released 1/8/85 |

*As of October 10, 1989. Source: U.S. Department of State and press reports. There were also a number of Lebanese hostages taken during this period. We have tried to be as complete as possible, but we do not exclude the possibility that some kidnappings may have been missed.

**Most of the abductions listed here as uncertain are believed to have been carried out by one or another of the Shiite terrorist groups.

| NAME/ NATIONALITY/ PROFESSION | DATE/PLACE ABDUCTED | ABDUCTORS | STATUS (10/89) |
|---|---|---|---|
| Fr. Lawrence Jenco/ U.S./Clergyman | 1/8/85 Beirut | Islamic Jihad | Released 7/26/86 |
| Fr. Nicolas Kluiters/ Dutch/Priest | 3/14/85 Beirut | Uncertain | **Body found 4/1/85** |
| Geoffrey Nash/British/ Businessman | 3/14/85 Beirut | Islamic Jihad Khaybar Brigades | Released 3/85 |
| Terry Anderson/U.S./ Journalist | 3/16/85 Beirut | Islamic Jihad | **Hostage** |
| Abd Al-Basit Al-Tarabulsi/Libyan/ Diplomat | 3/16/85 Beirut | *Amal* | **Unknown** |
| Michel Seurat/French/ Researcher/French Center | 3/22/85 Beirut | Islamic Jihad Khaybar Brigades | **Believed dead** |
| Marcel Fontaine/French/ Diplomat | 3/22/85 Beirut | Islamic Jihad Khaybar Brigades | Released 5/88 |
| Marcel Carton/French/ Diplomat | 3/22/85 Beirut | Islamic Jihad Khaybar Brigades | Released 5/88 |
| Giles Peyrolles/French/ Diplomat | 3/24/85 Tripoli | Lebanese Armed Revolutionary Faction | Released 4/2/85 |
| Alec Collett/British/UN relief worker | 3/26/85 Khaldah | Revolutionary Organiz. of Socialist Muslims | **Believed dead** |
| Jean-Paul Kauffman/ French/Journalist | 5/22/85 Beirut | Islamic Jihad | Released 5/88 |
| Denis Hill/British/Professor, Am. Univ. | 5/27/85 Beirut | Islamic Jihad | **Body found 5/29/85** |
| David Jacobsen/U.S./ Hospital administrator | 5/28/85 Beirut | Islamic Jihad | Released 11/2/86 |

| NAME/ NATIONALITY/ PROFESSION | DATE/PLACE ABDUCTED | ABDUCTORS | STATUS (10/89) |
|---|---|---|---|
| Thomas Sutherland/U.S./ Professor, Am. Univ. | 6/9/85 Beirut | Islamic Jihad | **Hostage** |
| Alfred Yaghobzadah/ Iranian/Photographer | 6/27/85 Beirut | Uncertain | Released 8/16/85 |
| Wajid Ahmad Dumani/ Kuwaiti/Diplomat | 7/11/85 Beirut | Uncertain | Released 8/10/85 |
| Robert Burkholder/ Canadian/ Relief worker | 8/8/85 Al-Nabatiyah | Uncertain | Released 8/8/85 |
| Alberto Molinari/Italian/ Businessman | 9/11/85 Beirut | Uncertain | **Believed dead** |
| Hazel Moss/British/ Businesswoman | 9/28/85 Beirut | Uncertain | Released 10/8/85 |
| Amanda McGrath/ British/Educator | 9/28/85 Beirut | Uncertain | Released 10/8/85 |
| Olig Spirin/Soviet/ Diplomat | 9/30/85 Beirut | Islamic Jihad/ Islamic Liberation Organization | Released 10/30/85 |
| Valeriy Mirikov/Soviet/ Diplomat | 9/30/85 Beirut | Islamic Jihad/ Islamic Liberation Organization | Released 10/30/85 |
| Arkady Katokov/Soviet/ Diplomat | 9/30/85 Beirut | Islamic Jihad/ Islamic Liberation Organization | **Died in captivity** |
| Nikolai Svirskiy/Soviet/ Diplomat | 9/30/85 Beirut | Islamic Jihad/ Islamic Liberation Organization | Released 10/30/85 |
| Pedro Sanchez/Spanish/ Diplomat | 1/17/86 Beirut | Black Banner- Organization | Released 2/19/86 |

| NAME/ NATIONALITY/ PROFESSION | DATE/PLACE ABDUCTED | ABDUCTORS | STATUS (10/89) |
|---|---|---|---|
| Do Chae Sung/ S. Korean/ Diplomat | 1/31/86 Beirut | *Hezbollah*, Org. of the Oppressed, plus 3 others | Released 10/26/87 |
| Marcel Coudari/French/ Businessman | 2/86 Beirut | Revolutionary Justice Organization | Released 11/10/86 |
| Camille Sontag/French/ Businesswoman | 2/86 Beirut | Revolutionary Justice Organization | Released 11/10/86 |
| Abdel-Ghani Khalil/ Palestinian/ U.N. worker | 2/25/86 Tripoli | Uncertain | Released 2/28/86 |
| Abdallah Kayal/ Palestinian/Doctor | 2/25/86 Tripoli | Uncertain | Released 2/28/86 |
| Phillipe Rochot/French/ TV cameraman | 3/8/86 Beirut | Islamic Jihad/ Organ.of Revolutionary Justice | Released 6/20/86 |
| George Hansen/French/ TV cameraman | 3/8/86 Beirut | Islamic Jihad/ Organ.of Revolutionary Justice | Released 6/20/86 |
| Aurel Cornea/French/ TV cameraman | 3/8/86 Beirut | Islamic Jihad/ Organ.of Revolutionary Justice | Released 12/24/86 |
| Jean-Huey Normandin/ French/TV cameraman | 3/8/86 Beirut | Islamic Jihad/ Organ. of Revolutionary Justice | **Unknown** |
| John Leigh Douglas/ Brit./Professor, Am. Univ. | 3/28/86 Beirut | Arab Revolutionary Cells | **Body found 4/17/86** |
| Philip Padfield/Brit./ Dir., Int. Lang. Center | 3/28/86 Beirut | Arab Revolutionary Cells | **Body found 4/17/86** |

| NAME/ NATIONALITY/ PROFESSION | DATE/PLACE ABDUCTED | ABDUCTORS | STATUS (10/89) |
|---|---|---|---|
| Michel Brian/French/ Educator | 4/8/86 Beirut | Islamic Seffine Organization | Released 4/12/86 |
| Brian Keenan/Irish/ Professor, Am. Univ. | 4/11/86 Beirut | Uncertain | **Hostage** |
| Raji Al-Najam/Palest./ PLO official | 4/11/86 Khaldeh | Uncertain | **Unknown** |
| John McCarthy/British/ Journalist | 4/17/86 Beirut | Arab Commando Cells | **Hostage** |
| Kirkas Panayiotis/ Cypriot/Student | 4/28/86 Beirut | Uncertain | Released 6/21/86 |
| Stavros Yiannaki/Cypriot/ Student | 4/28/86 Beirut | Uncertain | Released 6/21/86 |
| Frank Reed/U.S./ Dir.,Leb. Internat'l. School | 9/9/86 Beirut | Ba'th Cells Organiz./Arab Revolutionary Cells | **Hostage** |
| Joseph Cicippio/U.S./ Comptroller, Am. Univ. | 9/12/86 Beirut | Revolutionary Justice Organization | **Hostage** |
| David Hirst/British/ Journalist | 9/26/86 Beirut | Uncertain | Escaped 9/86 |
| Jean-Marc Sroussi/ French/TV cameraman | 9/28/86 Beirut | Uncertain | Escaped 10/1/86 |
| Edward Tracy/ U.S./Writer | 10/21/86 Beirut | Revolutionary Justice Organization | **Hostage** |
| Tawfiq Abu Khajil/ Jordanian/Diplomat | 1/8/87 Beirut | Uncertain | Released 1/10/87 |
| Bakr Damanhouri/Saudi/ Diplomat | 1/12/87 Beirut | Uncertain | Released 3/18/87 |

| NAME/ NATIONALITY/ PROFESSION | DATE/PLACE ABDUCTED | ABDUCTORS | STATUS (10/89) |
|---|---|---|---|
| Roger Auque/French/ Journalist | 1/13/87 Beirut | Uncertain | Released 11/27/87 |
| Rudolph Cordes/W. Ger./ Businessman | 1/17/87 Beirut | Strugglers for Freedom/Org. of Oppressed on Earth | Released 9/7/88 |
| Terry Waite/British/ Church of England envoy | 1/20/87 Beirut | Uncertain | **Hostage** |
| Alfred Schmidt/ W. German/ Businessman | 1/20/87 Beirut | Strugglers for Freedom/Org. of Oppressed on Earth | Released 9/7/88 |
| Robert Polhill/U.S./ Prof.,Beirut Univ. College | 1/24/87 Beirut | Oppressed of the Earth/ Islamic Jihad for Lib. of Palestine | **Hostage** |
| Alann Steen/U.S./ Prof.,Beirut Univ. College | 1/24/87 Beirut | Oppressed of the Earth/ Islamic Jihad for Lib. of Palestine | **Hostage** |
| Jesse Turner/U.S./ Prof.,Beirut Univ. College | 1/24/87 Beirut | Oppressed of the Earth/ Islamic Jihad for Lib. of Palestine | **Hostage** |
| Mithileshwar Singh/ Indian/Prof., Beirut Univ. College | 1/24/87 Beirut | Oppressed of the Earth/ Islamic Jihad for Lib. of Palestine | Released 10/88 |
| Khalid Deed/Saudi/ Businessman | 1/26/87 Beirut | Partisans of Islamic Jihad | Released 3/20/87 |
| Mohammad Khatemi/ Iranian/Embassy staff | 4/20/87 Beirut | Uncertain | **Unknown** |

| NAME/ NATIONALITY/ PROFESSION | DATE/PLACE ABDUCTED | ABDUCTORS | STATUS (10/89) |
|---|---|---|---|
| Charles Glass/U.S./ Journalist | 6/17/87 Beirut | Right Against Wrong/Org. for Defense of Free People | Escaped 8/17/87 |
| Badr Al-Fahoum/ Palestinian/Businessman | 10/27/87 Beirut | Oppressed People Forces | Released 11/5/87 |
| Fernand Houtekins/ Belgian/Traveler | 11/87 Offshore | Fatah Revolutionary Council | **Hostage** |
| Emmanuil Houtekins/ Belg./Traveler | 11/87 Offshore | Fatah Revolutionary Council | **Hostage** |
| Laurent Houtekins/Belg./ Traveler | 11/87 Offshore | Fatah Revolutionary Council | **Hostage** |
| Valire Houtekins/Belg./ Traveler | 11/87 Offshore | Fatah Revolutionary Council | **Hostage** |
| Godlieve Kets/Belgian/ Traveler | 11/87 Offshore | Fatah Revolutionary Council | **Hostage** |
| Jaqueline Valente/French/ Traveler | 11/87 Offshore | Fatah Revolutionary Council | **Hostage** |
| Baby Valente/French/ Child | Born in captivity | Fatah Revolutionary Council | **Hostage** |
| Marie Laure Betille/ French/Child | 11/87 Offshore | Fatah Revolutionary Council | Released 12/88 |
| Virginie Betille/French/ Child | 11/87 Offshore | Fatah Revolutionary Council | Released 12/88 |

| NAME/ NATIONALITY/ PROFESSION | DATE/PLACE ABDUCTED | ABDUCTORS | STATUS (10/89) |
|---|---|---|---|
| Ralph Schray/ W. German/ Businessman | 1/27/88 Beirut | Rev. Justice Organ./ Strugglers for Freedom | Released 3/88 |
| Muhammad Mu'atiyah/ Libyan/Businessman | 2/1/88 Beirut | Al-Sadr Brigades Organization | **Unknown** |
| Mohammad Mahmoud Al-Jiar/Egyptian/ Clergyman | 3/17/88 Near Tyre | Uncertain | **Unknown** |
| Ian Stening/Swedish/ U.N. relief worker | 2/5/88 near Sidon | Revolutionary Cells | Released 3/88 |
| William Jorgensen/ Norweigan/U.N. relief worker | 2/5/88 near Sidon | Revolutionary Cells | Released 3/88 |
| Lt.Col. William Higgins/ U.S./U.N. observer | 2/17/88 near Tyre | *Hezbollah* | **Announced dead 7/31/89** |
| Jan Cools/Belgian/ Doctor, Norweigan Aid | 5/21/88 near Tyre | Soldiers for the Right | Released 6/15/89 |
| Peter Winkler/Swiss/ Red Cross official | 11/17/88 Sidon | Uncertain | Released 12/88 |
| Jack Mann/British/ Retired | 5/13/89 Beirut | Armed Struggle Cells | **Reported dead 9/8/89** |
| Emanuel Cristen/Swiss/ Red Cross worker | 10/6/89 Sidon | Uncertain | **Unknown** |
| Elio Elliquez/Swiss/ Red Cross worker | 10/6/89 Sidon | Uncertain | **Unknown** |

# APPENDIX B
# SELECTED TERRORISM STATISTICS*

## TABLE B-1
## GLOBAL TERRORIST INCIDENTS, 1970–1984

|  | 1970–84 | 1985 | 1986 | 1987 | 1988 | TOTAL |
|---|---|---|---|---|---|---|
| Terrorist Incidents | 22,171 | 3,010 | 2,860 | 3,089 | 3,734 | 34,864 |
| Assassinations | 3,774 | 374 | 398 | 426 | 819 | 5,791 |
| Bombings | 10,207 | 1,527 | 1,498 | 1,501 | 1,622 | 16,355 |
| Hijackings | 142 | 10 | 6 | 2 | 9 | 169 |
| Kidnappings | 1,027 | 109 | 79 | 73 | 120 | 1,408 |
| Maimings | 137 | 0 | 0 | 0 | 1 | 138 |
| Facility Attacks | 6,884 | 990 | 879 | 1,087 | 1,163 | 11,003 |
| Deaths | 40,394 | 7,166 | 5,142 | 6,513 | 7,408 | 66,623 |
| Injuries | 24,588 | 5,181 | 5,618 | 6,779 | 7,682 | 49,848 |

*Source: Risks International Division, Business Risks International, Inc. Risks International has no "hostage" category, but all of the hijackings and many of the kidnappings would be found in such a category.

## TABLE B-2

# TERRORIST INCIDENTS, 1980–1988, BY REGION*

|                       | 1980  | 1981  | 1982  | 1983   | 1984  | 1985  | 1986  | 1987  | 1988  | TOTAL  |
|-----------------------|-------|-------|-------|--------|-------|-------|-------|-------|-------|--------|
| Total Incidents       | 2,755 | 2,701 | 2,492 | 2,838  | 3,525 | 3,010 | 2,860 | 3,089 | 3,734 | 27,004 |
| Latin America         | 1,566 | 1,711 | 1,700 | 1,857  | 2,257 | 1,933 | 1,702 | 1,868 | 1,615 | 16,209 |
| Europe                | 580   | 454   | 358   | 438    | 539   | 471   | 445   | 368   | 500   | 4,153  |
| Asia/Oceania          | 108   | 83    | 67    | 106    | 333   | 326   | 420   | 544   | 1,105 | 3,092  |
| N. America            | 27    | 22    | 31    | 14     | 10    | 10    | 7     | 0     | 0     | 121    |
| Mid-East/ N. Africa   | 426   | 352   | 294   | 352    | 289   | 171   | 212   | 211   | 257   | 2,564  |
| Sub-Sahara Africa     | 48    | 79    | 42    | 71     | 97    | 99    | 74    | 98    | 257   | 865    |
| Killed                | 4,843 | 5,611 | 6,166 | 10,159 | 9,614 | 7,166 | 5,142 | 6,513 | 7,408 | 62,622 |
| Injured               | 3,381 | 3,014 | 3,607 | 3,953  | 4,009 | 5,181 | 5,618 | 5,779 | 7,682 | 42,224 |

*Source: Risks International Division, Business Risks International, Inc. Note that these figures differ from official U.S. government statistics.

# TABLE B-3
# HIJACKINGS, 1979–1988, BY REGION*

|  | 1979 | 1980 | 1981 | 1982 | 1983 | 1984 | 1985 | 1986 | 1987 | 1988 | TOTAL |
|---|---|---|---|---|---|---|---|---|---|---|---|
| Total Incidents | 11 | 14 | 18 | 5 | 5 | 15 | 10 | 6 | 2 | 9 | 95 |
| Latin America | 1 | 4 | 9 | 3 | 0 | 1 | 1 | 2 | 0 | 5 | 26 |
| Europe | 3 | 2 | 3 | 0 | 1 | 1 | 3 | 0 | 1 | 0 | 14 |
| Asia/Oceania | 2 | 0 | 3 | 0 | 1 | 4 | 1 | 3 | 0 | 2 | 16 |
| N. America | 2 | 2 | 0 | 0 | 0 | 1 | 0 | 0 | 0 | 0 | 5 |
| Mid-East/N. Africa | 3 | 6 | 2 | 1 | 3 | 8 | 4 | 1 | 1 | 1 | 30 |
| Sub-Sahara Africa | 0 | 0 | 1 | 1 | 0 | 0 | 1 | 0 | 0 | 1 | 4 |

*Source: Risks International Division, Business Risks International, Inc. Note that these figures differ from official U.S. government statistics, and cover only **terrorist** incidents.

# TABLE B-4
# KIDNAPPINGS, 1979–1988, BY REGION*

|  | 1979 | 1980 | 1981 | 1982 | 1983 | 1984 | 1985 | 1986 | 1987 | 1988 | TOTAL |
|---|---|---|---|---|---|---|---|---|---|---|---|
| Total Incidents | 137 | 124 | 95 | 102 | 119 | 61 | 109 | 79 | 73 | 120 | 1,109 |
| Latin America | 66 | 98 | 65 | 79 | 93 | 37 | 64 | 33 | 33 | 68 | 636 |
| Europe | 44 | 18 | 18 | 10 | 12 | 1 | 5 | 6 | 4 | 5 | 123 |
| Asia/Oceania | 6 | 1 | 4 | 1 | 1 | 1 | 13 | 2 | 7 | 26 | 62 |
| N. America | 1 | 0 | 0 | 0 | 0 | 0 | 0 | 0 | 0 | 0 | 1 |
| Mid-East/N. Africa | 8 | 7 | 7 | 5 | 8 | 19 | 24 | 20 | 21 | 16 | 135 |
| Sub-Sahara Africa | 7 | 0 | 1 | 7 | 5 | 3 | 3 | 18 | 8 | 5 | 57 |

*Source: Risks International Division, Business Risks International, Inc.

# APPENDIX C
# PROS AND CONS OF RANSOM PAYMENTS

In the emotions of the moment, governments, businesses, and individuals are often tempted to concede to monetary demands made by terrorist hostage-takers. Frequently, they argue that human life is far more important than mere money, and that organizations or family members have a duty to the victim to pay up. We disagree with this as a general proposition, but we believe that any individual or business that considers payment of ransom weigh some additional factors before making such a payment.

Ransom demands have been sizeable over the years. It is impossible to ascertain exactly how much actually has been paid, but it is possible to get some sense of the dimensions of the problem by tracking the level of demands.[1] Between January 1,1970 and March 31, 1989, $739,696,461 in ransom demands were tracked by the Risks International Division of Business Risks International. Table C-1 provides a breakdown.

In a 1984 survey conducted by Mayer Nudell on the legality of ransom payments around the world, ten countries were identified as having legislation which was applicable to the physical act of making a ransom payment. The survey found that there were a number of countries which had such legislation, and we advised those who might be willing to make ransom payments to investigate the situation in the countries in which they had interest in order to ascertain the current situation.[2]

---

[1] Ransom demands are typically many, many times larger than ultimate settlements. Many analysts suggest that the factor is at least ten, so the figures presented here should be taken only as an indication of the problem.

[2] In addition to knowing whether such legislation exists, it is important to know how it is likely to be enforced. Not all countries can uniformly or vigorously enforce such laws.

During the preparation of this book, the survey was updated and expanded to ascertain the extent to which governments had legislation affecting the tax-deductibility of any ransom payments; that is, whether such payments are eligible for treatment as business expenses. The results were interesting.

As of September 1, 1989, nine countries had laws which expressly forbade the payment of ransoms in kidnapping or hostage-taking situations, or had laws which could be used by the government to block such payments. They are: Cyprus, Iraq, Italy, the Malagasy Republic, Malaysia, Singapore, Spain, Sri Lanka, and the United Kingdom. Thirty-two countries had laws and policies which either prohibited or could restrict consideration of ransom payments as business expenses. These are: Belize, Botswana, Canada, Chile, Costa Rica, Denmark, Finland, Honduras, India, Indonesia, Iraq, Israel, Italy, Jamaica, Laos, Malaysia, Mexico, the Netherlands, Oman, Peru, the Philippines, Singapore, South Korea, Spain, Sri Lanka, Sudan, Sweden, Thailand, Turkey, the United Kingdom, Uruguay, and West Germany.

As readers will note, not all of the countries which have laws prohibiting ransom payments have tax restrictions on such payments, suggesting that enforcement of the prohibition is inconsistent. It is also important that readers **not** assume that countries not listed here have no such prohibitions. In many cases, governments simply have not considered the matter and there is no certain way to predict a response during or after an incident.

Regardless of one's philosophical or political views concerning the payment of ransoms to terrorists, the consequences of such payments must not be overlooked. Businesses and individuals must take into account their legal position in the wake of any payment if they plan to remain in that country. And U.S. citizens and organizations should remember that U.S. government policy firmly precludes ransom payments—suggesting that no comfort can be expected from that quarter if legal proceedings are begun by a foreign government.

## TABLE C-1
## RANSOM DEMANDS, 1970–MARCH 1989*

| | |
|---|---|
| 1970–84 | $484,980,350 |
| 1985 | $ 17,621,540 |
| 1986 | $ 35,893,871 |
| 1987 | $ 99,855,200 |
| 1988 | $ 93,245,200 |
| 1989 (1st Quarter) | $ 8,100,000 |
| TOTAL | $739,696,461 |

*Source: Risks International Division, Business Risks International.

# APPENDIX D
# United Nations Conventions Regarding Hostage-Taking

There are a number of international agreements which deal with various facets of terrorism. Two with particular relevance to our subject matter have been developed under the auspices of the United Nations: the International Convention against the Taking of Hostages and the Convention on the Prevention and Punishment of Crimes against Internationally Protected Persons, including Diplomatic Agents. Both of these agreements currently are in force. The International Convention against the Taking of Hostages became effective on June 3, 1983. As of September 15, 1989, 27 countries had deposited ratifications, 28 had acceded to it, and there were 12 other signatories. The Convention on the Prevention and Punishment of Crimes against Internationally Protected Persons, including Diplomatic Agents became effective on February 20, 1977. As of September 15, 1989, 27 countries had deposited ratifications and 48 had acceded to it.

For the reader's information, following are the official texts of both treaties.[1]

---

[1]Texts supplied by the U.S. Department of State.

# INTERNATIONAL CONVENTION AGAINST THE TAKING OF HOSTAGES

**The States Parties to this Convention,**

**Having in mind** the purposes and principles of the Charter of the United Nations concerning the maintenance of international peace and security and the promotion of friendly relations and co-operation among States,

**Recognizing**, in particular, that everyone has the right to life, liberty and security of person, as set out in the Universal Declaration of Human Rights[1] and the International Covenant on Civil and Political Rights,[2]

**Reaffirming** the principle of equal rights and self-determination of peoples as enshrined in the Charter of the United Nations and the Declaration on Principles of International Law concerning Friendly Relations and Co-operation among States in accordance with the Charter of the United Nations,[3] as well as in other relevant resolutions of the General Assembly,

**Considering** that the taking of hostages is an offence of grave concern to the international community and that, in accordance with the provisions of this Convention, any person committing an act of taking of hostages shall be either prosecuted or extradited,

**Being convinced** that it is urgently necessary to develop international co-operation between States in devising and adopting effective measures for the prevention, prosecution and punishment of all acts of taking of hostages as manifestations of international terrorism,

**Have agreed** as follows:

## Article 1

1. Any person who seizes or detains and threatens to kill, to injure or to continue to detain another person (hereinafter referred to as the "hostage") in order to compel a third party, namely, a State, an international intergovernmental organization, a natural or juridical per-

---

[1]General Assembly resolution 217 A (III).

[2]General Assembly resolution 2200 A (XXI), annex.

[3]General Assembly resolution 2625 (XXV), annex.

son, or a group of persons, to do or abstain from doing any act as an explicit or implicit condition for the release of the hostage commits the offence of taking of hostages (''hostage-taking'') within the meaning of the Convention.

2. Any person who:

(a) Attempts to commit an act of hostage-taking, or

(b) Participates as an accomplice of anyone who commits or attempts to commit an act of hostage-taking likewise commits an offence for the purposes of this Convention.

## Article 2

Each State Party shall make the offences set forth in article 1 punishable by appropriate penalties which take into account the grave nature of those offences.

## Article 3

1. The State party in the territory of which the hostage is held by the offender shall take all measures it considers appropriate to ease the situation of the hostage, in particular, to secure his release and, after his release, to facilitate, when relevant, his departure.

2. If any object which the offender has obtained as a result of the taking of hostages comes into the custody of a State Party, that State Party shall return it as soon as possible to the hostage or the third party referred to in article 1, as the case may be, or to the appropriate authorities thereof.

## Article 4

States Parties shall co-operate in the prevention of the offences set forth in article 1, particularly by:

(a) Taking all practicable measures to prevent preparations in their respective territories for the commission of those offences within or outside their territories, including measures to prohibit in their territories illegal activities of persons, groups and organizations that encourage, instigate, organize or engage in the perpetration of acts of taking of hostages;

(b) Exchanging information and co-ordinating the taking of administrative and other measures as appropriate to prevent the commission of those offences.

## Article 5

1. Each State Party shall take such measures as may be necessary to establish its jurisdiction over any of the offences set forth in article 1 which are committed:

(a) In its territory or on board a ship or aircraft registered in that State;

(b) By any of its nationals or, if that State considers it appropriate, by those stateless persons who have their habitual residence in its territory;

(c) In order to compel that State to do or abstain from doing any act; or

(d) With respect to a hostage who is a national of that State, if that State considers it appropriate.

2. Each State party shall likewise take such measures as may be necessary to establish its jurisdiction over the offences set forth in article 1 in cases where the alleged offender is present in its territory and it does not extradite him to any of the States mentioned in paragraph 1 of this article.

3. This Convention does not exclude any criminal jurisdiction exercised in accordance with internal law.

## Article 6

1. Upon being satisfied that the circumstances so warrant, any State Party in the territory of which the alleged offender is present shall, in accordance with its laws, take him into custody or take other measures to ensure his presence for such time as is necessary to enable any criminal or extradition proceedings to be instituted. That State Party shall immediately make a preliminary inquiry into the facts.

2. The custody or other measures referred to in paragraph 1 of this article shall be notified without delay directly or through the Secretary-General of the United Nations to:

(a) The State where the offence was committed;

(b) The State against which compulsion has been directed or attempted;

(c) The State of which the natural or juridical person against whom compulsion has been directed or attempted is a national;

(d) The State of which the hostage is a national or in the territory of which he has his habitual residence;

(e) The State of which the alleged offender is a national or, if he is a stateless person, in the territory of which he has his habitual residence;

(f) The international intergovernmental organization against which compulsion has been directed or attempted;

(g) All other States concerned.

3. Any person regarding whom the measures referred to in paragraph 1 of this article are being taken shall be entitled:

(a) To communicate without delay with the nearest appropriate representative of the State of which he is a national or which is otherwise entitled to establish such communication or, if he is a stateless person, the State in the territory of which he has his habitual residence;

(b) To be visited by a representative of that State.

4. The rights referred to in paragraph 3 of this article shall be exercised in conformity with the laws and regulations of the State in the territory of which the alleged offender is present, subject to the proviso, however, that the said laws and regulations must enable full effect to be given to the purposes for which the rights accorded under paragraph 3 of this article are intended.

5. The provisions of paragraphs 3 and 4 of this article shall be without prejudice to the right of any State Party having a claim to jurisdiction in accordance with paragraph 1 (b) of article 5 to invite the International Committee of the Red Cross to communicate with and visit the alleged offender.

6. The State which makes the preliminary inquiry contemplated in paragraph 1 of this article shall promptly report its findings to the States or organization referred to in paragraph 2 of this article and indicate whether it intends to exercise jurisdiction.

## Article 7

The State Party where the alleged offender is prosecuted shall, in accordance with its laws, communicate the final outcome of the proceedings to the Secretary-General of the United Nations, who shall transmit the information to the other States concerned and the international intergovernmental organizations concerned.

## Article 8

1. The State party in the territory of which the alleged offender is found shall, if it does not extradite him, be obliged, without exception

whatsoever and whether or not the offence was committed in its territory, to submit the case to its competent authorities for the purpose of prosecution, through proceedings in accordance with the laws of that State. Those authorities shall take their decision in the same manner as in the case of any ordinary offence of a grave nature under the law of that State.

2. Any person regarding whom proceedings are being carried out in connexion with any of the offences set forth in article 1 shall be guaranteed fair treatment at all stages of the proceedings, including the enjoyment of all the rights and guarantees provided by the law of the State in the territory of which he is present.

### Article 9

1. A request for the extradition of an alleged offender, pursuant to this Convention, shall not be granted if the requested State Party has substantial grounds for believing:

(**a**) That the request for extradition for an offence set forth in article 1 has been made for the purpose of prosecuting or punishing a person on account of his race, religion, nationality, ethnic origin or political opinion; or

(**b**) That the person's position may be prejudiced:

(i) For any of the reasons mentioned in subparagraph (**a**) of this paragraph, or

   (ii) For the reason that communication with him by the appropriate
       authorities of the State entitled to exercise rights of protection
       cannot be effected.

2. With respect to the offences as defined in this Convention, the provisions of all extradition treaties and arrangements applicable between States Parties are modified as between States Parties to the extent that they are incompatible with this Convention.

### Article 10

1. The offences set forth in article 1 shall be deemed to be included as extraditable offences in any extradition treaty existing between States Parties. States Parties undertake to include such offences as extraditable offences in every extradition treaty to be concluded between them.

2. If a State Party which makes extradition conditional on the existence of a treaty receives a request for extradition from another State Party with which it has no extradition treaty, the requested State may at its option consider this Convention as the legal basis for extradition in respect of the offences set forth in article 1. Extradition shall be subject to the other conditions provided by the law of the requested State.

3. States Parties which do not make extradition conditional on the existence of a treaty shall recognize the offences set forth in article 1 as extraditable offences between themselves, subject to the conditions provided by the law of the requested State.

4. The offences set forth in article 1 shall be treated, for the purpose of extradition between States Parties, as if they had been committed not only in the place in which they occurred but also in the territories of the States required to establish their jurisdiction in accordance with paragraph 1 or article 5.

## Article 11

1. States Parties shall afford one another the greatest measure of assistance in connexion with criminal proceedings brought in respect of the offences set forth in article 1, including the supply of all evidence at their disposal necessary for the proceedings.

2. The provisions of paragraph 1 of this article shall not affect obligations concerning mutual judicial assistance embodied in any other treaty.

## Article 12

In so far as the Geneva Conventions of 1949 for the protection of war victims[4] or the Protocols Additional to those Conventions are applicable to a particular act of hostage-taking, and in so far as States Parties to this Convention are bound under those Conventions to prosecute or hand over the hostage-taker, the present Convention shall not apply to an act of hostage-taking committed in the course of armed conflicts as defined in the Geneva Conventions of 1949 and the Protocols thereto, including armed conflicts, mentioned in article 1,

---

[4]United Nations, *Treaty Series,* vol. 75, Nos. 970–973.

paragraph 4, of Protocol I of 1977,[5] in which peoples are fighting against colonial domination and alien occupation and against racist regimes in the exercise of their right of self-determination, as enshrined in the Charter of the United Nations and the Declaration on Principles of International Law concerning Friendly Relations and Co-operation among States in accordance with the Charter of the United Nations.

## Article 13

This Convention shall not apply where the offence is committed within a single State, the hostage and the alleged offender are nationals of that State and the alleged offender is found in the territory of that State.

## Article 14

Nothing in this Convention shall be construed as justifying the violation of the territorial integrity or political independence of a State in contravention of the Charter of the United Nations.

## Article 15

The provisions of this Convention shall not affect the application of the Treaties on Asylum, in force at the date of the adoption of this Convention, as between the States which are parties to those treaties; but a State Party to this Convention may not invoke those treaties with respect to another State Party to this Convention which is not a party to those treaties.

## Article 16

1. Any dispute between two or more States Parties concerning the interpretation or application of this convention which is not settled by negotiation shall, at the request of one of them, be submitted to arbitration. If within six months from the date of the request for arbitration the parties are unable to agree on the organization of the

---

[5]A/32/144, annex I.

arbitration, any one of those parties may refer the dispute to the International Court of Justice by request in conformity with the Statute of the Court.

2. Each State may at the time of signature or ratification of this Convention or accession thereto declare that it does not consider itself bound by paragraph 1 of this article. The other States Parties shall not be bound by paragraph 1 of this article with respect to any State Party which has made such a reservation.

3. Any State party which has made a reservation in accordance with paragraph 2 of this article may at any time withdraw that reservation by notification to the Secretary-General of the United Nations.

## Article 17

1. This Convention is open for signature by all States until 31 December 1980 at United Nations Headquarters in New York.

2. This Convention is subject to ratification. The instruments of ratification shall be deposited with the Secretary-General of the United Nations.

3. This Convention is open for accession by any State. The instruments of accession shall be deposited with the Secretary-General of the United nations.

## Article 18

1. This Convention shall enter into force on the thirtieth day following the date of deposit of the twenty-second instrument of ratification or accession with the Secretary-General of the United Nations.

2. For each State ratifying or acceding to the Convention after the deposit of the twenty-second instrument of ratification or accession, the Convention shall enter into force on the thirtieth day after deposit by such State of its instrument of ratification or accession.

## Article 19

1. Any State Party may denounce this Convention by written notification to the Secretary-General of the United Nations.

2. Denunciation shall take effect one year following the date on which notification is received by the Secretary-General of the United Nations.

## Article 20

The original of this Convention, of which the Arabic, Chinese, English, French, Russian and Spanish texts are equally authentic, shall be deposited with the Secretary-General of the United Nations, who shall send certified copies thereof to all States.

IN WITNESS WHEREOF, the undersigned, being duly authorized thereto by their respective Governments, have signed this Convention, opened for signature at New York on  . . . [6]

# CONVENTION ON THE PREVENTION AND PUNISHMENT OF CRIMES AGAINST INTERNATIONALLY PROTECTED PERSONS, INCLUDING DIPLOMATIC AGENTS

**The States Parties to this Convention,**

**Having in mind** the purposes and principles of the Charter of the United Nations[1] concerning the maintenance of international peace and the promotion of friendly relations and co-operation among States,

**Considering** that crimes against diplomatic agents and other internationally protected persons jeopardizing the safety of these persons create a serious threat to the maintenance of normal international relations which are necessary for co-operation among States,

**Believing** that the commission of such crimes is a matter of grave concern to the international community,

**Convinced** that there is an urgent need to adopt appropriate and effective measures for the prevention and punishment of such crimes,

**Have agreed** as follows:

## Article 1

For the purposes of this Convention:
1. "internationally protected person" means:

---

[6]The Convention was opened for signature on 18 December 1979.
[1]TS 993; 59 Stat. 1031.

(a) a Head of State, including any member of a collegial body performing the functions of a Head of State under the constitution of the State concerned, a Head of Government or a Minister for Foreign Affairs, whenever any such person is in a foreign State, as well as members of his family who accompany him;

(b) any representative or official of a State or any official or other agent of an international organization of an intergovernmental character who, at the time when and in the place where a crime against him, his official premises, his private accommodation or his means of transport is committed, is entitled pursuant to international law to special protection from any attack on his person, freedom or dignity, as well as members of his family forming part of his household;

2. "alleged offender" means a person as to whom there is sufficient evidence to determine *prima facie* that he has committed or participated in one or more of the crimes set forth in article 2.

## Article 2

1. The intentional commission of:

(a) a murder, kidnapping or other attack upon the person or liberty of an internationally protected person;

(b) a violent attack upon the official premises, the private accommodation or the means of transport of an internationally protected person likely to endanger his person or liberty;

(c) a threat to commit any such attack;

(d) an attempt to commit any such attack;

(e) an act constituting participation as an accomplice in any such attack

shall be made by each State Party a crime under its internal law.

2. Each State Party shall make these crimes punishable by appropriate penalties which take into account their grave nature.

3. Paragraphs 1 and 2 of this article in no way derogate from the obligations of States Parties under international law to take all appropriate measures to prevent other attacks on the person, freedom or dignity of an internationally protected person.

## Article 3

1. Each State Party shall take such measures as may be necessary to establish its jurisdiction over the crimes set forth in article 2 in the following cases:

(a) when the crime is committed in the territory of that State or on board a ship or aircraft registered in that State;

(b) when the alleged offender is a national of that State;

(c) when the crime is committed against an internationally protected person as defined in article 1 who enjoys his status as such by virtue of the functions which he exercises on behalf of that State.

2. Each State Party shall likewise take such measures as may be necessary to establish its jurisdiction over these crimes in cases where the alleged offender is present in its territory and it does not extradite him pursuant to article 8 to any of the States mentioned in paragraph 1 of this article.

3. This Convention does not exclude any criminal jurisdiction exercised in accordance with internal law.

## Article 4

States Parties shall co-operate in the prevention of the crimes set forth in article 2, particularly by:

(a) taking all practicable measures to prevent preparations in their respective territories for the commission of those crimes within or outside their territories;

(b) exchanging information and coordinating the taking of administrative and other measures as appropriate to prevent the commission of those crimes.

## Article 5

1. The State Party in which any of the crimes set forth in article 2 has been committed shall, if it has reason to believe that an alleged offender has fled from its territory, communicate to all other States concerned, directly or through the Secretary-General of the United Nations, all the pertinent facts regarding the crime committed and all available information regarding the identity of the alleged offender.

2. Whenever any of the crimes set forth in article 2 has been committed against an internationally protected person, any State Party which has information concerning the victim and the circumstances of the crime shall endeavour to transmit it, under the conditions provided for in its internal law, fully and promptly to the State Party on whose behalf he was exercising his functions.

## Article 6

1. Upon being satisfied that the circumstances so warrant, the State Party in whose territory the alleged offender is present shall take the appropriate measures under its internal law so as to ensure his presence for the purpose of prosecution or extradition. Such measures shall be notified without delay directly or through the Secretary-General of the United Nations to:

(a) the State where the crime was committed;

(b) the State or States of which the alleged offender is a national or, if he is a stateless person, in whose territory he permanently resides;

(c) the State or States of which the internationally protected person concerned is a national or on whose behalf he was exercising his functions;

(d) all other States concerned; and

(e) the international organization of which the internationally protected person concerned is an official or an agent.

2. Any person regarding whom the measures referred to in paragraph 1 of this article are being taken shall be entitled:

(a) to communicate without delay with the nearest appropriate representative of the State of which he is a national or which is otherwise entitled to protect his rights or, if he is a stateless person, which he requests and which is willing to protect his rights; and

(b) to be visited by a representative of that State.

## Article 7

The State Party in whose territory the alleged offender is present shall, if it does not extradite him, submit, without exception whatsoever and without undue delay, the case to its competent authorities for the purpose of prosecution, through proceedings in accordance with the laws of the State.

## Article 8

1. To the extent that the crimes set forth in article 2 are not listed as extraditable offenses in any extradition treaty existing between States Parties, they shall be deemed to be included as such therein. States Parties undertake to include those crimes as extraditable offenses in every future extradition treaty to be concluded between them.

2. If a State Party which makes extradition conditional on the existence of a treaty receives a request for extradition from another State Party with which it has no extradition treaty, it may, if it decided to extradite, consider this Convention as the legal basis for extradition in respect of those crimes. Extradition shall be subject to the procedural provisions and the other conditions of the law of the requested State.

3. States Parties which do not make extradition conditional on the existence of a treaty shall recognize those crimes as extraditionable offenses between themselves subject to the procedural provisions and the other conditions of the law of the requested State.

4. Each of the crimes shall be treated, for the purpose of extradition between States Parties, as if it had been committed not only in the place in which it occurred but also in the territories of the States required to establish their jurisdiction in accordance with paragraph 1 of article 3.

## Article 9

Any person regarding whom proceedings are being carried out in connection with any of the crimes set forth in article 2 shall be guaranteed fair treatment at all stages of the proceedings.

## Article 10

1. States Parties shall afford one another the greatest measure of assistance in connection with criminal proceedings brought in respect of the crimes set forth in article 2, including the supply of all evidence at their disposal necessary for the proceedings.

2. The provisions of paragraph 1 of this article shall not affect obligations concerning mutual judicial assistance embodied in any other treaty.

## Article 11

The State party where an alleged offender is prosecuted shall communicate the final outcome of the proceedings to the Secretary-General of the United Nations, who shall transmit the information to the other States Parties.

## Article 12

The provisions of this Convention shall not affect the application of the Treaties on Asylum, in force at the date of the adoption of this

Convention, as between the States which are parties to those Treaties; but a State Party to this Convention may not invoke those Treaties with respect to another State Party to this Convention which is not a party to those Treaties.

## Article 13

1. Any dispute between two or more States Parties concerning interpretation or application of this Convention which is not settled by negotiation shall, at the request of one of them, be submitted to arbitration. If within six months from the date of the request for arbitration the parties are unable to agree on the organization of the arbitration, any one of those parties may refer the dispute to the International Court of Justice by request in conformity with the Statute of the Court.

2. Each State Party may at the time of signature or ratification of this Convention or accession thereto declare that it does not consider itself bound by paragraph 1 of this article. The other States Parties shall not be bound by paragraph 1 of this article with respect to any State Party which has made such a reservation.

3. Any State Party which has made a reservation in accordance with paragraph 2 of this article may at any time withdraw that reservation by notification to the Secretary-General of the United Nations.

## Article 14

This Convention shall be open for signature by all States, until December 31, 1974 at United Nations Headquarters in New York.

## Article 15

This Convention is subject to ratification. The instruments of ratification shall be deposited with the Secretary-General of the United Nations.

## Article 16

This Convention shall remain open for accession by any State. The instruments of accession shall be deposited with the Secretary-General of the United Nations.

## Article 17

1. This Convention shall enter into force on the thirtieth day following the date of deposit of the twenty-second instrument of ratification or accession with the Secretary-General of the United Nations.

2. For each State ratifying or acceding to the Convention after the deposit of the twenty-second instrument of ratification or accession, the Convention shall enter into force on the thirtieth day after deposit by such State of its instrument of ratification or accession.

## Article 18

1. Any State Party may denounce this Convention by written notification to the Secretary-General of the United Nations.

2. Denunciation shall take effect six months following the date on which notification is received by the Secretary-General of the United Nations.

## Article 19

The Secretary-General of the United Nations shall inform all States, *inter alia*:

(a) of signatures to this Convention, of the deposit of instruments of ratification or accession in accordance with articles 14, 15 and 16 and of notifications made under article 18;

(b) of the date on which this Convention will enter into force in accordance with article 17.

## Article 20

The original of this Convention, of which the Chinese, English, French, Russian and Spanish texts are equally authentic, shall be deposited with the Secretary-General of the United Nations, who shall send certified copies thereof to all States.

IN WITNESS WHEREOF the undersigned, being duly authorized thereto by their respective Governments, have signed this Convention, opened for signature at New York on December 14, 1973.

# APPENDIX E
# MINIMANUAL OF THE URBAN GUERRILLA

Carlos Marighella's *Minimanual of the Urban Guerrilla* became the bible of revolutionaries and terrorists around the world during the 1970s. Marighella was not an original thinker; rather, he reduced to one small volume the collected wisdom of many theorists from Machiavelli to Mao and Ché, along with some homilies about initiative and flexibility. In fact, many of Marighella's formulations are reminiscent of a 1956 work, *Handbook for Volunteers of the Irish Republican Army*.

Marighella's book was translated into at least 15 languages and continues to influence the activities of contemporary terrorists. To a certain extent, this work might be considered a tradecraft manual prepared specifically for revolutionaries and terrorists.

While reading this document, we suggest that the reader make note of the inconsistencies and hypocrisy which are rife throughout the manuscript. For example, when Marighella distinguishes between an outlaw and an urban guerrilla by accusing the former of having "many ordinary men and women among his victims." Such sophistry is the hallmark of the terrorist.

Following is Marighella's complete text, which was first published in the Cuban revolutionary magazine, *Tricontinental*.

# MINIMANUAL OF THE URBAN GUERRILLA
## by Carlos Marighella

### A DEFINITION OF THE URBAN GUERRILLA

The chronic structural crisis characteristic of Brazil today, and its resultant political instability, are what have brought about the upsurge of revolutionary war in the country. The revolutionary war manifests itself in the form of urban guerrilla warfare, psychological warfare, or rural guerrilla warfare. Urban guerrilla warfare or psychological warfare in the city depends on the urban guerrilla.

The urban guerrilla is a man who fights the military dictatorship with arms, using unconventional methods. A political revolutionary and an ardent patriot, he is a fighter for his country's liberation, a friend of the people and of freedom. The area in which the urban guerrilla acts is in the large Brazilian cities. There are also bandits, commonly known as outlaws, who work in the big cities. Many times assaults by outlaws are taken as actions by urban guerrillas.

The urban guerrilla, however, differs radically from the outlaw. The outlaw benefits personally from the action, and attacks indiscriminately without distinguishing between the exploited and the exploiters, which is why there are so many ordinary men and women among his victims. The urban guerrilla follows a political goal and only attacks the government, the big capitalists, and the foreign imperialists, particularly North Americans.

Another element just as prejudicial as the outlaw and also operating in the urban area is the right-wing counterrevolutionary who creates confusion, assaults banks, hurls bombs, kidnaps, assassinates, and commits the worst imaginable crimes against urban guerrillas, revolutionary priests, students, and citizens who oppose fascism and seek liberty.

The urban guerrilla is an implacable enemy of the government and systematically inflicts damage on the authorities and on the men who dominate the country and exercise power. The principal task of the urban guerrilla is to distract, to wear out, to demoralize the militarists, the military dictatorship and its repressive forces, and also to attack and destroy the wealth and property of the North Americans, the foreign managers, and the Brazilian upper class.

The urban guerrilla is not afraid of dismantling and destroying the present Brazilian economic, political, and social system, for his aim is to help the rural guerrilla and to collaborate in the creation of a totally new and revolutionary social and political structure, with the armed people in power.

The urban guerrilla must have a certain minimal political understanding. To gain that he must read certain printed or mimeographed works such as:

*Guerrilla Warfare* by Ché Guevara
*Memories of a Terrorist*
*Some Questions about the Brazilian Guerrilla Operations and Tactics*
*On Strategic Problems and Principles*
*Certain Tactical Principles for Comrades Undertaking Guerrilla Operations*
*Organizational Questions*
*O Guerrilheiro*, newspaper of the Brazilian revolutionary groups.

## PERSONAL QUALITIES OF THE URBAN GUERRILLA

The urban guerrilla is characterized by his bravery and decisive nature. He must be a good tactician and a good shot. The urban guerrilla must be a person of great astuteness to compensate for the fact that he is not sufficiently strong in arms, ammunition, and equipment.

The career militarists or the government police have modern arms and transport, and can go about anywhere freely, using the force of their power. The urban guerrilla does not have such resources at his disposal and leans to a clandestine existence. Sometimes he is a convicted person or is out on parole, and is obliged to use false documents.

Nevertheless, the urban guerrilla has a certain advantage over the conventional military or the police. It is that, while the military and the police act on behalf of the enemy, whom the people hate, the urban guerrilla defends a just cause, which is the people's cause.

The urban guerrilla's arms are inferior to the enemy's, but from a moral point of view, the urban guerrilla has an undeniable superiority.

This moral superiority is what sustains the urban guerrilla. Thanks to it, the urban guerrilla can accomplish his principal duty, which is to attack and to survive.

The urban guerrilla has to capture or divert arms from the enemy to be able to fight. Because his arms are not uniform, since what he has are expropriated or have fallen into his hands in different ways, the urban guerrilla faces the problem of a variety of arms and a shortage of ammunition. Moreover, he has no place to practice shooting and marksmanship.

These difficulties have to be surmounted, forcing the urban guerrilla to be imaginative and creative, qualities without which it would be impossible for him to carry out his role as a revolutionary.

The urban guerrilla must possess initiative, mobility, and flexibility, as well as versatility and a command of any situation. Initiative especially is an indispensable quality. It is not always possible to foresee everything, and the urban guerrilla cannot let himself become confused, or wait for orders. His duty is to act, to find adequate solutions for each problem he faces, and not to retreat. It is better to err acting than to do nothing for fear of erring. Without initiative there is no urban guerrilla warfare.

Other important qualities in the urban guerrilla are the following: to be a good walker, to be able to stand up against fatigue, hunger, rain, heat. To know how to hide and to be vigilant. To conquer the art of dissembling. Never to fear danger. To behave the same by day as by night. Not to act impetuously. To have unlimited patience. To remain calm and cool in the worst conditions and situations. Never to leave a track or trail. Not to get discouraged.

In the face of the almost insurmountable difficulties of urban warfare, sometimes comrades weaken, leave, give up the work.

The urban guerrilla is not a businessman in a commercial firm nor is he a character in a play. Urban guerrilla warfare, like rural guerrilla warfare, is a pledge the guerrilla makes to himself. When he cannot face the difficulties, or knows that he lacks the patience to wait, then it is better to relinquish his role before he betrays his pledge, for he clearly lacks the basic qualities necessary to be a guerrilla.

## HOW THE URBAN GUERRILLA LIVES AND SUBSISTS

The urban guerrilla must know how to live among the people and must be careful not to appear strange and separated from ordinary city life.

He should not wear clothes that are different from those that other people wear. Elaborate and high fashion clothing for men or women may often be a handicap if the urban guerrilla's mission takes him into working class neighborhoods or sections where such dress is uncommon.

## THE URBAN GUERRILLA'S ARMS

The urban guerrilla's arms are light arms, easily exchanged, usually captured from the enemy, purchased, or made on the spot.

Light arms have the advantage of fast handling and easy transport. In general, light arms are characterized as short barrelled. This includes many automatic arms.

Automatic and semiautomatic arms considerably increase the fighting power of the urban guerrilla. The disadvantage of this type of arm for us is the difficulty in controlling it, resulting in wasted rounds or in a prodigious use of ammunition, compensated for only by optimal aim and firing precision. Men who are poorly trained convert automatic weapons into an ammunition drain.

Experience has shown that the basic arm of the urban guerrilla is the light machine gun. This arm, in addition to being efficient and easy to shoot in an urban area, has the advantage of being greatly respected by the enemy. The guerrilla must know thoroughly how to handle the machine gun, now so popular and indispensable to the Brazilian urban guerrilla.

The ideal machine gun for the urban guerrilla is the Ina 45 calibre. Other types of machine guns of different calibres can be used—understanding, of course, the problem of ammunition. Thus it is preferable that the industrial potential of the urban guerrilla permit the production of a single machine gun so that the ammunition used can be standardized.

Each firing group of urban guerrillas must have a machine gun managed by a good marksman. The other components of the group must be armed with .38 revolvers, our standard arm. The .32 is also useful for those who want to participate. But the .38 is preferable since its impact usually puts the enemy out of action.

Hand grenades and conventional smoke bombs can be considered light arms, the defensive power for cover and withdrawal.

Long barrel arms are more difficult for the urban guerrilla to transport and attract much attention because of their size. Among the long barrel arms are the FAL, the Mauser guns or rifles, hunting guns such as the Winchester, and others.

Shotguns can be useful if used at close range and point blank. They are useful even for a poor shot, especially at night when precision isn't much help. A pressure air gun can be useful for training in marksmanship. Bazookas and mortars can also be used in action but the conditions for using them have to be prepared and the people who use them must be trained.

The urban guerrilla should not try to base his actions on the use of heavy arms, which have major drawbacks in a type of fighting that demands lightweight weapons to insure mobility and speed.

Homemade weapons are often as efficient as the best arms produced in conventional factories, and even a cut-off shotgun is a good arm for the urban guerrilla.

The urban guerrilla's role as gunsmith has a fundamental importance. As a gunsmith he takes care of the arms, knows how to repair them, and in many cases can set up a small shop for improvising and producing efficient small arms.

Work in metallurgy and on the mechanical lathe are basic skills the urban guerrilla should incorporate into his industrial planning, which is the construction of homemade weapons.

This construction and courses in explosives and sabotage must be organized. The primary materials for practice in these courses must be obtained ahead of time to prevent an incomplete apprenticeship— that is to say, so as to leave no room for experimentation.

Molotov cocktails, gasoline, homemade contrivances such as catapults and mortars for firing explosives, grenades made of tubes and cans, smoke bombs, mines, conventional explosives such as dynamite and potassium chloride, plastic explosives, gelatine capsules, ammunition of every kind are indispensable to the success of the urban guerrilla's mission.

The method of obtaining the necessary materials and munitions will be to buy them or to take them by force in expropriation actions especially planned and carried out.

The urban guerrilla will be careful not to keep explosives and materials that can cause accidents around for very long, but will try always to use them immediately on their destined targets.

The urban guerrilla's arms and his ability to maintain them constitute his fire power. By taking advantage of modern arms and introducing innovations in his fire power and in the use of certain arms, the urban guerrilla can change many of the tactics of city warfare. An example of this was the innovation made by the urban guerrillas in Brazil when they introduced the machine gun in their attacks on banks.

When the massive use of uniform machine guns becomes possible, there will be new changes in urban guerrilla warfare tactics. The firing group that utilizes uniform weapons and corresponding ammunition, with reasonable support for their maintenance, will reach a considerable level of efficiency. The urban guerrilla increases his efficiency as he improves his firing potential.

## THE SHOT: THE URBAN GUERRILLA'S REASON FOR EXISTENCE

The urban guerrilla's reason for existence, the basic condition in which he acts and survives, is to shoot. The urban guerrilla must know how to shoot well because it is required by his type of combat.

In conventional warfare, combat is generally at a distance with long range arms. In unconventional warfare, in which urban guerrilla is included, the combat is at close range, often very close. To prevent his own extinction, the urban guerrilla has to shoot first and he cannot err in his shot. He cannot waste his ammunition because he doesn't have large amounts, so he must save it. Nor can he replace his ammunition quickly, since he is part of a small group in which each guerrilla has to take care of himself. The urban guerrilla can lose no time and must be able to shoot at once.

One fundamental fact which we want to emphasize fully and whose particular importance cannot be overestimated is that the urban guerrilla must not fire continuously, using up his ammunition. It may be that the enemy is not responding to the fire precisely because he is waiting until the guerrilla's ammunition is used up. At such a moment, without having time to replace his ammunition, the urban guerrilla faces a rain of enemy fire and can be taken prisoner or be killed.

In spite of the value of the surprise factor which many times makes it unnecessary for the urban guerrilla to use his arms, he cannot be allowed the luxury of entering combat without knowing how to shoot. And face to face with the enemy, he must always be moving from one position to another, because to stay in one position makes him a fixed target and, as such, very vulnerable.

The urban guerrilla's life depends on shooting, on his ability to handle his arms well and to avoid being hit. When we speak of shooting, we speak of marksmanship as well. Shooting must be learned until it becomes a reflex action on the part of the urban guerrilla.

To learn how to shoot and to have good aim, the urban guerrilla must train himself systematically, utilizing every apprenticeship method, shooting at targets, even in amusement parks and at home.

Shooting and marksmanship are the urban guerrilla's water and air. His perfection of the art of shooting makes him a special type of urban guerrilla—that is, a sniper, a category of solitary combatant indispensable in isolated actions. The sniper knows how to shoot, at close range and at long range, and his arms are appropriate for either type of shooting.

## THE FIRING GROUP

In order to function, the urban guerrillas must be organized in small groups. A group of no more than four or five is called *the firing group*.

A minimum of two firing groups, separated and sealed off from other firing groups, directed and coordinated by one or two persons, this is what makes a *firing team*.

Within the firing group there must be complete confidence among the comrades. The best shot and the one who best knows how to manage the machine gun is the person in charge of operations.

The firing group plans and executes urban guerrilla actions, obtains and guards arms, studies and corrects its own tactics.

When there are tasks planned by the strategic command, these tasks take preference. But there is no such thing as a firing group without its own initiative. For this reason it is essential to avoid any rigidity in the organization in order to permit the greatest possible initiative on the part of the firing group. The old-type hierarchy, the style of the traditional left doesn't exist in our organization.

That means that, except for the priority of objectives set by the strategic command, any firing group can decide to assault a bank, to kidnap or to execute an agent of the dictatorship, a figure identified with the reaction, or a North American spy, and can carry out any kind of propaganda or war of nerves against the enemy without the need to consult the general command.

No firing group can remain inactive waiting for orders from above. Its obligation is to act. Any single urban guerrilla who wants to establish a firing group and begin action can do so and thus become a part of the organization.

This method of action eliminates the need for knowing who is carrying out which actions, since there is free initiative and the only important point is to increase substantially the volume of urban guerrilla activity in order to wear out the government and force it onto the defensive.

The firing group is the instrument of organized action. Within it, guerrilla operations and tactics are planned, launched, and carried through to success.

The general command counts on the firing groups to carry out objectives of a strategic nature, and to do so in any part of the country. For its part, it helps the firing groups with their difficulties and their needs.

The organization is an indestructible network of firing groups, and of coordinations among them, that functions simply and practically with a general command that also participates in the attacks; an organization which exists for no purpose other than pure and simple revolutionary action.

## CHARACTERISTICS OF THE URBAN GUERRILLA'S TECHNIQUE

The technique of the urban guerrilla has the following characteristics:

(a) it is an aggressive technique, or in other words, it has an offensive character. As is well known, defensive action means death for us. Since we are inferior to the enemy in fire power and have neither his resources nor his power force, we cannot defend ourselves against an offensive or a concentrated attack by the gorillas. And that is the reason why our urban technique can never be permanent, can never defend a fixed base nor remain in any one spot waiting to repel the circle of reaction;

(b) it is a technique of attack and retreat by which we preserve our forces;

(c) it is a technique that aims at the development of urban guerrilla warfare, whose function will be to wear out, demoralize, and distract the enemy forces, permitting the emergence and survival of rural guerrilla warfare which is destined to play the decisive role in the revolutionary war.

## ON THE TYPES AND NATURE OF ACTION MODELS FOR THE URBAN GUERRILLA

In order to achieve the objectives previously enumerated, the urban guerrilla is obliged, in his technique, to follow an action whose nature is as different and as diversified as possible. The urban guerrilla does not arbitrarily choose this or that action model. Some actions are simple, others are complicated. The urban guerrilla without experience must be incorporated gradually into actions and operations that run from the simple to the complex. He begins with small missions and tasks until he becomes a completely experienced urban guerrilla.

Before any action, the urban guerrilla must think of the methods and the personnel at his disposal to carry out the action. Operations and actions that demand the urban guerrilla's technical preparation cannot be carried out by someone who lacks that technical skill. With these cautions, the action models which the urban guerrilla can carry out are the following:

(a) assaults;

(b) raids and penetrations;

(c) occupations;

(d) ambush;

(e) street tactics;

(f) strikes and work interruptions;

(g) desertions, diversions, seizures, expropriations of arms, ammunition, explosives;

(h) liberation of prisoners;

(i) executions;

(j) kidnappings;

(k) sabotage;

(l) terrorism;

(m) armed propaganda;

(n) war of nerves.


## ASSAULTS

Assault is the armed attack which we make to expropriate funds, liberate prisoners, capture explosives, machine guns, and other types of arms and ammunition.

Assaults can take place in broad daylight or at night.

Daytime assaults are made when the objective cannot be achieved at any other hour, as for example, the transport of money by the banks, which is not done at night.

Night assault is usually the most advantageous to the urban guerrilla. The ideal is for all assaults to take place at night when conditions for a surprise attack are most favorable and the darkness facilitates flight and hides the identity of the participants. The urban guerrilla must prepare himself, nevertheless, to act under all conditions, daytime as well as nighttime.

The most vulnerable targets for assault are the following:

(a) credit establishments;

(b) commercial and industrial enterprises, including the production of arms and explosives;

(c) military establishments;

(d) commissaries and police stations;

(e) jails;

(f) government property;

(g) mass communication media;

(h) North American firms and properties;

(i) government vehicles, including military and police vehicles, trucks, armored vehicles, money carriers, trains, ships, and planes.

The assaults on establishments are of the same nature because in every case the property and buildings represent a fixed target.

Assaults on buildings are conceived as guerrilla operations, varied according to whether they are against banks, a commercial enterprise, industries, military camps, commissaries, prisons, radio stations, warehouses for imperialist firms, etc.

The assaults on vehicles—money-carriers, armored cars, trains, ships, airplanes—are of another nature since they are moving targets. The nature of the operations varies according to the situation and the possibility—that is, whether the target is stationary or moving.

Armored cars, including military cars, are not immune to mines. Obstructed roads, traps, ruses, interception of other vehicles, Molotov cocktails, shooting with heavy arms, are efficient methods of assaulting vehicles.

Heavy vehicles, grounded planes, anchored ships can be seized and their crews and guards overcome. Airplanes in flight can be diverted from their course by guerrilla action or by one person.

Ships and trains in movement can be assaulted or taken by guerrilla operations in order to capture the arms and munitions or to prevent troop deployment.

## THE BANK ASSAULT AS A POPULAR MODEL

The most popular assault model is the bank assault. In Brazil, the urban guerrilla has begun a type of organized assault on the banks as a guerrilla operation. Today this type of assault is widely used and has served as a sort of preliminary examination for the urban guerrilla in his apprenticeship for the techniques of revolutionary warfare.

Important innovations in the technique of assaulting banks have developed, guaranteeing flight, the withdrawal of money, and the anonymity of those involved. Among these innovations we cite shooting the tires of cars to prevent pursuit; locking people in the bank bathroom, making them sit on the floor; immobilizing the bank guards and removing their arms, forcing someone to open the coffer or the strong box; using disguises.

Attempts to install bank alarms, to use guards or electronic detection devices of U.S. origin, prove fruitless when the assault is political and is carried out according to urban guerrilla warfare technique. This technique tries to utilize new resources to meet the enemy's tactical changes, has access to a fire power that is growing every day, becomes increasingly astute and audacious, and uses a larger number of revolutionaries every time; all to guarantee the success of operations planned down to the last detail.

The bank assault is a typical expropriation. But, as is true in any kind of armed expropriatory action, the revolutionary is handicapped by a two-fold competition:

(a) competition from the outlaw;

(b) competition from the right-wing counterrevolutionary.

This competition produces confusion, which is reflected in the people's uncertainty. It is up to the urban guerrilla to prevent this from happening, and to accomplish this he must use two methods:

(a) he must avoid the outlaw's technique, which is one of unnecessary violence and appropriation of goods and possessions belonging to the people;

(b) he must use the assault for propaganda purposes, at the very moment it is taking place, and later distribute material, leaflets, every possible means of explaining the objectives and the principles of the urban guerrilla as expropriator of the government, the ruling classes, and imperialism.

## RAIDS AND PENETRATION

Raids and penetrations are quick attacks on establishments located in neighborhoods or even in the center of the city, such as small military units, commissaries, hospitals, to cause trouble, seize arms, punish and terrorize the enemy, take reprisal, or rescue wounded prisoners, or those hospitalized under police vigilance.

Raids and penetrations are also made on garages and depots to destroy vehicles and damage installations, especially if they are North American firms and property.

When they take place on certain stretches of the highway or in certain distant neighborhoods, the raids can serve to force the enemy to move great numbers of troops, a totally useless effort since he will find nobody there to fight.

When they are carried out in certain houses, offices, archives, or public offices, their purpose is to capture or search for secret papers and documents with which to denounce involvements, compromises, and the corruption of men in government, their dirty deals and criminal transactions with the North Americans.

Raids and penetrations are most effective if they are carried out at night.

## OCCUPATIONS

Occupations are a type of attack carried out when the urban guerrilla stations himself in specific establishments and locations for a temporary resistance against the enemy or for some propaganda purpose.

The occupation of factories and schools during strikes or at other times is a method of protest or of distracting the enemy's attention.

The occupation of radio stations is for propaganda purposes.

Occupation is a highly effective model for action but, in order to prevent losses and material damage to our ranks, it is always a good idea to count on the possibility of withdrawal. It must always be meticulously planned and carried out at the opportune moment.

Occupation always has a time limit and the faster it is completed the better.

## STREET TACTICS

Street tactics are used to fight the enemy in the streets, utilizing the participation of the masses against him.

In 1968 the Brazilian students used excellent street tactics against police troops, such as marching down streets against traffic, utilizing slings and marbles as arms against the mounted police.

Other street tactics consist in constructing barricades; pulling up paving blocks and hurling them at the police; throwing bottles, bricks, paper-weights, and other projectiles from the tops of apartment and office buildings against the police; using buildings under construction for flight, for hiding, and for supporting surprise attacks.

It is equally necessary to know how to respond to enemy tactics. When the police troops come protected with helmets to defend themselves against flying objects, we have to divide ourselves into two teams: one to attack the enemy from the front, the other to attack him in the rear, withdrawing one as the other goes into action to prevent the first from becoming a target for projectiles hurled by the second.

By the same token it is important to know how to respond to the police net. When the police designate certain of their men to go into the masses to arrest a demonstrator, a larger group of urban guerrillas must surround the police group, disarming and beating them and at the same time letting the prisoner escape. This urban guerrilla operation is called the *net within the net.*

When the police net is formed at a school building, a factory, a place where the masses assemble, or some other point, the urban guerrilla must not give up or allow himself to be taken by surprise. To make his net work the enemy is obliged to transport the police in vehicles and special cars to occupy strategic points in the streets in order to invade the building or chosen locale. The urban guerrilla, for his part, must never clear a building or an area and meet in it without first knowing its exits, the way to break the circle, the strategic points that the police might occupy, and the roads that inevitably lead into the net, and he must hold other strategic points from which to strike at the enemy.

The roads followed by the police vehicles must be mined at key points along the way and at forced stopping points. When the mines explode, the vehicles will fly into the air. The police will be caught in the trap and will suffer losses or will be victims of ambush. The net must be broken by escape routes unknown to the police. The rigorous planning of the retreat is the best way of frustrating any encircling effort on the part of the enemy.

When there is no possibility of a flight plan, the urban guerrilla must not hold meetings, assemblies, or do anything else since to do so will prevent him from breaking through the net the enemy will surely try to throw around him.

Street tactics have revealed a new type of urban guerrilla, the urban guerrilla who participates in mass demonstrations. This is the type we designate as the urban guerrilla demonstrator, who joins the ranks and participates in popular marches with specific and definite aims.

These aims consist in hurling stones and projectiles of every type, using gasoline to start fires, using the police as a target for their fire arms, capturing police arms, kidnapping agents of the enemy and provocateurs, shooting with careful aim at the henchmen torturers and the police chiefs who come in special cars with false plates in order not to attract attention.

The urban guerrilla demonstrator shows groups in the mass demonstration the flight route if that is necessary. He plants mines, throws Molotov cocktails, prepares ambushes and explosions.

The urban guerrilla demonstrator must also initiate the net within the net, going through government vehicles, official cars, and police vehicles before turning them over or setting them on fire, to see if any of them have money and arms.

Snipers are very good for mass demonstrations and, along with the urban guerrilla demonstrators, can play a valuable role.

Hidden at strategic points, the snipers have complete success, using shotguns, machine guns, etc. whose fire and ricocheting easily cause losses among the enemy.

## STRIKES AND WORK INTERRUPTIONS

The strike is a model of action employed by the urban guerrilla in work centers and schools to damage the enemy by stopping work and study activities. Because it is one of the weapons most feared by the exploiters and oppressors, the enemy uses tremendous fighting power and incredible violence against it. The strikers are taken to prison, suffer beatings, and many of them wind up assassinated.

The urban guerrilla must prepare the strike in such a way as to leave no tracks or clues that identify the leaders of the action. A strike is successful when it is organized through the action of a small group, if it is carefully prepared in secret and by the most clandestine methods.

Arms, ammunition, Molotovs, homemade weapons of destruction and attack, all this must be supplied beforehand in order to meet the enemy. So that it can do the greatest possible damage, it is a good idea to study and put into effect a sabotage plan.

Work and study interruptions, although they are of brief duration, cause severe damage to the enemy. It is enough for them to crop up at different points and in different sections of the same area, disrupting daily life, occurring endlessly one after the other, in authentic guerrilla fashion.

In strikes or simple work interruptions, the urban guerrilla has recourse to occupation or penetration of the locale or can simply make a raid. In that case his objective is to take hostages, to capture prisoners, or to kidnap enemy agents and propose an exchange for the arrested strikers. In certain cases, strikes and brief work interruptions can offer an excellent opportunity for preparing ambushes or traps whose aim is the physical liquidation of the cruel, bloody police.

The basic fact is that the enemy suffers losses and material and moral damage, and is weakened by the action.

## DESERTIONS, DIVERSIONS, SEIZURES, EXPROPRIATIONS OF ARMS, AMMUNITION, EXPLOSIVES

Desertion and the diversion of arms are actions effected in military camps, ships, military hospitals, etc. The urban guerrilla soldier, chief, sergeant, subofficial, and official must desert at the most opportune moment with modern arms and ammunition to hand them over for the use of the Brazilian revolution.

One of the opportune moments is when the military urban guerrilla is called upon to pursue and to fight his guerrilla comrades outside the military quarters. Instead of following the orders of the guerrillas, the military urban guerrilla must join the revolutionaries by handing over the arms and ammunition he carries, or the military plane he pilots.

The advantage of this method is that the revolutionaries receive arms and ammunition from the army, the navy, and the air force, the military police, the civilian guard, or the firemen without any great work, since it reaches their hands by government transport.

Other opportunities may occur in the barracks, and the military urban guerrilla must always be alert to this. In case of carelessness on the part of the commanders or in other favorable conditions, such as bureaucratic attitudes and behavior or relaxation of discipline on the part of sublieutenants and other internal personnel, the military urban guerrilla must no longer wait but must try to advise the organizations and desert alone or accompanied, but with as large a supply of arms as possible.

With information from and participation of the military urban guerrilla, raids on barracks and other military establishments for the purpose of capturing arms can be organized.

When there is no possibility of deserting and taking arms and ammunition, the military urban guerrilla must engage in sabotage, starting explosions and fires in munitions and gunpowder.

This technique of deserting with arms and ammunition, of raiding and sabotaging the military centers, is the best way of wearing out and demoralizing the gorillas and of leaving them confused.

The urban guerrilla's purpose in disarming an individual enemy is to capture his arms. These arms are usually in the hands of sentinels or others whose task is guard duty or repression.

The capture of arms may be accompanied by violent means or by astuteness and by tricks or traps. When the enemy is disarmed, he must be searched for arms other than those already taken from him. If we are careless, he can use the arms that were not seized to shoot the urban guerrilla.

The seizure of arms is an efficient method of acquiring machine guns, the urban guerrilla's most important arms.

When we carry out small operations or actions to seize arms and ammunition, the material captured may be for personal use or for armaments and supplies for the firing groups.

The necessity to provide firing power for the urban guerrilla is so great that in order to take off from zero point we often have to purchase one weapon, divert or capture a single arm. The basic point is to begin, and to begin with a great spirit of decisiveness and of boldness. The possession of a single arm multiplies our forces.

In a bank assault, we must be careful to seize the arm or arms of the bank guard. The remainder of the arms we find with the treasurer, the bank teller, or the manager must also be seized ahead of time.

The other method we can use to capture arms is the preparation of ambushes against the police and the cars they use to move around in.

Quite often we succeed in capturing arms in the police commissaries as a result of raids from outside.

The expropriation of arms, ammunition, and explosives is the urban guerrilla's goal in assaulting commercial houses, industries, and quarries.

## LIBERATION OF PRISONERS

The liberation of prisoners is an armed operation designed to free the jailed urban guerrilla. In daily struggle against the enemy, the urban guerrilla is subject to arrest and can be sentenced to unlimited years in jail. This does not mean that the revolutionary battle stops here. For the guerrilla, his experience is deepened by prison and continues even in the dungeons where he is held.

The imprisoned urban guerrilla views jail as a terrain he must dominate and understand in order to free himself by a guerrilla operation. There is no prison, either on an island, in a city penitentiary, or on a farm, that is impregnable to the slyness, the cleverness, and the firing potential of the revolutionaries.

The urban guerrilla who is free views the penal establishments of the enemy as the inevitable site of guerrilla action designed to liberate his ideological brothers from prison.

It is this combination of *the urban guerrilla in freedom and the urban guerrilla in jail* that results in the armed operations we refer to as the liberation of prisoners.

The guerrilla operations that can be used in liberating prisoners are the following:

(a) riots in penal establishments, in correctional colonies and islands, or on transport or prison ships;

(b) assaults on urban or rural penitentiaries, houses of detention, commissaries, prisoner depots, or any other permanent, occasional, or temporary place where prisoners are held;

(c) assaults on prisoner transport trains and cars;

(d) raids and penetrations of prisons;

(e) ambushing of guards who are moving prisoners.


## EXECUTION

Execution is the killing of a North American spy, of an agent of the dictatorship, of a police torturer, of a fascist personality in the government involved in crimes and persecutions against patriots, of a stool pigeon, informer, police agent, or police provocateur.

Those who go to the police of their own free will to make denunciations and accusations, who supply clues and information and finger people, must also be executed when they are caught by the urban guerrilla.

Execution is a secret action in which the least possible number of urban guerrillas are involved. In many cases, the execution can be carried out by one sniper, patiently, alone and unknown, and operating in absolute secrecy and in cold blood.

## KIDNAPPING

Kidnapping is capturing and holding in a secret spot a police agent, a North American spy, a political personality, or a notorious and dangerous enemy of the revolutionary movement.

Kidnapping is used to exchange or liberate imprisoned revolutionary comrades, or to force suspension of torture in the jail cells of the military dictatorship.

The kidnapping of personalities who are known artists, sports figures, or are outstanding in some other field, but who have evidenced no political interest, can be useful form of propaganda for the revolutionary and patriotic principles of the urban guerrilla provided it occurs under special circumstances, and the kidnapping is handled so that the public sympathizes with it and accepts it.

The kidnapping of North American residents or visitors in Brazil constitutes a form of protest against the penetration and domination of United States imperialism in our country.

## SABOTAGE

Sabotage is a highly destructive type of attack using very few persons and sometimes requiring only one to accomplish the desired result. When the urban guerrilla uses sabotage the first phase is isolated sabotage. Then comes the phase of dispersed and generalized sabotage, carried out by the people.

Well-executed sabotage demands study, planning, and careful execution. A characteristic form of sabotage is explosion using dynamite, fire, and the placing of mines.

A little sand, a trickle of any kind of combustible, a poor lubrication, a screw removed, a short circuit, pieces of wood or of iron, can cause irreparable damage.

The objective of sabotage is to hurt, to damage, to make useless, and to destroy vital enemy points such as the following:

(a) the economy of the country;

(b) agricultural or industrial production;

(c) transport and communication systems;

(d) the military and police systems and their establishments and deposits;

(e) the repressive military-police system;

(f) the firms and properties of North Americans in the country.

The urban guerrilla should endanger the economy of the country, particularly its economic and financial aspects, such as its domestic and foreign commercial network, its exchange and banking systems, its tax collection systems, and others.

Public offices, centers of government services, government warehouses, are easy targets for sabotage.

Nor will it be easy to prevent the sabotage of agricultural and industrial production by the urban guerrilla, with his thorough knowledge of the local situation.

Industrial workers acting as urban guerrillas are excellent industrial saboteurs since they, better than anyone, understand the industry, the factory, the machine, or the part most likely to destroy an entire operation, doing far more damage than a poorly informed layman could do.

With respect to the enemy's transport and communications systems, beginning with railway traffic, it is necessary to attack them systematically with sabotage arms.

The only caution is against causing death and fatal injury to passengers, especially regular commuters on suburban and long-distance trains.

Attacks on freight trains, rolling or stationary stock, stoppage of military transport and communication systems, these are the major sabotage objectives in this area.

Sleepers can be damaged and pulled up, as can rails. A tunnel blocked by a barrier after an explosion, an obstruction by a derailed car, cause tremendous harm.

The derailment of a cargo train carrying fuel is of major damage to the enemy. So is dynamiting railway bridges. In a system where the weight and the size of the rolling equipment is enormous, it takes months for workers to repair or rebuild the destruction and damage.

As for highways they can be obstructed by trees, stationary vehicles, ditches, dislocation of barriers by dynamite, and bridges blown up by explosion.

Ships can be damaged at anchor in seaports and river ports or in the shipyards. Airplanes can be destroyed or sabotaged on the ground.

Telephonic and telegraphic lines can be systematically damaged, their towers blown up, and their lines made useless.

Transport and communications must be sabotaged at once because the revolutionary war has already begun in Brazil and it is essential to impede the enemy's movement of troops and munitions.

Oil lines, fuel plants, depots for bombs and ammunition, powder magazines and arsenals, military camps, commissaries must become targets par excellence in sabotage operations, while vehicles, army trucks, and other military and police cars must be destroyed wherever they are found.

The military and police repression centers and their specific and specialized organs, must also claim the attention of the urban guerrilla saboteur.

North American firms and properties in the country, for their part, must become such frequent targets of sabotage that the volume of actions directed against them surpasses the total of all other actions against vital enemy points.

## TERRORISM

Terrorism is an action, usually involving the placement of a bomb or fire explosion of great destructive power, which is capable of effecting irreparable loss against the enemy.

Terrorism requires that the urban guerrilla should have an adequate theoretical and practical knowledge of how to make explosives.

The terroristic act, apart from the apparent facility with which it can be carried out, is no different from the other urban guerrilla acts and actions whose success depends on the planning and determination of the revolutionary organization. It is an action the urban guerrilla must execute with the greatest cold bloodedness, calmness, and decision.

Although terrorism generally involves an explosion, there are cases in which it may also be carried out by execution and the systematic burning of installations, properties, and North American depots, plantations, etc. It is essential to point out the importance of fires and the construction of incendiary bombs such as gasoline bombs in the technique of revolutionary terrorism. Another thing is the importance of the material the urban guerrilla can persuade the people to expropriate in moments of hunger and scarcity resulting from the greed of the big commercial interest.

Terrorism is an arm the revolutionary can never relinquish.

## ARMED PROPAGANDA

The coordination of urban guerrilla actions, including each armed action, is the principal way of making armed propaganda.

These actions, carried out with specific and determined objectives inevitably become propaganda material for the mass communications system.

Bank assaults, ambushes, desertions and diverting of arms, the rescue of prisoners, executions, kidnappings, sabotage, terrorism, and the war of nerves, are all cases in point.

Airplanes diverted in flight by revolutionary action, moving ships and trains assaulted and seized by guerrillas, can also be solely for propaganda effects.

But the urban guerrilla must never fail to install a clandestine press and must be able to turn out mimeographed copies using alcohol or electric plates and other duplicating apparatus, expropriating what he cannot buy in order to produce small clandestine newspapers, pamphlets, flyers, and stamps for propaganda and agitation against the dictatorship.

The urban guerrilla engaged in clandestine printing facilitates enormously the incorporation of large numbers of people into the revolutionary struggle, by opening a permanent work front for those willing to carry on revolutionary propaganda, even when to do so means acting alone and risking their lives as revolutionaries.

With the existence of clandestine propaganda and agitational material, the inventive spirit of the urban guerrilla expands and creates catapults, artifacts, mortars, and other instruments with which to distribute the antigovernment pamphlets at a distance.

Tape recordings, the occupation of radio stations, and the use of loud speakers, drawings on walls and in other inaccessible places are other forms of propaganda.

In using them, the urban guerrilla should give them the character of armed operations.

A consistent propaganda by letters sent to specific addresses, explaining the meaning of the urban guerrilla's armed actions, produces considerable results and is one method of influencing certain segments of the population.

Even this influence exercised in the heart of the people by every possible propaganda device revolving around the activity of the urban guerrilla does not indicate that our forces have everyone's support.

It is enough to win the support of a part of the people and this can be done by popularizing the following slogan: "Let he who does not wish to do anything for the revolutionaries, do nothing against them."

## URBAN GUERRILLA WARFARE, SCHOOL FOR SELECTING THE GUERRILLA

Revolution is a social phenomenon that depends on men, arms, and resources. Arms and resources exist in the country and can be taken and used, but to do this it is necessary to count on men. Without them, the arms and the resources have no use and no value. For their part, the men must have two basic and indispensable obligatory qualities:

(a) they must have a politico-revolutionary motivation;

(b) they must have the necessary technical-revolutionary preparation.

Men with a politico-revolutionary motivation are found among the vast and clearheaded contingents of enemies of the military dictatorship and of the domination of U.S. imperialism.

Almost daily such men gravitate to urban guerrilla warfare, and it is for this reason that the reaction no longer announces that it has thwarted the revolutionaries and goes through the unpleasantness of seeing them rise up again out of their own ashes.

The men who are best trained, most experienced, and dedicated to urban guerrilla warfare and at the same time to rural guerrilla warfare, constitute the backbone of the revolutionary war and, therefore, of the Brazilian revolution. From this backbone will come the marrow of the revolutionary army of national liberation, rising out of guerrilla warfare. This is the central nucleus, not the bureaucrats and opportunists hidden in the organizational structure, not the empty conferees, the cliched writers of resolutions that remain on paper, but rather the men who fight. The men who from the very first have been determined and ready for anything, who personally participate in revolutionary actions, who do not waver or deceive.

This is the nucleus indoctrinated and disciplined with a long-range strategic and tactical vision consistent with the application of Marxist theory, of Leninism, and of Castro-Guevara developments applied to the specific conditions of the Brazilian situation. This is the nucleus that will lead the rebellion through its guerrilla phase.

From it will come men and women with politico-military development, one and indivisible, whose task will be that of future leaders after the triumph of the revolution, in the construction of the new Brazilian society.

As of now, the men and women chosen for urban guerrilla warfare are workers; peasants whom the city has attracted as a market for

manpower and who return to the countryside indoctrinated and politically and technically prepared: students, intellectuals, priests. This is
the material with which we are building—starting with urban guerrilla warfare—the armed alliance of workers and peasants, with students, intellectuals, priests.

Workers have infinite knowledge in the industrial sphere and are
best for urban revolutionary tasks. The urban guerrilla worker participates in the struggle by constructing arms, sabotaging and preparing
saboteurs and dynamiters, and personally participating in actions involving hand arms, or organizing strikes and partial paralysis with the
characteristics of mass violence in factories, workshops, and other
work centers.

The peasants have an extraordinary intuition for knowledge of the
land, judgment in confronting the enemy, and the indispensable ability to communicate with the humble masses. The peasant guerrilla is
already participating in our struggle and it is he who reaches the
guerrilla core, establishes support points in the countryside, finds
hiding places for individuals, arms, munitions, supplies, organizes
the sowing and harvesting of grain for use in the guerrilla war,
chooses the points of transport, cattle-raising posts, and sources of
meat supplies, trains the guides that show the rural guerrillas the
road, and creates an information service in the countryside.

Students are noted for being politically crude and coarse and thus
they break all the taboos. When they are integrated into urban guerrilla warfare, as is now occurring on a wide scale, they show a special talent for revolutionary violence and soon acquire a high level of
political-technical-military skill. Students have plenty of free time on
their hands because they are systematically separated, suspended, and
expelled from school by the dictatorship and so they begin to spend
their time advantageously, on behalf of the revolution.

The intellectuals constitute the vanguard of resistance to arbitrary
acts, social injustice, and the terrible inhumanity of the dictatorship
of the gorillas. They spread the revolutionary call and they have great
influence on people. The urban guerrilla intellectual or artist is the
most modern of the Brazilian revolution's adherents.

Churchmen—that is to say, those ministers or priests and religious
men of various hierarchies and persuasions—represent a sector that
has special ability to communicate with the people, particularly with
workers, peasants, and the Brazilian woman. The priest who is an
urban guerrilla is an active ingredient in the ongoing Brazilian revo-

lutionary war, and constitutes a powerful arm in the struggle against military power and North American imperialism.

As for the Brazilian woman, her participation in the revolutionary war, and particularly in urban guerrilla warfare, has been marked by an unmatched fighting spirit and tenacity, and it is not by chance that so many women have been accused of participation in guerrilla actions against banks, quarries, military centers, etc., and that so many are in prison while others are sought by the police.

As a school for choosing the guerrilla, urban guerrilla warfare prepares and places at the same level of responsibility and efficiency the men and women who share the same dangers fighting, rounding up supplies, serving as messengers or runners, as drivers, sailors, or airplane pilots, obtaining secret information, and helping with propaganda and the task of indoctrination.

# SELECTED BIBLIOGRAPHY

Alix, Ernest Kahlar, *Ransom Kidnapping in America, 1874–1974*, Southern Illinois University Press, Carbondale, Illinois, 1978.

Asencio, Diego and Nancy, with Ron Tobias, *Our Man is Inside*, Little, Brown and Company, Boston, 1983.

Aston, Clive C., "Political Hostage-Taking in Western Europe," *Conflict Studies*, Number 157, 1984.

Blum, Dr. Robert, "Hostage Negotiations," unpublished manuscript.

Bolz, Frank A., Jr., *How To Be a Hostage and Live*, Lyle Stuart, Secaucus, New Jersey, 1987.

———— and Edward Hershey, *Hostage Cop*, Rawson, Wade Publishers, Inc., New York, 1979.

Carlson, Kurt, *One American Must Die*, Congdon & Weed, Inc., New York, 1986.

Cassese, Antonio, *Terrorism, Politics and Law*, Princeton University Press, Princeton, New Jersey, 1989.

Cassidy, William L., *Political Kidnapping: An Introductory Overview*, Sycamore Island Books, Boulder, Colorado, 1978.

Cohen, Herb, *You Can Negotiate Anything*, Bantam Books, New York, 1980.

Crelinsten, Ronald D. and Denis Szabo, *Hostage-Taking*, Lexington Books, Lexington, Massachusetts, 1979.

Christopher, Warren, et. al., *American Hostages in Iran: The Conduct of a Crisis*, Yale University Press, New Haven, Connecticut, 1985.

Daraul, Arkon, *A History of Secret Societies*, Citadel Press, Secaucus, New Jersey, 1961.

Debray, Regis, *Revolution in the Revolution?*, Grove Press, New York, 1967.

Fitzpatrick, Robert, "Hostage Negotiations," FBI Academy, Quantico, Virginia, n.d.

Francis, Dick, *The Danger*, Fawcett Crest, New York, 1984.

Friedland, William H., et. al., *Revolutionary Theory*, Allenheld, Osmun & Co., Totowa, New Jersey, 1982.

Fuselier, G. Dwayne and Clinton R. VanZandt, "A Practical Overview of Hostage Negotiations," FBI Academy, Quantico, Virginia, n.d.

Fuselier, G. Dwayne, Clinton R. VanZandt, and Frederick J. Lance-
ley, "Negotiating the Protracted Incident: The Oakdale and Atlanta
Prison Sieges," *FBI Law Enforcement Bulletin*, Vol. 58, No. 7,
July 1989.

Hacker, Frederick J., M.D., *Crusaders, Criminals, Crazies: Terror
and Terrorism in Our Time*, W.W. Norton & Company, Inc., New
York, 1976.

Hassel, Conrad V., "Law Enforcement and Behavioral Science: Closing the Gap," FBI Academy, Quantico, Virginia, n.d.

Herz, John H., "Rise and Demise of the Territorial State," *World
Politics*, vol. IX, July 1957.

Irish Republican Army, *Handbook for Volunteers of the Irish Republican Army*, IRA Headquarters, 1956.

Lanceley, Frederick J., "The Antisocial Personality as a Hostage-
Taker," FBI Academy, Quantico, Virginia, June 1979.

Little, Lt. M.R., "The Evolution and Future of Revolutionary Guerrilla Warfare and Terrorism," *RUSI*, London, June 1984.

Marighella, Carlos, "Minimanual of the Urban Guerrilla," *Tricontinental*, Havana, n.d.

Messick, Hank and Burt Goldblatt, *Kidnapping: The Illustrated History*, The Dial Press, New York, 1974.

Mueller, G.O.W. and Freda Adler, *Outlaws of the Ocean*, Hearst Marine Books, New York, 1985.

Nudell, Mayer and Norman Antokol, *The Handbook for Effective
Emergency and Crisis Management*, Lexington Books, Lexington,
Massachusetts, 1988.

Reid, Major Pat and Maurice Michael, *Prisoner of War*, Beaufort
Books, New York, 1884.

Salewski, Wolfgang, "Conduct and Negotiations in Hostage Situations," *International Summaries*, vol. 3, National Institute of Law
Enforcement and Criminal Justice, Washington, D.C., 1979.

Santoro, Victor, *Disruptive Terrorism*, Loompanics Unlimited, Port
Townsend, Washington, 1984.

Saunders, Herbert, *The American Hostage . . . to be or not to be*,
Varicon International, Falls Church, Virginia, 1988.

Sickmann, Rocky, *Iranian Hostage: A Personal Diary of 444 Days in
Captivity*, Crawford Press, Topeka, Kansas, 1982.

Special Operations and Research Unit, "Abnormal Psychology for
Hostage Negotiations," FBI Academy, Quantico, Virginia, n.d.

Strentz, Thomas, "The Stockholm Syndrome: Law Enforcement Policy and the Ego Defenses of the Hostage," FBI Academy, Quantico, Virginia, n.d.

———, "The Inadequate Personality as a Hostage Taker," FBI Academy, Quantico, Virginia, n.d.

———, "A Statistical Analysis of American Hostage Situations," FBI Academy, Quantico, Virginia, n.d.

Office of Security, *Hostage Taking: Preparation, Avoidance, and Survival*, United States Department of State, Washington, D.C., 1984.

———, *Hostage Negotiation: A Matter of Life and Death*, United States Department of State, Washington, D.C., 1983.

———, *Hostage Negotiation in Incidents Involving International Terrorism*, United States Department of State, Washington, D.C., 1984.

Queller, Donald E., *The Office of Ambassador in the Middle Ages*, Princeton University Press, Princeton, New Jersey, 1967.

Quigley, Carroll, *The Evolution of Civilizations*, The Macmillan Company, New York, 1961.

Thompson, Leroy, *The Rescuers: The World's Top Anti-Terrorist Units*, Paladin Press, Boulder, Colorado, 1986.

VanZandt, Clinton R. and David A. Soskis, M.D., "Hostage Negotiation: Law Enforcement's Most Effective Non-Lethal Weapon," FBI Academy, Quantico, Virginia, n.d.

# INDEX